U.S. GRANT'S
FAILED PRESIDENCY

U.S. GRANT'S
FAILED PRESIDENCY

PHILIP LEIGH

SHOTWELL PUBLISHING
COLUMBIA, SOUTH CAROLINA

Produced in the Republic of South Carolina by

Shotwell Publishing, LLC
Post Office Box 2592
Columbia, South Carolina 29202

www.ShotwellPublishing.com

Cover Design: Hazel's Dream

ISBN-13: 978-1-947660-18-2
ISBN-10: 1-947660-18-7

10 9 8 7 6 5 4 3 2 1

If I don't see things your way, well, why should I? — Will Rogers

CONTENTS

ILLUSTRATIONS

PREFACE

ULYSSES GRANT'S PRESIDENCY deserves a fresh analysis because modern historians and biographers have lifted him too high. Initially, their rehabilitation of his previously mixed reputation concentrated on his military performance during the Civil War, but more lately it has included his presidency. In 1948, for example, Grant ranked near the bottom at twenty-eighth out of thirty presidents. But a 2017 survey ranked him in the middle of the pack at twenty-second out of forty-one.[1]

The ranking improvement reflects two factors. First is an increasing focus on his civil rights policies on behalf of blacks, if not other minorities. Historians who came of age during, or after, the 1960s civil rights movement tend to concentrate on the racial aspects of Reconstruction. In a 2018 interview, for example, Ron Chernow proclaimed Grant to be "the single most important president in terms of civil rights between Abraham Lincoln and Lyndon B. Johnson . . ." Second is a tenacious tendency among modern historians to minimize the corruption that plagued his presidency as well as an inclination to dismiss suspicions that he may have been personally culpable.[2]

Regarding the first point, today's historians too often fail to critically evaluate Grant's motives for supporting black civil rights, particularly voting rights. His policy is commonly portrayed as a

---

[1] Gary Maranell, "The Evaluation of Presidents: An Extension of the Schlesinger Polls." *The Journal of American History*, v. 57, no. 1 (104-113); C-Span, "Presidential Historians Survey: 2017" Available: http://cs.pn/2lomfHW [Accessed: February 1, 2018]

[2] Ron Chernow, "Restoring Grant to Greatness," *America's Civil War*, v. 31, no. 1 (March 2018), 58-59

noble stand for racial equality. They fail to adequately examine evidence that his prime motive may have been to gain the political power that a routinely obedient voting bloc could provide to Republican candidates. Consider, for example, that only a minority of America's whites voted for Grant when he was first elected President in 1868, despite his popularity as a war hero. His 300,000 popular vote majority resulted from winning about 90% of the votes among the mostly illiterate ex-slaves.[3]

More importantly, President Grant may have limited his voting rights advocacy to blacks since they composed the solitary minority group that could be politically significant. He did nothing for smaller racial minorities such as Indians, Chinese Americans and other immigrant groups. In fact, at the end of the Civil War Grant *opposed* black suffrage, even for those who were Union veterans. His move toward black suffrage over the next three years paralleled his increasing intimacy with Radical Republicans and fully solidified with his nomination for President on the Republican ticket in May 1868.[4]

Similarly, Indians generally could not vote during Grant's Administration. Moreover, in 1875-76 he secretly provoked a war with tribes in the Northern Great Plains. He wanted to give white men access to doubtfully valuable gold deposits in the Black Hills in order to help America's economy recover from the depression that followed the Panic of 1873. Although the war is best known for the fight at Custer's Last Stand the U. S. Supreme Court ruled a century later that it was illegal and awarded over $100 million in damages to tribal descendants.[5]

---

[3] J. G. Randall and David Donald *The Civil War and Reconstruction*, (Boston: D. C. Heath and Company, 1961), 640

[4] Joseph Rose, *Grant Under Fire*, (New York: Alderhanna Publishing, 2015), 558-59, n717

[5] Nathaniel Philbrick, *The Last Stand* (New York: Viking, 2010), 3-4; Peter Cozzens, *The Earth is Weeping: The Epic Story of the Indian Wars for the American West* (New York: Alfred Knopf, 2016), Kindle Location, 4087-4092, 4143, 4159, 4179-4184; John S. Gray, *Centennial Campaign: The 1876 Sioux War* (Norman: University of Oklahoma Press, 1988), 23; Frederic Frommer, *The Los Angeles Times*, "Black Hills Are Beyond Price to Sioux" Available: http://lat.ms/2yo096M [Accessed: September 19, 2017] (August 19, 2001)

Chinese Americans were also generally denied the opportunity to become citizens and vote. Not until 1943 would they be eligible to become naturalized citizens. Even though they never numbered more than ten percent of California's population, they represented about two-thirds of the state's lynch victims between 1849 and 1902. In fact, the biggest lynching in American history took place in Los Angeles during Grant's first presidential term in 1871. The nineteen victims were Chinese Americans.

Since the Fourteenth Amendment only granted citizenship to persons born in America, Grant signed the 1870 Naturalization Act in order to enable blacks born elsewhere to become citizens. But the act deliberately excluded Chinese Americans and other "non-whites." In 1875 he signed the Page Act that sharply restricted entry into America of Chinese women at a time when 96% of Chinese Americans were male and interracial marriage was rare. That effectively blocked the Fourteenth Amendment's birthright citizenship for Asian Americans. The 1875 Civil Rights Act also failed to include Chinese Americans. In *Driven Out: The Forgotten War Against Chinese Americans*, Jean Paelzer explained the effect of such restrictions and omissions: "The Civil Rights Act and the Page Act of 1875 . . . removed the right of Chinese immigrants to ever become citizens and banned the immigration of most Chinese women."[6]

As for the dubious ethics displayed by Grant's Administration there were at least ten incidents of malfeasance connected to it during his eight-year presidency. The sheer number and frequency that repeatedly signified Grant's association with men of questionable character may also hint at his own potential culpability. Consider, for example, the President's conduct during the Whisky Ring Scandal, which involved tax evasion and bribery in the distilled spirits industry, which was the top source of domestic federal tax revenue.

---

[6] Jean Pfaelzer, *Driven Out: The Forgotten War Against Chinese Americans* (Berkeley: University of California Press, 2008), 45, 52, 58, 102; John Soennichsen, *The Chinese Exclusion Act of 1882* (Santa Barbara, Calif.: Greenwood, 2011), Kindle Loc. 74

Ultimately the treasury's investigation led to the threshold of the presidency when Grant's personal secretary, Orville Babcock, was indicted as a leading Ring conspirator. Grant responded by first trying to move the trial to a friendly military court since Babcock was also an army officer. But a justice department prosecutor blocked the move by noting that it would violate procedural rules against removing evidence from the court of jurisdiction. Second, he hired a spy to infiltrate the prosecutor's office, but the mole eventually sided with the prosecution. Third, he fired an assistant prosecutor whose comments during a jury summation personally offended Grant. Fourth, he forbade prosecutors to plea bargain with low-level conspirators as a means to convict high-level participants. Along with other evidence Grant's obstruction were so suspicious that the treasury department's chief clerk wrote a future Supreme Court justice two days before Babcock's trial, "What has hurt [Treasury Secretary] Bristow worst of all & most disheartened him is the final conviction that Grant himself is in the Ring and knows all about [it.]"[7]

Grant also used a law commonly associated with protecting black civil rights in the South to police voter registrations in big Northern cities where growing immigrant populations were steadily strengthening the Democratic Party. When the wife of Attorney General George Williams accused Grant of using secret service funds to benefit Republican candidates in New York City, the President explained that the money was spent in compliance with the 1871 Ku Klux Klan Acts to supervise voter registrations.[8]

Grant was also an eager recipient of valuable gifts which he reciprocated with patronage appointments. Between 1865 and 1869

---

[7] Charles Calhoun, *The Presidency of Ulysses S*. Grant, 521, 524-25; Timothy Rives, "Grant, Babcock & the Whiskey Ring: Part 2" *Prologue Magazine* Vol. 32, No. 3 (Fall 2000) Available: http://bit.ly/2iIEVJy [Accessed: January 2, 2018]; Max Skidmore, *History? Because its Here* "General Grant, General Babcock, and Journalist Colony: A Study in Scandal & Friendship" Available: http://bit.ly/2EsU5wV [Accessed: January 1, 2018]

[8] Charles Calhoun, *The Presidency of Ulysses S. Grant*, 435; Allan Nevins, *Hamilton Fish: The Inner History of the Grant Administration*, Vol. 2 (New York: Fred Ungar Publishing, 1937), 663; William Gillette, *Retreat From Reconstruction* (Baton Rouge: Louisiana State University Press, 1979), 48-49

inclusive, donors bought—or gave him enough money to buy—a total of four homes. One each in Galena, Illinois, Philadelphia, Washington City and Long Branch, New Jersey.

One of the seven donors of the 27-room Long Branch "cottage" was Thomas Murphy who was a notorious supplier of shoddy merchandise to the Union army during the Civil War. Grant later appointed Murphy as customs collector for the Port of New York where the treasury collected three-fourths of America's tariffs. It was the most lucrative patronage assignment available in the federal government.

Similarly, Grant assigned General Daniel Butterfield to New York's sub-treasury office in exchange for raising a fund enabling General William T. Sherman to buy Grant's Washington home at a price that was more than double the price Grant paid only three years earlier. Soon after his appointment, Butterfield took a bribe to join Jay Gould's attempted corner of the gold market in September 1869.[9]

Historians specializing in the Civil War and Reconstruction era are sometimes too easily persuaded by Grant's words, while ignoring his contradictory actions. But, as J. P. Morgan once remarked, "A man always has two reasons for the things he does—a good one and the real one." Morgan was implying that the good reason is a false, benevolent explanation that conceals the real self-serving one. For example, Grant justified restricting the immigration of Chinese women by implying that he wanted to avoid forcing them into prostitution. In his 1875 annual presidential message he wrote, "few . . . are brought to our shores to pursue honorable or useful occupations." But Chinese American history specialist Jean Paelzer concludes that the true purpose of the act was "to force thousands of men to return to China" since only four percent of Asian Americans in 1875 were women. [10]

---

[9] William Hesseltine, *Grant the Politician* (New York: Dodd & Meade, 1935), 212-13; William McFeely, *Grant* (New York: W. W. Norton, 1981), 232, 303, 322-23; Joseph Rose, *Grant Under Fire*, 570-71

[10] Matthew Josephson *The Robber Barons*, (New York: Harcourt, Brace & Company, 1934), 294; Jean Pfaelzer, *Driven Out: The Forgotten War Against Chinese Americans*, 102; Ulysses

Similarly, Grant initially adopted a benevolent attitude toward Indians. In his first annual message in December 1869 he announced that he had put Quakers in charge of several reservations because the sect had long coexisted peaceably with Indians: "From the foundation of the Government to the present, management of the . . . Indians . . . has been a subject of embarrassment and . . . attended with continuous robberies, murders, and wars. I do not hold . . . the conduct of the whites . . . blameless . . . [and] have attempted a new [Quaker managed] policy . . . with fair results so far . . . which I hope will be [a] great success." Yet, his professions of good feelings proved false when he launched the Centennial War in the North Plaines noted earlier.[11]

When a group of African Americans visited the White House to congratulate him for winning reelection in 1872, Grant told them what they wanted to hear: "I wish that everyman in the United States would stand in all respects alike." But, to Grant, "everyman" did not include Indians and Chinese Americans, among other non-black minorities.[12]

Since Grant sometimes contradicted himself, his true intent must be deduced from his actions, not his words. Yet some modern biographers too readily accept the statements that reflect upon him favorably and ignore the contradictory ones. Charles Calhoun does so when suggesting that Grant supported labor over capital in the 1877 railroad strike during the first year of Rutherford Hayes's presidency. While complaining that the press had been overly critical of his use of federal troops in the South, Calhoun cites Grant as complaining, "Now [during the 1877 railroad strike], however, there is no hesitation about exhausting the whole power of the government

---

S. Grant, *Seventh Annual Message* (December 7, 1875) Available: http://bit.ly/2soNVSq [Accessed: February 3, 2018]

[11] Ulysses S. Grant, *First Annual Message: December 6, 1869*; Ulysses S. Grant, *First Inaugural Address: March 6, 1869* Available: http://bit.ly/2wQtXH4 [Accessed: September 24, 2017]

[12] Charles Calhoun, *The Presidency of Ulysses S. Grant*, 392

to suppress a strike on the slightest intimation that danger threatens."[13]

But in an August 27, 1877 letter to brother-in-law Abel Corbin Grant displayed a hard, and contradictory, stance toward labor. He wrote, "My judgment is that [the strike] should have been put down with a strong hand and so summarily as to prevent a like occurrence for a generation."[14]

Finally, even though Grant's fundamental interest in black civil rights may have reflected the power of the group's voting bloc more than the morality of racial equality, it ultimately failed to be enough to sustain his support. The moment-of-truth came during the autumn 1875 elections in Mississippi and Ohio.

Mississippi carpetbag governor Adelbert Ames twice asked Grant for federal troops to police the polls on Election Day but was turned down. It would be another forty years before former Republican Mississippi Congressman John Lynch revealed that Grant confessed to him in November 1875 that Ohio politicians convinced the President that Mississippi intervention would likely cause Republicans to lose Ohio. Basically, Grant traded a Republican victory in Mississippi for a bigger one in Ohio. Thereafter, the Republican Party steadily lost interest in Southern blacks.[15]

Understanding Grant's roller-coaster reputation begins with a study of contrasts. In a mere seven years he rose from obscurity to the presidency, only to generally skid downward from his inauguration day to the end of his second term.

---

[13] *Ibid.*, 571

[14] Ulysses S. Grant, *Letters of Ulysses S. Grant to His Father and His Youngest Sister, 1857-78*, Edited by Jesse Grant Cramer, Available: http://bit.ly/2GJ5NEP [Accessed: February 3, 2018]

[15] Ron Chernow, *Grant,* (New York: Random House, 2017), 816-817

CHAPTER 1: INTRODUCTION

PERHAPS NO NINETEENTH CENTURY American won a greater triumph than did Ulysses Grant when he received the surrender of Robert E. Lee's Confederate Army of Northern Virginia on April 9, 1865, bringing an end to the Civil War. Few Americans today appreciate the scope of that war. About seven hundred thousand soldiers died at a time when the country had but thirty-one million people. If America were to sustain such losses in a war today the dead would exceed seven million. Moreover, Grant's success was all the more significant given his low personal status only four years before Lee's surrender.

In April 1861 the thirty-nine-year-old Grant was working under his two younger brothers at a leather goods store in Galena, Illinois a short distance from the Mississippi River west of Chicago. The job was basically a gift from his father, Jesse, who owned the store but lived near Cincinnati, Ohio where he had related businesses. During the preceding seven years Ulysses had resigned from the army in disgrace and thereafter failed at various commercial and farming ventures despite significant aid from his prosperous father-in-law, Frederick Dent. Mr. Dent believed that his daughter had married beneath her station, while Jesse bluntly concluded, "West Point spoiled one of my boys [Ulysses] for business."[16]

After graduating from West Point in 1843 Grant soon compiled a good record during the 1846-48 Mexican War. Upon returning from Mexico, he married Julia Dent in 1848. Although starting as a Pittsburgh merchant, Julia's dad had moved to St. Louis where he

---

[16] Brooks Simpson *Ulysses S. Grant: Triumph Over Adversity, 1822-1865*, (Boston: Houghton Mifflin, 2000), 64

1

Jesse Grant, Father of Ulysses

became a slaveholder, accumulated a thousand-acre farm and accepted the honorary title of "Colonel" within the family. It was at that farm, White Haven, where Grant met Julia who was a sister of his senior year West Point roommate.

Over the next four years husband and wife had two sons and mostly shared a roving army life although Julia found excuses to return to White Haven for extended visits. In 1852 the army ordered Grant to a beautiful, but isolated, outpost near Portland, Oregon. Julia declined to follow. In autumn of 1853 he won promotion from lieutenant to captain and transferred to Eureka, California. Despite the promotion Julia still chose to remain in St. Louis. Consequently, Grant became lonely and yielded to alcoholism.

By 1854 he could no longer abide the loneliness and resigned from the army although he had no other means for supporting his family. He arrived in New York City in July but hesitated to return to White Haven without knowing whether he would be welcome. Thus, he borrowed money from a friend, who would become a future Confederate enemy, to pay his hotel bill before heading to Ohio where Grant would visit his father prior to heading to St. Louis. He received a chilly greeting in Ohio but continued on to White Haven in August after a letter from Julia assured him of her love. Colonel Dent, however, remained cool.

After Grant's return, Julia's father gave her a sixty-acre farm that eventually grew to three hundred acres including rented land. Notwithstanding diligent efforts and the assistance of three male slaves, Grant could never make it profitable. Near his nadir in 1857 he pawned a pocket watch for $22 two days before Christmas. In 1859 he sold the farm to join one of Julia's cousins in a St. Louis real estate partnership but was forced out when he proved unable to collect rents.

Ultimately, he experienced nothing but failure in St. Louis. According to biographer William Hesseltine when Grant drank with army comrades whom he occasionally met in the town "it was evident [to them] that he was not fitted to succeed in the world of business. To his family it was equally evident." Consequently, he swallowed his pride and accepted the fifty-dollar a month job at his dad's Galena leather store. Jesse's oldest child had basically returned home as a financial dependent. Memory of the humiliation would haunt the son, and influence his decisions, ever after.[17]

The outbreak of the Civil War rescued Grant from a frustrating life. After Fort Sumter surrendered in April 1861, Galena enthusiastically welcomed President Lincoln's national call for 75,000 volunteers to put down the rebellion. When town leaders realized that Captain Grant was the only resident that understood military drills, they offered to let him lead Galena's new volunteer company. He declined because he hoped to get a bigger command by applying to the Illinois governor.

His appeals had no success until Governor Richard Yates became eager to find a new commander for the Twenty-First Illinois Infantry Regiment that was in virtual revolt against the militarily incompetent politician that was originally assigned to lead it. Grant became the replacement with a colonel's commission. At about the same time President Lincoln asked for brigadier general nominations from Illinois congressmen. Since Ulysses was then the only high-ranking

---

[17] The Ulysses S. Grant Homepage, *Chronology,* Available: http://bit.ly/1QNXvhe [Accessed: August 11, 2017], William McFeely, *Grant,* (New York: W. W. Norton, 1981), 57; Ronald C. White, *American Ulysses: A Life of U. S. Grant* (New York: Random House, 2016), Kindle location 2791; William B. Hesseltine, *Ulysses Grant Politician,* (New York: Dodd Meade & Company, 1935), 13-17

officer in the Galena congressman's district, Colonel Grant got that nod as well. After seven lean years the newly promoted Brigadier General Grant found himself on a path that would lead through seven fat years culminating in 1868 with his election as President of the United States.[18]

By 1868, Grant had become the latest incarnation of the proverbial American folk hero—at least in the North. He drew upon that vast reservoir of popular devotion to easily win the Republican nomination in May. The closing sentence of his acceptance letter became a campaign slogan: "Let us have peace."

His Party, however, was too shrewd to pin their election hopes on a mere slogan. By overriding the vetoes of President Andrew Johnson in 1867, Republicans forced universal black suffrage in the former Confederate states for the election of delegates to conventions empowered to form new state governments that could qualify for readmission to the Union. Of the eleven applicable states, all but Virginia, Mississippi, and Texas had been readmitted under such terms by the 1868 general election. Only two of the readmitted eight voted for Grant's opponent, New York Democratic governor Horatio Seymour.[19]

Grant would serve two terms as President ending in March 1877. On 10 May of the preceding year in Philadelphia, he addressed a group of 4,000 dignitaries at America's Centennial Exposition that showcased such inventions as the typewriter and the telephone, while another 180,000 common visitors toured the exhibits on opening day. According to historian Nathaniel Philbrick, the silence that greeted the President's ten-minute speech ". . . was astonishing [evidence of] how far Grant had plummeted. After winning the war for Lincoln, he seemed on the brink of even greater accomplishments

---

[18] Hesseltine, *Ulysses Grant Politician*, 18-21

[19] James Randall and David Donald, *The Civil War and Reconstruction*, (Boston: D. C Heath & Company, 1961), 640; C. Vann Woodward *American Heritage* "The Lowest Ebb" Volume 8, Number 3 (April 1957) Available: http://bit.ly/2ydpIdA [Accessed: October 11, 2017]

as president." Despite only fair auditorium acoustics, "it must have been sad and infuriating [for Grant] to see America's celebration of its centennial come down to this: the rude derisive silence of several thousand people withholding their applause."[20]

---

[20] Nathaniel Philbrick, *The Last Stand* (New York: Viking, 2010), 9

CHAPTER 2: NEW NORMAL

ROBERT E. LEE SURRENDERED ON Palm Sunday 1865. President Lincoln was shot on Good Friday and died on Easter. After Lincoln's death no American was more popular than Ulysses S. Grant, although that wasn't his real name. It was actually Hiram Ulysses Grant, but the true name did not match the admissions roster when the seventeen- year-old arrived at West Point on July 1, 1839. Rather than return home he acquiesced to the Ulysses S. Grant name that appeared on the list of incoming plebes. Classmates often called him Sam because the U. S. initials on the class roll suggested the obvious, and simpler, nickname. Nonetheless, the man with multiple names would enjoy unrivaled popularity for most of his remaining twenty-one years after earning a promotion to Lieutenant General in 1864. His reputation among historians, however, would fluctuate.

Grant avoided the Ford's Theater assassination in Washington— for which he may have also been a target—because Julia insisted that the couple decline Lincoln's invitation to join the presidential couple at the performance of *Our American Cousin*. Julia disliked Mrs. Lincoln. Officially Grant declined the invitation by explaining that Mrs. Grant was anxious to return to their children in Burlington, New Jersey, which was near Philadelphia. The couple no longer depended upon Jesse's charity for a home. Grant's military rank paid enough salary to enable an independent and comfortable living. He and Julia would strive ever after to sustain, or improve, the family's economic and social status as their new normal. Public adulation soon resulted in gifts that only intensified the couple's appetite for more possessions and honorariums.

A month following Lincoln's assassination wealthy Philadelphians gave Grant's family a grand home at 2009 Chestnut Street. It included closets full of snowy linen and dining tables set with fine silver. Grant planned to commute to Washington, but the five-hour train ride quickly rendered the plan impracticable. As a result, he temporarily accepted an offer from Henry Halleck, who was his predecessor as Army General-in-Chief, to use Halleck's Georgetown Heights home. Still wanting a Washington residence of his own, in October he purchased a four-story structure for $30,000. A future brother-in-law, Abel Corbin, actually bought the home and gave Grant title in exchange for a note to pay Corbin $30,000 over ten years.

Four months later former Major General Daniel Butterfield led a subscription for Grant among rich New Yorkers that resulted in a purse of $105,000, which was equivalent to about $1.7 million in 2018. Grant first used the money to repay his debt to Corbin. He then invested $55,000 in government bonds and took the last $20,000 in cash. Bostonians similarly gave him a personal library valued at $75,000. While living in Halleck's home during the summer of 1865 he also accepted a $16,000 gift home back in Galena, Illinois. Four years later Butterfield and Corbin would teach Grant that there is no such thing as a free home.[21]

Early in 1866 Horace Greeley's *New York Tribune* humorously wrote, "Since Richmond's capitulation the stern soldier [Grant] spent his days . . . in conjugating the transitive verb *to receive*, in all its moods and tenses, but always in the first person singular . . . " Soon thereafter the *Georgetown Courier* continued in form by adding that Grant had conjugated the verb for a total of $175,000, which biographer Hesseltine concluded was "obviously too low."[22]

---

[21] William McFeely, *Grant*, 232; Ronald C. White, *American Ulysses: A Life of U. S. Grant*, Kindle Location, 8490-8501; William Hesseltine, *Ulysses S. Grant Politician*, 51, 57, 63; Federal Reserve Bank of Minneapolis, *Consumer Price Index*, Available: http://bit.ly/1FTcHOC [Accessed: August 12, 2017]

[22] William Hesseltine, *Ulysses S. Grant Politician*, 63

Grant learned by telegram around midnight on Good Friday 1865 while waiting at an intermediate Philadelphia stop to switch trains for Burlington, that Lincoln had been shot and was dying. After escorting Julia to Burlington, he complied with Secretary of War Edwin Stanton's summons to Washington.

Many leaders in the capital city wrongly supposed that the assassination was a high-level Confederate conspiracy. Initially the same suspicions infected Grant. He ordered the Union commander in occupied Richmond to arrest an official Confederate peace negotiator—Rebel armies were still in the field beyond Virginia—and all "paroled [Confederate] officers." When the Richmond commander reminded Grant that such an order would include Lee and others surrendered at Appomattox presently living in Richmond, Grant rescinded the order. He also soon thereafter concluded that there had been no Confederate conspiracy.[23]

The new President was Tennessee's Andrew Johnson, the only senator from a Confederate state to remain Union-loyal during the Civil War. As a reward he became Lincoln's vice-presidential running mate in the 1864 election and was inaugurated as VP only six weeks before Lincoln was killed. Although Johnson was a former slaveholder, he was born into poverty and disliked Southern aristocrats.

Immediately after Lincoln's death, his disdain for the antebellum gentry provoked Johnson to make comments that implied he would align with the Radical wing of the Republican Party—a wing that wanted strict and vindictive Reconstruction terms, beyond those intended by Lincoln. For example, he wrote Indiana's Governor Oliver Morton, "Treason must be made odious . . . traitors must be punished . . . [and] their social power destroyed. I say as to the [Southern] leaders, punishment. I say leniency . . . and amnesty to the thousands they have misled. . . " The day after Lincoln died,

---

[23] Brooks Simpson, *Ulysses S. Grant: Triumph and Adversity, 1822-1865*, 443-44

Johnson told Michigan Senator Zack Chandler, "Treason must be made infamous and traitors must be impoverished."[24]

After the rest of the Confederate armies surrendered, former politically-appointed general and erstwhile Massachusetts Congressman Benjamin Butler hastened to Washington to advise Johnson that ex-Confederate soldiers could legitimately be charged with treason. They could not, in his legal opinion, rely upon the protection of the surrender terms that assured them that upon returning home they were "not to be disturbed by United States authority so long as they observe[d] their paroles and the laws in force where they may reside." Butler simply reasoned that they were no longer soldiers and therefore presently subject to civil, not martial, law.[25]

On June 7, 1865 Butler's rationalizations prompted a Virginia federal court to indict Robert E. Lee for treason. Lee wrote Grant for advice and Grant urged Lee to apply for a pardon. Lee sent his application to Grant who took the papers to Johnson.

"When can these men [former Rebel soldiers] be tried," asked Johnson?

Grant replied, "Never, unless they violate their paroles. If I had told [Lee] and his army . . . they would be open to arrest, trial, and execution for treason, Lee would never have surrendered, and we should have lost many lives in destroying him." After returning to his office Grant told his staff, "I will not stay in the army if they break the pledges that I made. I will keep my word."

Johnson realized he could not successfully override the wishes of the popular Grant no matter how clever were Butler's contrary legal arguments. As a result, the federal government made no further

---

[24] Avery Craven *Reconstruction: The Ending of the Civil War* (New York: Holt, Reinhart & Winston, 1969) 84; Kenneth Stampp *The Era of Reconstruction,* (New York: Alfred A. Knopf, 1965), 52

[25] Ulysses S. Grant, *Memoirs* (New York, De Capo Press, 1982), 557; Hesseltine, *Grant the Politician,* 53

efforts to charge Confederate soldiers with treason, although former Confederate government officials remained vulnerable. Among them was President Jefferson Davis who was indicted for treason several times, lastly in May 1866. A year later federal prosecutors said they were unprepared to try Davis's case. He was, therefore, released on bond. He never asked for a pardon because he wanted to prove his innocence in court, but never got the chance.[26]

After blocking treason charges against Lee, Grant turned his attention to a couple of immediate objectives. First was to demobilize the federal army. From May to November 1865 eight hundred thousand soldiers returned home and they were disproportionately white. Blacks composed 11% of the Union army at the end of the war. By November they represented 36% and the ratio would trend even higher as the volunteer army continued to demobilize. Blacks tended to remain in uniform because even the low pay of an enlisted man was comparatively attractive to their alternative occupations.

Grant recommended that selected federal garrisons temporarily remain in the South because the civil chaos that accompanied the end of the war meant that, "The white and black require the protection of the federal government." But he urged that blacks not be among the occupying soldiers. "The presence of black troops, lately slaves, demoralizes labor both by their advice and by furnishing in their camps a resort for [surrounding] freedmen . . . White troops generally excite no opposition and therefore a small number . . . can maintain order in a given district." He also presciently noted that the presence of black troops might trigger guerrilla attacks.[27]

Secondly, General Grant wanted to promptly expel a French-backed puppet regime in Mexico. Several European powers were hostile to the 1823 Monroe Doctrine by which the United States declared the Western Hemisphere to be off limits to further

---

[26] Ronald C. White, *Grant,* Kindle location 8334; William C. Davis, *Jefferson Dais: The Man and His Hour* (New York: HarperCollins, 1991), 655-57

[27] William McFeely, *Grant*, 239-40; Ronald C. White, *Grant,* Kindle location 8411-17

European colonization. France, especially, felt that the Doctrine was merely a fig leaf to permit America's "Manifest Destiny" to dominate the hemisphere.

Ever since Napoleon I sold New Orleans and the Louisiana Territory about sixty years earlier in 1803 France had been shut out of the Western hemisphere. Since then the United States absorbed half of Mexico, first by annexing Texas and next by way of the Mexican Cession that followed the end of the Mexican War. During the American Civil War the reigning French monarch, Louis-Napoleon, reasoned that Lincoln might be too focused on suppressing the Confederacy to risk opposing an armed French presence in Mexico. If Louis were successful, the Monroe Doctrine would become impotent and the Western hemisphere might once again become fertile territory for European colonies.[28]

Led by France, several European nations sent an expeditionary force to Mexico's chief port of Veracruz in order to collect customs duties and thereby repay the Europeans for debts owed to them by Mexico. But after the coalition army occupied the port, it became clear that Louis-Napoleon's intent was to install a vassal government under the rule of the Austrian monarch's younger brother, Maximilian. As a pretense, the French Monarch claimed he wanted to re-establish Roman Catholic faith, ethics, and authority in the Central American country. Thereafter, the other Europeans in the expedition left the country in protest. Maximilian became Emperor of Mexico in 1864 under the protection of a French occupying army.

Grant was aware that Lincoln and many in Congress objected to the regime. After Appomattox he sent a 50,000-man force under Major General Philip Sheridan to the Texas border as a demonstration of American military power. He also prompted Sheridan to send 30,000 rifles to the Mexican guerrilla leader opposing Maximilian. Finally, Grant planned to send Major General John Schofield into Mexico to recruit an army of American

---

[28] Donald Miles, *Cinco de Mayo*, (Lincoln, Nebraska: iUniverse, 2006), 7-8

expatriates—including former Rebels—and others to overthrow Mexico's Austrian Emperor.

While the show of force on the border conformed to Secretary of State William H. Seward's diplomatic efforts, the unauthorized weapons shipment and plan to raise an army in Mexico did not. They threatened to put America unnecessarily at war with a major European power. Therefore, Seward sent Schofield on a diplomatic errand to France and continued to negotiate with Louis-Napoleon for a voluntary French withdrawal. In April 1866 the French ambassador in Washington notified Seward that Napoleon had agreed to a three-stage withdrawal, which was completed in 1867. After the last of the French army left, Maximilian's government collapsed, and Mexico regained home rule. The Emperor was executed.[29]

Historian Albert Castel reasons that if Grant's bellicose approach had prevailed, Andrew Johnson would have been the chief political beneficiary even though the President backed the Secretary of State's more measured policy.

> Grant's [warlike approach] would have been
> highly popular and in all probability successful . . .
> [I]t most likely would have assured the acceptance of
> Johnson's Reconstruction program by a nation and
> Congress preoccupied with the possibility of war.
> Indeed, fear of a conflict with France would divert
> Republican attention from "guarding the poor
> freedmen" and would lead to immediate readmission
> of the Southern states . . . [thereby blocking the
> Radical Reconstruction that later ensued.][30]

---

[29] Hesseltine, *Grant the Politician*, 53; Philip Leigh, *Trading With the Enemy* (Yardley, Pa.: Westholme Publishing, 2013), 103-04, 107; Albert Castel, *The Presidency of Andrew Johnson* (Lawrence: University Press of Kansas, 1979), 41

[30] Albert Castel, *Andrew Johnson*, 42

Since Johnson once identified Lincoln as "the greatest American that has ever lived" he came to regard it as his duty to be the trustee of the martyred President's legacy. Johnson resolved that his Reconstruction policies would follow in the great man's footsteps or try to. Among Lincoln's clearest signals was that Reconstruction should proceed promptly and under the authority of the federal executive branch before Congress was scheduled to reconvene in early December 1865. Johnson quickly settled on such a plan and discussed it thoroughly with his Lincoln-inherited cabinet on 9 May. None of the members voiced "[any] doubt of the power of the executive branch . . . to reorganize [the former Confederate] state governments without the aid of Congress."[31]

Johnson disclosed the two-step plan near the end of May, only a month-and-a-half after Lincoln's death. First, former qualified Rebels were invited to apply for pardon and amnesty. Such persons would have their non-slave property rights restored. Second, each former Confederate state was to hold a convention to create a new state constitution. Tennessee, Arkansas and Louisiana were exempted because they had already formed state governments recognized by Lincoln during the war.

Pardon and amnesty required that each applicant take an oath to "henceforth faithfully support . . . the Constitution . . . and abide by . . . all laws . . . made during the existing rebellion . . . [involving] . . . the emancipation of slaves." Significantly, it did not require applicants to say that they had *never* rebelled against the Union. Some former Rebels, however, could not qualify merely by taking the oath. Most notable among them were persons with more than $20,000 in property. They were required to apply directly to the

---

[31] J. G. Randall and David Donald *Civil War and Reconstruction*, 561-2; Avery Craven *Reconstruction*, 80; Albert Castel *President Johnson*, 25

President who would judge their applications on a case-by-case basis.[32]

Johnson set three basic conditions for the new state constitutions. First, they must outlaw slavery. Second, they must renounce secession. Third, they must repudiate all Confederate debts. The conventions were also authorized to set dates to elect state officers and congressional representatives. Once the legislatures were chosen the Southern states were called upon to—and did—supply the incremental votes needed to ratify the Thirteenth Amendment abolishing slavery throughout the nation. According to historians J. G. Randall and David Donald martial law ruled during the (1865) transition process "without any of the attributes of terrorism, violence or menace to the tranquility of the people." Such would prove to be a contrast to the experience during the carpetbag era when groups such as the Ku Klux Klan resisted the Radical Republican state governments.[33]

By December 1865 all of the former Rebel states except Texas had fulfilled Johnson's requirements. They had also elected federal senators and congressmen, ready to take their seats when Congress reconvened on 4 December.[34]

Grant officially endorsed Johnson's Reconstruction plan on June 7, 1865 when he appeared at a pro-Johnson rally in New York City. During the morning he steadily exchanged handshakes with attendees for two hours. By noon the reception line was even longer than when he started. When he entered the rally hall that evening, the crowd interrupted the speaker who had called the meeting to order with chants of "Grant! Grant! Grant! Grant! Grant!" After he took a seat on the stage the audience could not see him. As a result, he rose and started walking to a better position as the crowd cheered

---

[32] Avery Craven *Reconstruction*, 88-9; J. G. Randall and David Donald *The Civil War and Reconstruction*, 560-1

[33] Randall and Donald, *The Civil War and Reconstruction*, 562-3

[34] *Ibid.*, 560

his every step. The reception could leave nobody doubtful about the general's potential to influence voters more than any other American.[35]

Shortly after Grant bought his Washington home in November three staff officers joined him on a tour of the South requested by President Johnson. They visited only Virginia, the Carolinas and Georgia. Other observers had already toured the former Confederacy. One example was Major General Carl Schurz who was financially supported by Johnson's opponents. A case in point was the *Boston Advertiser*, which paid Schurz to write articles about his findings that were mostly at odds with Johnson's plan. Schurz concluded that Southerners were recalcitrant and determined to abuse the freedmen. But Schurz's motives may have been chiefly political. For example, the *New York Herald* wrote, "During [Schurz'] recent trip through the Southern states . . . his time was largely spent in efforts to organize the Republican Party in that region."

Grant's conclusions were generally opposite those of Schurz. "The mass of thinking men in the South", said Grant, "accept the present situation in good faith. [T]hey are in earnest in wishing to do what is required of them by the government." Along with his assistants, Grant suggested that freedmen in Virginia and North Carolina were delaying the region's economic recovery by refusing to work. Upon returning he met with Johnson's cabinet where he indicated that prompt reunification was the correct policy. Although Schurz's report was published at public expense in December and widely distributed by Johnson's opponents, Grant's popularity temporarily carried the day for the President.

New England journalist Benjamin Truman may have written the most objective and authoritative report on the early post war conditions in the South. He spent seven months in the region from September 1865 to March 1866, and visited every state except

---

[35] Albert Castel *President Johnson*, 31; William McFeely *Grant*, 233-34

Virginia and North Carolina, which were two included in Grant's tour. Truman's report also generally supported President Johnson.[36]

In the winter of 1865 when Congress and President Johnson locked horns over conflicting Reconstruction plans, Radical Republicans intensified efforts to win Grant to their side. Although present in New York on the same day in February 1866 as a rally supporting Presidential Reconstruction, Grant did not attend. He instead concentrated on trying to avoid giving offense to either Congress or the President so that they would enact a bill that would promote him from Lieutenant General to full General with a $20,000 annual salary. Only George Washington had previously held the rank.

Since the military rank bill was not enacted until July, and he also disliked War Secretary Edwin Stanton, Grant showed little interest in allying with the Radical wing of the Republican Party for most of 1866. To the contrary, he attended the nominating convention for Johnson's National Union Party. He also agreed to accompany the President on an eighteen-day railroad tour of Northern states to promote the Party's candidates and Johnson's Reconstruction plan. The President referred to the trip as "the swing around the circle."

The train left Washington for its first stop at Baltimore on August 28, 1866. Johnson was initially received enthusiastically in Baltimore, Philadelphia and New York. Nonetheless, everywhere the public was more interested in seeing Grant than the President.

Six days into the trip the stop at Cleveland proved to be a turning point. The crowd included hecklers, who may have been paid by Radical Republicans to provoke Johnson into reckless remarks. When a large crowd assembled outside his hotel, Johnson felt compelled to address them even though he did not have a speech planned. He should have simply acknowledged the greeting and returned to his hotel room. Instead, however, he responded to a

---

[36] Hesselltine *Grant the Politician*, 59-61; Curt Anders, *Powerlust* (Garrison, N.Y.: Highland Outpost Press, 2010), 329-30

heckler's "Hang Jeff Davis!" shout by remarking that as President he did not have the power to bypass the judiciary on such matters. He went on to criticize Congress for "trying to break up the Government."

Despite his personal popularity, the trip demoralized Grant. He fell into a drunken state on the railroad ride from Buffalo to Cleveland where he departed for Detroit on a sobering-up cruise via a Lake Erie steamer before rejoining Johnson in Chicago. Nonetheless, audiences interrupted Johnson with shouts for Grant and Admiral David Farragut, also on the tour. At St. Louis Grant wrote Julia that the trip had descended into a "national disgrace."

From St. Louis onward the journey was dismal. A riot prevented the President from speaking at Indianapolis. Grant left the train in Cincinnati, announcing that he wanted to visit his father. Johnson was also shouted down in Steubenville and Pittsburgh. At the end of the trip, it was the President—not the Radical Republicans—that impressed the public as revolutionary and intemperate.[37]

The failure of the swing around the circle led the infant GOP to solidify veto-proof majorities in both the Senate and House. Even though the Democrats won a Senate seat in Maryland, the Republicans picked up one each in Pennsylvania, California and Oregon. They also got two new seats after Nebraska was admitted as a state. Finally, a vacant Senate seat in New Jersey also went to the Republicans. The Party increased its majority in the House of Representatives as well. President Johnson's National Union Party coalition collapsed. Thereafter, control of the federal government would evolve into contests between two parties: Democrats and Republicans.

President Johnson transformed the 1866 elections into a referendum on his Reconstruction polices when he requested that an

---

[37] Hesselltine, *Grant the Politician*, 68-75; Albert Castel, *President Johnson*, 89-95; William McFeely, *Grant*, 252; Howard K. Beale *The Critical Year* (New York: Frederick Unger, 1958), 308

allied Wisconsin senator, James Doolittle, ask cabinet members to endorse his Reconstruction Program shortly before the National Union Party convention in August. The navy, state, and treasury secretaries promptly agreed. In contrast, the attorney general, postmaster general, and interior secretary resigned. Although War Secretary Edwin Stanton did not reply to Doolittle, his remarks to others indicate that he opposed Johnson. Although Stanton remained in the cabinet, Johnson was correctly skeptical of his loyalty.

When Chief Justice Salmon P. Chase handed down the Supreme Court's April 1866 *Ex-Parte Milligan* ruling, Johnson saw a chance to push his Presidential plan despite the recent election losses. The Court decision stipulated that civilians could not be tried in a military court in areas where civil courts were also operating. Although it involved a wartime Indiana incident, Johnson could presently use the decision to enable Southerners to be tried in civil courts instead of the military courts that had been the earlier practice under the authority of the 1865 Freedmen's Bureau Act. Thus, Johnson began dissolving the military courts.[38]

Two months earlier, in February 1866, Congress had passed a new version of the Freedmen's Bureau Act. It considerably extended the Bureau's power over economic and civil affairs and specifically authorized federal and military enforcement. It also extended the Bureau's activities into the previous Union-loyal slave states where it could be used to enlarge Republican influence. Johnson vetoed the bill, which the Thirty-Ninth Congress initially fell two votes short of overriding. But five months later congressional Republicans were able to garner enough support to pass a modified version over a second Johnson veto.[39]

---

[38] Brooks Simpson *The Reconstruction Presidents* (Lawrence: University Press of Kansas, 1998), 104-05, 111-12; Howard K. Beale, *The Critical Year*, 127-28

[39] J. G. Randall and David Donald *The Civil War and Reconstruction*, 577-8; Ludwell Johnson *Division and Reunion,* (New York: John Wiley & Sons, 1978), 209-10

The Fortieth Congress began in March 1867 with a series of Reconstruction Acts to replace President Johnson's Reconstruction plan with one crafted by Radical Republicans. The Republican plan ultimately became known as Congressional Reconstruction.

The first act, which passed on the first day of the Fortieth Congresses, declared that no lawful state governments existed in the former Confederacy except Tennessee, which was already ruled by Radical Republicans. The rest of the South was to be governed by martial law and divided into five military districts.

A second act passed three weeks later. It required each military occupation commander to compile a roster of voters based upon eligibility standards within the act. It disfranchised about 150,000 previous Confederates but provided for universal suffrage among black adult males. Upon completion, about 1.3 million men were declared legal voters. Blacks outnumbered whites by 703,000 to 627,000 (53%-to-47%) although blacks represented only about 40% of the region's population. African-Americans were the majority of voters in Mississippi, South Carolina, Louisiana, Florida, and Alabama.[40]

Voters thus declared legal were to elect delegates to constitutional conventions in each state. Such constitutions were required to provide for universal black suffrage. They could, however, restrict white voters and office holders. Ultimately Alabama, Arkansas, and Louisiana restricted both white voters and office holders. The remaining seven states did not constrain white voters, but Virginia and Mississippi blocked former Confederates from holding public office.

The resulting constitutions were to be submitted to a statewide voter referendum. After passing the referendums, the constitutions were to be presented to the U. S. Congress where they might be accepted or rejected. Following acceptance of a state's constitution

---

[40] Merton Coulter *The South During Reconstruction* (Baton Rouge: LSU Press, 1947), 132-133

by Congress, each Southern state had to ratify the Fourteenth Amendment. Its representatives could not join the U. S. Congress until the Fourteenth Amendment had been ratified nationally *and* the applicable state also its endorsed ratification. The Fourteenth Amendment granted American-born blacks citizenship and was basically an intermediate step toward the soon-to-be-adopted Fifteenth Amendment, which would provide for black suffrage throughout the country instead of just the South.

The third act, passed in July 1867, provided for liberal interpretation of the first two acts.[41]

In addition to the two Reconstruction Acts passed in March, Congress enacted two bills that same month, also over Johnson's vetoes, to limit the President's powers.

First, was the Command of the Army Act, which required that all of the President's orders to military officers be delivered through the General-in-Chief, Ulysses Grant at the time. Furthermore, the General-in-Chief could not be ordered away from Washington without his consent. The act made it illegal for any other military officer to accept orders directly from the President. The provisions basically insured that President Johnson could not unilaterally direct actions in the Southern states while they were under martial law. He would need Grant's agreement.

Second, was the Tenure of Office Act, which stipulated that civil officers appointed by the President with the consent of the Senate could not be dismissed without the Senate's consent. The main purpose of the Tenure Act was to prevent Johnson from removing War Secretary Stanton who had become an ally of the congressional Republicans and basically their spy in the President's cabinet. It might also prevent Johnson from replacing lesser federal officers in the South who were implementing Congressional Reconstruction. In combination the two acts were designed to increase congressional

---

[41] Merton Coulter *The South During Reconstruction* 118-120, 133, 136; Ludwell Johnson *Division and Reunion*, 226-27

authority over the military and correspondingly weaken the President's influence over it.[42]

When the arrest of a Mississippi newspaperman in November 1867 suggested that his attorney could use the Supreme Court's *Ex-Parte Milligan* decision to get his case moved from a military court to a civilian one, the Fortieth Congress sensed a legal threat to their plans. Any court ruling favorable to the newspaperman could cause Congressional Reconstruction to unravel by neutering Southern military courts. After the Supreme Court took up the newspaperman's case, Congress muddied the waters in March 1868 by repealing the 1867 Habeas Corpus Act shortly before the court ended its hearings. The repealed act was the very law the Mississippian used to appeal his case.

Although most legal scholars, then and now, might conclude that Congress could not pull the legs out from under a case by retroactively nullifying the law upon which it was based, that was undeniably their intent. The 1868 Supreme Court interpreted the repeal-during-litigation tactic as a shot across the bow by one branch of the federal government against another, with the Court being the target. The justices worried that Congress might take even more restrictive action against the Court if they ruled in favor of the newspaperman. Therefore, the judges made no ruling at all on the Mississippi case by claiming the repeal denied them jurisdiction.[43]

After passing the Reconstruction Acts, Congress focused on crafting and adopting a Fourteenth Amendment that would insure that provisions of the acts could not be challenged as unconstitutional. Foremost among them was that federally imposed black suffrage be limited to the former Confederate states. Without such an amendment, ultimately a federal court would likely have ruled that Congress did not have the constitutional power to impose voting qualifications on any state. Since Republicans were doubtful

---

[42] Ludwell Johnson *Division and Reunion*, 228

[43] Albert Castel, *President Johnson*, 183-85

that three-fourths of the states would ratify an amendment that required black suffrage in all the states, the Fourteenth Amendment was worded in a way that would penalize the Southern states for failing to approve black suffrage but have little effect on the Northern states that declined to do so.

Specifically, the amendment stipulated that those states failing to authorize black suffrage would have their congressional representation and electoral votes cut by the same percentage of their population that was black. Since blacks represented forty percent of the population in the former Confederacy and only one percent of the population in the pre-war "free" states of the North, the amendment would have little impact above the Mason-Dixon line but considerable impact below it.

Due to his wide popularity, both the congressional Republicans and President Johnson wanted General Grant as an ally. Although the swing around the circle soured him on Johnson, he recognized that as General-in-Chief of the army he had obligations to the President and his fellow citizens to act in the country's best interests. Thus, when the President decided to suspend Edwin Stanton from office in August 1867, Grant agreed to Johnson's request that he temporarily replace Stanton as secretary of war until Congress reconvened in November 1867.

Grant's status as war secretary was officially termed *ad interim* because of the stipulations in the Tenure Act explained earlier. Specifically, it specified that no President could replace an executive officer—including cabinet members—who had previously met the "advice and consent" of the U. S. Senate during the same administration.

The true object was to keep Secretary Stanton in the cabinet as a Radical Republican mole even though the secretary himself doubted the bill's constitutionality when it was introduced in March. Johnson intended to challenge the act's constitutionality if the Senate rejected his attempt to replace Stanton after Congress reconvened. Like most historians, author Gene Davis concluded that Grant had agreed to

23

Edwin M. Stanton

cooperate with Johnson's *ad interim* appointment: "If it came to a fight with the Senate, he [Grant] would probably hang on. If he [Grant] should change his mind, he would resign and let the President appoint someone else."[44]

But as early as the first cabinet meeting after moving into Stanton's office, Grant tended to side with the Republicans. Contrary to the President's viewpoint, he defended the Reconstruction Acts as constitutional and voiced his reluctance to replace any of the Southern military governors Stanton had installed while the latter held the office. Johnson, nonetheless, instructed Grant to replace Major General Philip Sheridan who was in charge of the military districts of Louisiana and Texas and whom Johnson considered to be a tyrant. Grant objected, but eventually complied.

The odd year 1867 elections favored the Democrats. Although Northerners would support black suffrage in the South, they did not want it in their own states. It was overwhelmingly rejected in all Northern states where it was on the ballot. Democrats made gains in New York and Pennsylvania and the Republican vote margins relative to 1866 narrowed in Ohio, Massachusetts and Maine.[45]

---

44 Brooks Simpson, *The Reconstruction Presidents*, 113; Gene Davis, *High Crimes and Misdemeanors* (New York: William Morrow, 1977), 213; William Hesseltine, *Grant the Politician*, 128

45 William B. Hesselltine, *Grant the Politician*, 95-98

After the elections Johnson perceived that he might be impeached if he refused to restore Stanton should a reconvened Senate demand Stanton's reinstatement. He therefore went to see Grant in order to learn whether the general would obey his orders, instead of the urgings of Congress. According to Navy Secretary Gideon Welles's diary entry for October 10, 1867 "[Grant] said he should expect to obey [the President's] orders; that should he (Grant) change his mind he would advise the President in season, that he might have time to make other arrangements." Basically, Grant was saying that if he resigned he would do so with enough advance notice for Johnson to replace him with someone else who would hold the office so that the Supreme Court—then in session—could rule on whether the Tenure Act was even constitutional.[46]

Grant began to squirm on Friday January 10, 1868 after a Senate committee recommended that the chamber reject Stanton's suspension. On Saturday he told Major General William T. Sherman that he would give up the war office if the Senate refused to authorize Stanton's suspension. Sherman advised him to first inform Johnson. Grant went to the White House and stated his intent. The two men debated the legal status of the situation. Johnson asked Grant to return to continue the discussion on Monday 13 January. Grant agreed that he would.

On Sunday Grant met with General Sherman again and the two agreed that Grant should suggest that Johnson appoint Ohio Governor and former Civil War General Jacob Cox to replace Grant in the war office. Sherman's foster father, who was an elder statesman, wrote a note to the President that Senator Reverdy Johnson carried to the White House on Monday. The note said that the Senate would likely accept the Cox appointment thereby avoiding a constitutional crisis. But it also warned that Cox's appointment had to be announced that very day. Since Andrew Johnson believed that

---

[46] Gideon Welles, *Diary Volume 3* (Boston: Houghton Mifflin, 1911), 234; Albert Castel, *President Johnson*, 150

Grant's pledge to give the President a chance to replace him with a substitute of Johnson's own choosing would be honored, he ignored the note's advice.

That very evening the Senate voted 36-to-6 to refuse Stanton's removal. On Tuesday morning 14 January Grant locked the war office door and turned the key over to an administrator. After returning to his General-in-Chief office he had a messenger carry a letter to the White House stating that he was no longer war secretary. Stanton preemptively reoccupied the war department before Johnson could intervene. [47]

Later that same Tuesday Grant attended a cabinet meeting where Johnson asked whether Grant had agreed to their plan of 10 October. The general affirmed that he did—at the time. He added, however, that he disclosed during their Saturday 11 January discussion that he had changed his mind after learning that he could be fined for disobeying the Tenure Act. Johnson then asked if the two had not agreed to continue the Saturday discussion on Monday. Grant affirmed that he had so agreed.

As an excuse for missing the Monday meeting, however, Grant hesitatingly explained that he had been too busy with military matters. After the general left, Navy Secretary Welles wrote that Grant's "manner . . . was almost abject." Treasury Secretary Hugh McCullough felt that Grant appeared to be drunk. Grant would later claim that when he vacated the war office, he no longer believed he had an agreement with Johnson to either hold the office or give the President time to appoint a replacement before resigning.[48]

Thereafter, each man accused the other of lying. Among the factors favoring Grant's accusation is his insistence that he told Johnson on Saturday 11 January of his intent to vacate the office if

---

[47] Albert Castel, *President Johnson*, 156-58; Brooks Simpson, *Reconstruction Presidents*, 121; Gene Davis, *High Crimes and Misdemeanors*, 221

[48] Albert Castel, *President Johnson*, 160

the Senate voted to reject Stanton's suspension, which it did the following Monday evening.

On Johnson's side of the balance-scale is Grant's admission during the Tuesday 14 January cabinet session that he had agreed to continue Saturday's discussion with the President on Monday and yet failed to do so. Also, weighing on Johnson's side was Grant's failure to tell the President at the White House reception on Monday night that the general would vacate the office the next morning, even though the two men spoke together at the event. Finally, Grant's claim that he "had not expected" that Stanton would promptly reoccupy the office is suspect. Grant had known for at least three months that he was party to a plan to keep Stanton out of the war office until the Supreme Court could decide whether the Tenure Act was legal.[49]

Whether through misunderstanding or deceit, the consequence of the imbroglio would be a first attempt to impeach a United States President. It evolved into a national trauma, which might have been avoided if Johnson and/or Grant had earned their salaries. The stage was finally set for a showdown with Congress on February 21, 1868 when Johnson appointed Adjutant General Lorenzo Thomas as his new *ad interim* war secretary, but—with Grant's encouragement—Stanton refused to yield the office. The face-off did not take long. The House voted on 24 February to impeach Johnson. A week later it formally presented eleven impeachment articles to the Senate for trial. Alleged violation of the Tenure Act was central to the bulk of them.[50]

Massachusetts Representative Benjamin Butler directed the prosecution. He paid spies to search the trash baskets of defense counsel William Evarts's hotel room. Out of the courtroom he

---

[49] Brooks Simpson, *Reconstruction Presidents*, 121; Gideon Welles, *Diary Volume 3*, 234, Albert Castel, *President Johnson*, 160; William Hesseltine, *Grant the Politician*, 103-09

[50] Gene Davis, *High Crimes and Misdemeanors*, 221-3; William Hesseltine, *Grant the Politician*, 113-114

denounced Johnson as the soul of corruption, assassination, cowardice and murder thereby falsely implying that Johnson was involved in Lincoln's assassination.[51]

Since conviction required a two-thirds majority the Radicals guarded every presumed "yea" vote and attempted to seize others. Even though the President Pro Tempore of the Senate would replace Johnson upon a conviction because there was no Vice President, the applicable senator refused to abstain from voting despite his conflict of interest. The Republicans also attempted to add two likely conviction votes before the trial with a surprise move to admit Colorado as a state, but they were unable to gather the required two-thirds majority needed to override Johnson's likely veto of a statehood bill. Even after the trial was underway another prosecution leader, Thaddeus Stevens, made a similar failed effort to admit the senators from the newly formed Republican administration in Arkansas.[52]

The President engaged five good lawyers out of his own pocket. Most notable among them was New York Republican William Evarts who otherwise opposed the President's policies. Although Grant lobbied certain senators to vote against Johnson, the President survived the impeachment attempt. On 16 May Johnson was acquitted on a 35-to-19 affirmative vote, which was one short of the necessary two-thirds majority. Radical Republicans manipulatively adjourned the Senate for ten days in hopes of persuading at least one acquittal vote to switch sides, but they failed. Johnson survived a second, and last, conviction attempt on 26 May, again by a single vote.[53]

---

[51] Gene Davis, *High Crimes and Misdemeanors*, 237, 243-4, 258, 268

[52] Gene Davis, *High Crimes and Misdemeanors*, 244, 265; Robert Selph Henry, *The Story of Reconstruction* (Indianapolis, In.: Bobbs-Merrill, 1938), 304

[53] Robert Selph Henry, *The Story of Reconstruction*, 308; William Hesseltine *Grant the Politician*, 116; Joseph Rose, *Grant Under Fire*, 560

Grant's break with Johnson thrust the general into the forefront of likely Republican presidential candidates for the 1868 election by convincing the Radicals that he was on their side. While Grant was in Washington the Republican convention in Chicago gave him the nomination on 20 May, six days before Johnson survived the second impeachment vote. Indiana's Schuyler Colfax, who was Speaker of the House, became his running mate.

Although Grant was certain to be a popular candidate, the Party was anxious to get the Fourteenth Amendment ratified so that the resulting puppet governments in the Southern states could be relied upon to throw their votes behind him. When impeachment proceedings started in late February, the Fourteenth Amendment still needed to be ratified in at least six more states. By the process of elimination, at least several would have to be former slave states. All the former Confederate states, except Tennessee, had yet to ratify it. As a result, Congress adopted an act in March 1868 that made it easier for Republican minorities in the former Confederate states to ratify the amendment by obtaining a simple majority of the votes cast as opposed to a majority of registered voters.

On 3 April Arkansas became the first Southern state to ratify the Fourteenth Amendment under the new act. Six more Southern states followed suit by the end of July, which was the month when Secretary of State Seward declared the amendment ratified.[54]

The Republicans reasoned correctly about the need for Southern black votes. Despite his popularity, Grant received only a minority of the white popular vote. He picked up forty-one electoral votes from former Confederate states as compared to only sixteen for his Democratic opponent, Horatio Seymour. Although Grant won a lopsided Electoral College victory, the national popular vote was much closer with 3.0 million for Grant and 2.7 million for Seymour. Grant's popular total included about 450,000 black votes as

---

[54] Robert Selph Henry, *The Story of Reconstruction*, 310-2

compared to only 50,000 for Seymour. The general's African American popular votes were overwhelmingly from the South.[55]

Grant finished the Civil War at the top of his military profession. Four years later the forty-seven-year-old was at the head of his country in the White House. Success appeared to be becoming the Grant family's new normal station in life.

---

[55] J. G. Randall and David Donald *The Civil War and Reconstruction*, 640-1

CHAPTER 3: CORRUPTION CULTURE

SINCE MUCH OF GRANT'S PRESIDENCY is tainted by scandal, fairness requires a discussion of how a culture of corruption progressively infected the Republican Party even before he moved into the White House. To be sure, Democrats of the era were also prone to corruption, as prominently exemplified by New York's Tammany Hall. Nonetheless, bribe payers seeking federal favors were more likely to deal with Republicans because the infant GOP controlled all three branches of the federal government. Washington's low ethical standards had a pernicious impact on the morality of the entire country. They perhaps most conspicuously affected the carpetbag regimes of the Southern states, which were the stepchildren of the national Republican Party.

The culture of dishonesty started during the Civil War when Lincoln was President. The enormous expenditures required to supply the victorious Union military and the profits available via inter-belligerent cotton trade were tempting ways for the politically well-connected to profit. Such practices were rife in Grant's district prior to his first major victory at Fort Donelson in February 1862. Thereafter, his higher ascending public profile led him to sometimes condemn such activities although they continued to varying degrees until the end of the war. President Lincoln's first attorney general, Edward Bates, wrote, "The demoralizing effect of this civil war is plainly visible in every department of life. The abuse of official powers and the thirst for dishonest gain are now so common that they cease to shock."[56]

During the war from 1861 to 1865, annual federal spending increased over 1600% from $80 million to more than $1.3 billion. By exploiting the army's rush to get needed supplies, unscrupulous manufacturers were able to sell the federal government poor quality uniforms, guns that didn't shoot, and ill-fitting shoes, among other faulty and overpriced items. Similarly, as cotton prices increased from a low of $0.10 a pound prior to the war to a peak of almost $1.90 before the fighting stopped, adroit Northern speculators made fortunes buying cotton at below-market prices from the enemy and selling it at full price on the New York and London exchanges.[57]

Thus, historian C. Vann Woodward concluded that the war "combined heroism with shabby expedience and laid a terrible toll upon public morals as well as upon lives. For some it was the road to sudden and unscrupulously gained riches and for many the path from deserved obscurity to high office and power. It was the heyday of the claim agent, the speculator, the subsidy-seeker, the government contractor, and the all-purpose crook. The war left this priceless crew with power and influence, and they turned from military to other fields—politics among them."[58]

In his analysis of Civil War profiteering historian Ron Soodalter concluded, "government representatives awarded contracts based not on the best product, or the fairest price, but on the highest bribe . . . It would be easy to excuse a little corruption, or even a lot, if the result was high-quality equipment. But much of the contactors' profit came from cutting corners." From the beginning of the war, uniform and shoe suppliers provided some of the most egregious examples. Their clothing gave birth to the slang term "shoddy," a superficially acceptable material that would disintegrate like Papier-mâché the

---

[56] Jeffrey R. Hummel, *Emancipating Slaves, Enslaving Free Men* (Chicago: Open Court, 1996), 314; Joseph Rose *Grant Under Fire*, 58-62

[57] Philip Leigh, *Trading With the Enemy* (Yardley, Pa.: Westholme Publishing, 2013), 13, 141

[58] C. Vann Woodward, "The Lowest Ebb" *American Heritage Vol. 8, No. 3* (April, 1957) Available: http://bit.ly/2AttHDS [Retrieved: November 30, 2017]

first time it got wet. In fact, shoddy cloth was assembled much like Papier-mâché.

Only two weeks after the outbreak of the war, Brooks Brothers won a contract to supply 12,000 uniforms and filled orders for three times that number during the first eight months of the war. Many of the uniforms were so hurriedly manufactured that they had no buttons or buttonholes. Due to a wool shortage, "Brooks Brothers glued together shredded, often decaying rags, pressed them into a semblance of cloth, and sewed the pieces into cloth" that would fall apart in the first rain. Similarly, some suppliers provided shoes that were composed of glued-together wood chips that shredded after less than an hour of marching.

Wool mills sprang up in the North like mushrooms after a summer rain. While many operated conscientiously, they typically enjoyed enviable profit margins. Federal procurement attempts to import less costly wool from Europe instantly prompted domestic producers to demand high protective tariffs, which virtually assured continued prosperity in the domestic sector.

From Fort Sumter to Appomattox such practices enabled many suppliers to become millionaires. Before the war New York had only a few dozen millionaires, but by the end they numbered in the hundreds. Eighteen months before Lee's surrender, the *New York Herald* characterized many of them as "Shoddy Aristocrats." One example was George Opdyke who was elected New York's mayor in 1862 on the Republican ticket. Not only was he the city's largest clothing manufacturer, he also approved the shoddy Brooks Brothers shipments under his authority as an official inspector. His vigorous support for Lincoln and the war provided the political cover that permitted his unsavory conduct to escape reprimand.[59]

The poor quality of early military supply shipments prompted Congress to form its Select Committee on Government Contracts less than three months after the war started. During the rest of the war it produced over three thousand pages of findings and disclosed

---

[59] Ron Soodalter, *New York Times Opinionator: Disunion* "The Union's 'Shoddy' Aristocracy" (May 9, 2011) Available: http://nyti.ms/2ANwOa8 [Accessed: December 4, 2017]

numerous frauds. Since it was composed of political moderates, however, the steadily strengthening Radical wing of the Republican Party was suspicious of its motives and often opposed its work.

Early in the war, for example, the committee discovered extensive fraud in the department of Major General John C. Fremont in St. Louis, including General Grant's district at Cairo. Fremont was the Party's first presidential candidate in 1856. A year before Lincoln's preliminary Emancipation Proclamation in September 1862, General Fremont issued a directive in an attempt to free Missouri's slaves. Lincoln overruled it because he felt it could drive Missouri into the Confederacy at the time.

John C. Fremont

Simon Stevens, who was a protégé of Radical Republican Congressman Thaddeus Stevens, also objected to the committee after it began investigating a fraud that became known as the Hall Carbine Affair. Although Hall Carbines were obsolete, an arms merchant named Eastman agreed to buy 5,000 of them from the army's Ordnance Bureau at $3.50 each. After Eastman rifled the barrels at a cost of $0.75 he sold them to Simon Stevens for $12.50. Stevens had previously arranged to resell them to General Fremont for $22.00. A youthful J. P. Morgan financed the original $20,000 required to purchase and refurbish the arms. Simon Stevens complained to anyone who would listen that the committee had "no honest purpose to know the truth" except to go "scandal hunting."[60]

---

[60] Mark Greenbaum, *New York Times Opinionator: Disunion* "The Civil War's War on Fraud" (March 7, 2013) Available: http://nyti.ms/2zPQplW [Accessed: December 4, 2017]; Matthew Josephson, *The Robber Barons*, (San Diego, Ca.: Harcourt Brace & Co., 1962), 61- 62; Ron Chernow, *The House of Morgan* (New York: Grove Press, 2001), 22

After the war ended, no single factor shaped America's economy more than the railroad industry. When Lee's Confederate army surrendered the country had 35,000 miles of track but by 1900 the total was almost 200,000, which represented about forty percent of the world's total mileage. Among the catalysts that drove the expansion, none were more important than the federal subsidies provided by the Pacific Railroad Acts passed during the Civil War.[61]

After the 1849 gold rush, talk of an independent California Republic gained traction out west. Since most Americans wanted to maintain a single continental United States, both the Republican and Democratic Parties favored a transcontinental railroad, which would help economically tie California to the eastern part of the country. But the Parties differed over two factors. First, as a Northern sectional Party the Republicans wanted the eastern terminal in the upper Mississippi Valley. In contrast, the Democrats were divided. Their Southern wing desired the eastern terminus to be in the lower Mississippi Valley. Second, Republicans were generally more willing to provide land grants and other federal subsidies to finance construction of the railroad.

The temporary sectional split caused by the Civil War enabled Lincoln and a truncated Republican-dominated Congress to act. Lincoln signed the First Pacific Railway Act on July 1, 1862. It provided subsidies to the Central Pacific (CP) and the Union Pacific (UP) railroads, which were basically paper companies at the time. Their chief occupation for years thereafter would be to complete construction.

Organized in Sacramento, California, the Central Pacific was responsible for building a line eastward over the Sierra Nevada Mountains into Nevada. The Union Pacific was to simultaneously build a road from Omaha, Nebraska westward. The two would either connect at an undetermined point in between, or a third railroad would be organized to join them.[62]

---

[61] Walter Webb, *Divided We Stand* (New York: Farrar & Reinhart, 1937), 11
[62] H. W. Brands, *American Colossus* (New York: Anchor Books, 2010), 46-9

The Union Pacific's initial stock capitalization hinted at the project's enormous size. The company was authorized to issue a hundred thousand shares with a par value of $1,000 each. Thus, stock capitalization alone (excluding debt) could total as much as $100 million. As a point of reference, the entire federal budget in fiscal 1861 was only $80 million. The speculative nature of the venture is underscored by the fact that only forty-five shares were sold in 1861. Furthermore, only the five purchased by Mormon Church leader Brigham Young were paid in full. The other buyers subscribed to the remaining forty shares by initially paying only ten percent up-front with the balance to be paid through future assessments.[63]

In addition to the Union Pacific's large stock capitalization, the transcontinental railroads were granted generous federal subsidies. Aside from a 400-foot right of way along its route each railroad was to be given land grants in a checkerboard pattern totaling five square miles (6,400 acres) for each mile of track completed. The checkerboard design was intended to ensure that the applicable public lands gained value in direct proportion to the railroad properties granted along the track.

To visualize the pattern, imagine a folding checkerboard with the crease down the middle representing the path of the track. The checkerboard is composed of alternating red and black squares extending for ten miles on each side of the track. The railroad gets the red squares whereas the black squares remain public lands. Ultimately the UP received lands equal to the total area of the combined states of New Jersey and New Hampshire while the CP got acreage that totaled slightly more than the area of the state of Maryland.

Additionally, each company received financial aid in the form of government bonds, which could be resold to investors. The CP and UP were expected to repay the bonds by selling the red square portions of the checkerboard land grants, or through their future

---

[63] Philip Leigh *Trading With the Enemy* (Yardley, Pa.: Westholme, 2013), 142; Stephen Ambrose *Nothing Like It In The World* (New York: Touchstone, 2000), 80, 86

operating revenues after the lines were completed and hauling traffic. Nonetheless, the federal government guaranteed both the principal and interest of the bonds.

The amount of government bonds granted depended upon the miles of track completed in one of three terrain categories. The rate was $16,000 per mile on flat land, $32,000 per mile in the high plains and $48,000 per mile in the mountains. The sums eventually totaled about $65 million. The railroads were also given land for sidings and stations. During construction they were also allowed to use whatever was needed in the way of timber or stone.[64]

Despite its generous appropriations, the '62 Act was merely the industry's opening bid for subsidies. Two years later the Second Pacific Railroad Act increased the largess. Land grants were doubled to 12,800 acres per mile and included the mineral rights, which had previously been excluded. The companies were also given the right to issue first mortgage bonds of their own, which enjoyed superior creditor status over the government bonds. Thus, if either the UP or CP went bankrupt, first mortgage bondholders would be repaid by the applicable railroad before it had to repay the holders of the government-guaranteed bonds.

The Pacific Railroad Acts triggered three lasting unintended consequences.

First, the large subsidies encouraged a culture of bribery and fraud. As the second bill was under consideration one Union Pacific lobbyist distributed $250,000 in bonds among influence peddlers. For example, twenty thousand dollars went to Charles Sherman for "professional services." He was the eldest brother of Union Major General William T. Sherman and Ohio Senator John Sherman. The New York lawyer who wrote the bill also got $20,000 in bonds. One

---

[64] Richard White, *The Republic for Which it Stands*, (Oxford: Oxford University Press, 2017) 118-20; Stephen Ambrose, *Nothing Like It In The World*, 80-1; Robert S. Henry, "The Railroad Land Grant Legend in American History Texts" *The Mississippi Valley Historical Review* Vol. 32 No. 2, (Sep. 1945), 182-3; "Railroads: Federal Land Grants" *Gale Encyclopedia of U.S. Economic History* 2000. *Encyclopedia.com*. (January 19, 2016) http://www.encyclopedia.com/doc/1G2-3406400787.html

of the UP's New York investors visited Omaha, charging $4,000 for "expenses and services."[65]

Second, the Railroad Acts prompted an increasing tendency toward government subsidization of politically connected industries. Capitalists outside the railroad sector demanded that they also be invited to The Great Barbecue. Radical Republican Congressman Thaddeus Stevens insisted that the acts require that all of the rails and other iron works of the CP and UP be "of American manufacture of the best quality"— meaning the highest price. Aside from being a persistent advocate for high tariffs, Congressman Stevens owned a Pennsylvania iron foundry.[66]

Third, the entire railroad industry was soon obsessed with getting subsidies from all levels of government. Other transcontinental roads that were hardly beyond the planning stages would also be granted federal aid to build their lines. Examples include the Northern Pacific, the Santa Fe and the Southern Pacific. The Northern Pacific alone was ultimately granted forty-four million acres, which approximates an area the size of the state of Missouri.[67]

Although the CP and the UP would link the eastern and western parts of the country, the railroads would need traffic to generate revenues and would therefore be unprofitable during the early years of operation until population density increased. Thus, privileged shareholders arranged matters so that they could profit during the construction phase. Consequently, the leading shareholders of each railroad set up construction companies to build the tracks. If the railroads could not be immediately profitable, the linked construction contractors could be because they were able to charge

---

[65] Stephen Ambrose, *Nothing Like It In The World*, 95-6; Walter R. Borneman, *Rival Rails* (New York: Random House, 2010), Kindle Location 913; Louis Hacker and Benjamin Kendrick, *The United States Since 1865* (New York: Appleton-Century-Crofts, 1949), 113

[66] Stephen Ambrose, *Nothing Like It In The World*, 78; Kenneth Stampp, *The Era of Reconstruction*, 106; Ludwell Johnson, *Division and Reunion*, 110

[67] Samuel Morison and Henry Commager, *The Growth of the American Republic: Volume Two*, Fourth Edition (New York: Oxford Press, 1950), 112

their affiliated railroads whatever fees were required in order to turn a profit.

Charles Crocker, Mark Hopkins, Leland Stanford, and Collis Huntington (the Big Four) were the sole owners of the Central Pacific and its construction arm, the Contract & Finance Company. The railroad paid about $79 million in cash, bonds, and stock to Contract & Finance. Experts estimate that reasonable construction costs should have totaled about $40 million thereby implying that the excess $39 million lined the pockets of

Collis Huntington

the Big Four. When an 1873 congressional investigating committee asked to see the Contract & Finance Company records, Huntington explained that Hopkins had destroyed them because the railroad's construction phase had ended four years previously.[68]

The Union Pacific's construction arm became infamous because it involved many more shareholders, including leading politicians. Early UP shareholder George Train had been assigned the job of persuading new investors to buy stock. He was largely unsuccessful until he stumbled upon the construction company concept. The Boston-based Train had earlier founded a clipper ship line, which yielded overseas business acquaintances. He learned of two French brothers that had been successful in similar circumstances with construction companies named Crédit Mobilier and Crédit Foncier.

In order to attract investors into a UP construction company, Train realized the affiliate must provide limited liability. He located such a corporation in Pennsylvania that was comparatively inactive

---

[68] Walter Borneman, *Iron Horse* (Boston, Little Brown & Co. 2014), 98; Matthew Josephson, *The Robber Barons*, 87

and bought it for a moderate sum. He changed its name to Crédit Mobilier of America.

Like the CP's Contract's & Finance Company, Crédit Mobilier was certain to be immediately profitable. By one estimate it ultimately earned a profit of $40 million, nearly identical to the estimated $39 million of the Big Four's Contract & Finance Company noted above. Thus, bargain-priced sales of the Crédit Mobilier shares would essentially become donations of a stream of reliable dividends to the buyers over the period of years that the UP remained under construction. Consequently, it was not long before shares of Crédit Mobilier were sold at below-market prices to key politicians. The distributor was Republican Massachusetts Congressman Oakes Ames.

Oakes Ames

Oakes, and his brother Oliver, had earned a fortune supplying shovels and similar instruments during the California Gold Rush and the Civil War. They also furnished shovels for railroad construction, which led them to become involved with the Union Pacific. Oakes started distributing shares of Crédit Mobilier to influential politicians in 1867 because, "We want more friends in this Congress. There is no difficulty getting men to look after their own property."[69]

Five years later a newspaper blew his cover during President Ulysses Grant's 1872 re-election campaign. The anti-Grant paper discovered a partial list of recipients disclosed in testimony involving a Crédit Mobilier lawsuit. The list

---

[69] Matthew Josephson, *The Robber Barons,* 92-3; Edward Martin, *A Complete and Graphic Account of the Credit Mobilier Investigations: Chapter 7* (New York: Continental and National Publishing Companies, 1873) Available: http://bit.ly/2nzA57q [Accessed: December 6, 2017]

included Grant's previous Vice President, Schuyler Colfax, his current running mate, Henry Wilson and his former Treasury Secretary, George Boutwell. Other senators and congressmen on the list, or that were soon disclosed, included John Logan, Roscoe Conkling, Henry Dawes, James Brooks, James Harlan, Glenni Scofield, William "Pig Iron" Kelley, John Bingham, James Patterson, and William Allison, as well as future President James Garfield and sitting Speaker of the House James G. Blaine. All but Brooks were Republicans. None were Southerners. Brooks, however, was the federal government's representative on the UP's board of directors. As shall be explained in chapter seven the revelations would cause a loss of public confidence in the federal government and big business, which would trigger an economic collapse.[70]

---

[70] Matthew Josephson, *The Robber Barons*, 92-3; Edward Martin, *A Complete and Graphic Account of the Credit Mobilier Investigations: Chapter 7* Available: http://bit.ly/2nzA57q [Accessed: December 6, 2017]

Chapter 4: Money and Imperialism

ALTHOUGH MOST MODERN biographies attribute the corruption in Grant's Administration to venal advisors who took advantage of the President's innocent naivety, they tend to ignore early examples of Grant's own dubious conduct that set low ethical standards for others in his Administration to follow.

One incident was the sale of his "I" Street residence in Washington shortly before he moved into the White House on the March 4, 1869 inauguration day. He had purchased the four-story structure only three years earlier for $30,000 with part of a $100,000 purse raised on subscription for him by wealthy New Yorkers arranged by former General Daniel Butterfield. His wife, however, was angry about the sale because she anticipated the home would be their permanent residence after Grant's presidency ended. She also seemed to be annoyed at the $40,000 sales price.

In response, at Grant's urging, Butterfield and treasury secretary designee Alexander Stewart led a subscription to buy the furnished house for General William T. Sherman at a price of $65,000. Once the money was raised, Grant repudiated his written agreement with the first buyer, pocketed the $35,000 profit, and appointed Butterfield as an assistant treasurer in the department's vital New York City office where he would soon become involved in the Administration's first major scandal. Although Grant returned his $1,000 deposit, the first buyer of the home felt cheated and threaten to embarrass the President with a breach of contract suit during Grant's second election campaign in 1872.

Grant set a second bad example of taking a genteel form of bribery when he accepted a vacation home as a gift only a few months after becoming President. During his first six months in office he spent at least two months on vacation. One of his favorite spots was the seaside village of Long Branch, New Jersey where seven donors bought him a $35,000 "cottage" with twenty-seven rooms.

One of the donors owned a Philadelphia newspaper and another owned the Pullman Company, which manufactured railroad cars. Grant would later appoint a third donor, Thomas Murphy, to the notoriously lucrative and corrupt post of New York's customs collector. Even when he was in his White House office he worked only an estimated four hours daily. He was on vacation when the Administration's first big scandal was secretly hatched, and on another vacation when it publicly climaxed.[71]

IIe even approached his inauguration with a petty resentment. A day earlier the *New York Times* reported that Andrew Johnson had sent a courteous note to Grant proposing that they ride to the Capitol together. When the reporter asked Grant about the note, the President-elect said he never received it. Despite being thus told of the note he nevertheless made no effort to contact Johnson. As a result, Johnson invited several cabinet members to the White House on the morning of the inauguration to finish administrative matters instead of going to Grant's ceremony. When Grant's carriage unexpectedly stopped at the White House he was told that Johnson was too busy to get away.[72]

About two weeks after assuming office, President Grant signed the first bill Congress sent him, which became the Public Credit Act. His endorsement put him on the side of conservative monetary interests, which many residents in his home states of Ohio, Illinois and Missouri opposed. Specifically, the act pledged to redeem the Civil War public debt in gold although nearly all holders of such bonds

---

[71] William McFeely, *Grant*, 303; Joseph Rose, *Grant Under Fire*, 570-71; William Hesseltine, *Grant the Politician*, 142; Ronald White, *American Ulysses*, Kindle Location 9544-49
[72] William McFeely, *Grant*, 286

(including Grant) purchased them with paper currency that traded at a fluctuating discount to gold.[73]

Since there was not enough gold to support the federal spending required to finance the war, the government went into deficit spending, thereby increasing the national debt from $65 million to $2.7 billion between 1861 and 1865. It also issued a new fiat paper currency, termed greenbacks, which could not be redeemed for gold at face value. Nonetheless, the greenbacks were otherwise legal tender.

Because gold was required to pay for imports and customs duties New Yorkers organized an exchange where greenback holders could purchase gold at fluctuating prices, but always below parity to gold. During the war, greenbacks traded as low as $0.33 in relation to each gold dollar. As a result, bondholders overwhelmingly used them to buy their bonds. Even though greenbacks had advanced to $0.75 a few months after the Public Credit Act, redeeming war bonds at face value in gold was still a significant windfall to Northern bondholders. In contrast, it was a burden to the taxpayers who had to earn more than a dollar in greenbacks to pay for each dollar of bonds thus redeemed.

But the Public Credit Act also adversely impacted the economies of the Western and Southern states by a collateral effect. Specifically, it encouraged the treasury to retire greenbacks from circulation in order to reduce the amount of discounted currency. This had comparatively little impact in the North and East where a surplus of currency was banked and circulated. But the South, and to a lesser extent the West, suffered chronic currency shortages.

As a result, Westerners and Southerners wanted the government to increase the supply of greenbacks. Their stance became known as

---

[73] To be accurate, the act required that the public debt be redeemed in specie, which could be either gold or silver coins. In March 1869, however, the bullion value of silver was greater than its monetary value. Thus, as a pragmatic matter, the bonds would be redeemed in gold, unless the market value of silver dropped below its monetary value.

an inflationary monetary policy. In contrast, Northerners and Easterners urged a deflationary program. They euphemistically termed their position as a "sound money" policy because it would eventually make greenbacks "as good as a gold." The conflicting monetary policies would remain a political hot potato until about 1900.

Grant was personally familiar with the hardships that the tenets of the "sound money" could impose. As a commander early in the Civil War he complained in a letter to his congressman that banks in cash-strapped areas always discounted his drafts. In modern terms, the general could not "cash a check" at face value. Area banks always gave him a smaller amount of cash in exchange for his checks. The discount tended to be directly proportional to the intensity of the applicable region's cash shortage. Despite such experiences, President Grant sided with the moneyed interests of the Northeast where cash shortages were uncommon. It is difficult to avoid concluding that the residential, and other, gifts he received from prominent men in the banking centers may have influenced his choice of monetary policy.[74]

Grant's initial cabinet nominees are listed in Table 1 below. The first three were announced before he took office, while the last four were publicly identified when he sent their names to the Senate for advice and consent. Experienced politicians, particularly in the Senate, were shocked that the new President had not consulted them prior to making his choices. Even some of the nominees, such as Borie and Cox, were surprised to learn that they had been selected.

---

[74] William McFeely, *Grant*, 288; H. W. Brands *Greenback Planet* (Austin: University of Texas Press, 2011), 13-4; Irwin Unger *The Greenback Era* (Princeton, N. J.: Princeton University Press, 1964), 152; Walter Nugent *Money and American Society: 1865-1880* (New York: The Free Press, 1968), 168; Henry Adams, *Historical Essays*, "The New York Gold Conspiracy" (New York: C. Scribner's & Sons, 1891), 319

Table 1
President Ulysses S. Grant
Initial Cabinet Member Nominations
March 1869

Name	State	Appointment Post
Alexander Stewart	New York	Secretary of the Treasury
Elihu Washburne	Illinois	Secretary of State
John Rawlins	Illinois	Secretary of War
E. Rockwood Hoar	Massachusetts	Attorney General
General Jacob Cox	Ohio	Secretary of the Interior
J. A. J. Creswell	Maryland	Posmaster General
Adolph Borie	Pennsylvania	Secretary of the Navy

It became apparent in a matter of days that Stewart could not be confirmed because an eighteenth-century law prohibited anyone "concerned . . . in trade or commerce" from being treasury secretary. Stewart owned the country's largest retail business and was an importer. As noted earlier, he had also been a major contributor to financial aid subscriptions for General Grant. By mid-March Grant withdrew Stewart's name and substituted Massachusetts's George Boutwell. Since Boutwell was a financial conservative, his nomination prompted a rise in the market price of federal war bonds.

Most everyone was baffled by the inexperienced Elihu Washburne's nomination of secretary of state. Apparently, Grant only intended that he hold the post temporarily in order to gain a credential that might justify giving Washburne a diplomatic spot in Paris. After Washburne promptly resigned, Grant accepted the First Lady's suggestion that he nominate former New York Senator Hamilton Fish to the post because she was friendly with Fish's wife. Ebenezer Hoar became Grant's first attorney general. Four more would follow him including one who would resign under suspicion of corruption. Cox would be one of three interior secretaries, and one of his successors would resign under clouds of bribery.

John Rawlins had been the general's key military aide during the Civil War. He is commonly credited with helping Grant manage alcoholism. But Rawlins suffered from tuberculosis and would only hold the post six months before dying. He would, however, become promptly involved in attempts to overthrow Spanish rule of Cuba. His successor would resign to avoid impeachment for accepting bribes. Postmaster General Creswell would last for one-and-a-half of Grant's two presidential terms. After only three months on the job, Navy Secretary Borie, a Philadelphia businessman, resigned

War Secretary John Rawlins

unexpectedly. Grant replaced him the same day with George Robeson who would later be accused of corruption, partly by taking kickbacks from a Philadelphia supplier of provender to the Navy.

As personal White House aides, Grant drew mostly from earlier military friendships. Generals Horace Porter, Cyrus Comstock, and Orville Babcock were officially placed on the staff of William T. Sherman who was the new General-in-Chief. But Sherman cooperatively assigned the men to the White House. Adam Badeau got a room in the mansion where his primary job was to finish a Grant hagiography. The President's West Point roommate and brother in law, Frederick T. Dent, became an aide-de-camp to perform ceremonial duties. Finally, Grant appointed a son of the famous, but deceased, Stephen A. Douglas as an assistant personal secretary.[75]

Babcock was especially influential. He was one of only a few men with daily access to President Grant. His office was in a second-floor room of the White House that led to Grant's private office. He opened and answered most of the President's mail. His office location enabled Babcock to be a gatekeeper to most anyone wanting to visit Grant. Historian Allan Nevins averred that Babcock had more influence on Grant than most cabinet members.[76] Another historian, C. Vann Woodward, added that Babcock:

> . . . was constantly at his [Grant's] side for eight years . . . A subtle and unscrupulous Iago, Babcock shrewdly implanted suspicions of his betters in the President's mind, plotted their downfall, and sought to replace them with pliant tools of his own. He succeeded in these tactics repeatedly and thereby gained indirect control of whole departments of the government. Once a prejudice or a plan was firmly implanted in Grant's mind, he would cling to it with all the tenacity that had toppled the strongholds of the Confederacy. Babcock was at once the leader of the political gangsters and the stumbling block in the way of the talent and ability that might have saved the President. Grant's unshakable confidence in his betrayer was pathetic and all but incredible.[77]

Even as early as his presidential campaign only months after Johnson avoided impeachment for violating the Tenure Act, candidate Grant urged that the act be repealed. While he felt that it

---

[75] William Hesseltine, *Grant the Politician*, 139-40, 145-49

[76] Ralph Kirshner, *The Class of 1861: Custer, Ames, and Their Classmates After West Point* (Carbondale: Southern Illinois University, 1999), 133

[77] C. Vann Woodward *American Heritage* "The Lowest Ebb" Volume 8, Number 3 (April, 1957) Available: http://bit.ly/2ydpIdA [Accessed: October 11, 2017]

was okay to shackle Johnson with the act's restrictions, he had no tolerance for its limitations when applied to his own presidency. Thus, when forced as a candidate to take a non-partisan viewpoint, he had to admit that the act took too much power away from the President's office. Since the Senate had used the law as an excuse for its failed effort to remove former President Andrew Johnson, the chamber was too embarrassed to abolish it. Instead they modified it enough to satisfy the new President. He would be permitted to remove appointed officeholders and replace them with nominees that the Senate would be asked to approve. Soon after the act was altered Grant sent hundreds of nominations to replace Johnson appointees in various offices across the country, thereby immediately endorsing the political spoils system.[78]

The role that money would play in Grant's presidency was first highlighted six months after he took office with the collapse of the gold market in September 1869. It resulted from an attempt to corner the gold market that began three months earlier in June when President Grant and his wife took a holiday trip to New York City to visit his sister and her husband, Abel Corbin. Corbin, it will be recalled, had earlier sold Grant the "I Street" home in Washington. This time Corbin introduced Grant to Jay "The Mephistopheles of Wall Street" Gould, who together with Jim Fisk controlled the Erie Railroad. Together with the New York Central, the Erie was one of two trunk lines between New York and Chicago. Thus, began a series of conversations involving Gould, Fisk, Grant, and Corbin superficially focused on boosting the economy and helping the western farmer. In reality it concentrated on lining the pockets of Gould, Fisk and their cooperating syndicate members.

Gould's plan had a core of merit, if not corrupted for personal gain. He argued, correctly, that the vast majority of domestic transactions were unaffected by the price of gold in terms of greenbacks. Since greenbacks were legal tender they were widely accepted at face value

---

[78] William Hesseltine, *Grant the Politician*, 152, 155

among Americans transacting commerce with one another. Except in selected port cities where goods were imported, greenbacks had driven specie (gold and silver coins) out of circulation. Even in port cities, greenbacks were the major form of currency.

Conversely, international buyers purchased—imported into their countries—American goods by paying with specie. Therefore, the greenback-to-gold exchange ratio was inconsequential to overseas buyers *per se.* Put another way, the price of grain in London was immune to the gold-to-greenback ratio in New York. Therefore, Gould reasoned, manipulation of the gold-to-greenback exchange rate might offer an opportunity to help the economy and the western farmer. Here's how it could work.

When he proposed the scheme, gold dollars traded at a value of about 130% of greenbacks. Therefore, if he could induce gold to rise to 145% each shipload of grain sold in London would net American farmers about 12% (145/130) more in greenbacks, even though the amount of gold Londoners would use to purchase the shipload would not change.

Gould explained that he had enough money to execute his plan as long as the U. S. Treasury did not enter the New York gold market as a seller. He would simply buy gold on the exchange until it reached 145%. Since only about $20 million in gold was normally available to trade on the exchange, only sales from the $100 million treasury reserve could disrupt Gould's intentions.

In a partial "what-I-get-out-of-it" confession, Gould admitted that the plan would increase freight traffic for the Erie Railroad as grain was shipped from western states to the port of New York. He said nothing, however, about the capital gains he'd make as his gold holdings increased in price. It is likely he also realized that there was a good chance the premium would rise well above 145% as speculators began to comprehend that Gould had purchased all of the available market supply in a classic corner operation. Gould originally discussed the plan with Grant on 15 June when he was invited to meet the President at the Corbin household. Fisk joined

Financier Jay Gould

Gould and Grant in a second discussion over dinner aboard a Fisk-owned Long Island Sound steamer the following evening.

Grant would later tell a newspaper reporter, "I don't know but I should have felt insulted by such a proposal had it come from any other but a person like Fisk. But coming from a man so destitute of moral character, I didn't think it worth noticing." The remark dismayed historian Alan Nevins who wrote, "This must have left readers breathless. Why should the President of the United States associate with a man destitute of moral character? Why, above all, accept favors from him?"

Although Fisk concluded from the conversation that Grant would not cooperate, Gould remained unconvinced. Together with Corbin the pair successfully advised Grant to appoint Major General Daniel Butterfield to head the New York sub-treasury office on 1 July where he could provide the conspirators with advance warning should Treasury Secretary George Boutwell send orders from Washington to sell gold. Grant made another visit to Corbin's house on 3 August and dined there on 9 August with Secretary of State Fish. He visited again on 2 September when he wrote a letter to Boutwell explaining that it was "undesirable to force down the price of gold."[79]

Gould had been buying gold since 20 August with little effect on the market price, but Grant's letter to Boutwell implied the market would soon do Gould's bidding since the treasury would not be a

---

[79] Henry Adams, *Historical Essays*, "The Gold Conspiracy", 334, 338, 340-41, 343; William Hesseltine, *Grant the Politician*, 166; William McFeely, *Grant*, 322-23

seller. Nonetheless, since Jay Gould understood he was playing for big stakes he sought every possible advantage. Thus, using his own money he purchased $1.5 million in gold for the account of Abel Corbin. He intended to sell the contract later at a higher price, letting Corbin keep the profit while allocating the original $1.5 million back to his own account.

Next Gould started buying gold aggressively on 3 September. But on 7 September a member in his original conspiracy syndicate abandoned the operation and sold his holdings at 138, putting pressure on the price. Gould responded by purchasing $1.5 million in gold for the account of Daniel Butterfield. That gave the New York sub-treasury officer a powerful incentive to warn Gould of any signs that Washington was on the verge of selling gold. Gould also offered a $500,000 contract to White House staff member Horace Porter who claimed he declined it. Seven years later, however, an investigation into presidential staff member Orville Babcock indicated that Babcock also had a gold contract but lost money when he sold it. Contrary to his earlier denial, evidence from the same investigation suggested that Porter also held gold contracts during the corner attempt.

By 14 September Gould concluded it was necessary to inform Fisk of the scheme and admit him into the pool because Fisk's resources could finance enough gold purchases to lift the market price. According to historian Hesseltine, "Fisk, went to Corbin, who whisperingly assured him that Mrs. Grant was in on the scheme. Gould had purchased gold for her at 131 and sold it at 137. Corbin himself had about $2 million in the market. Five hundred thousand of that was Mrs. Grant's and a like amount belonged to General Porter. Gould confirmed that he had recently given Corbin a check for $25,000 and Corbin asserted that he had sent the money to Washington." Basically, Fisk was led to believe that some of the gold contracts Corbin held in his name were really for the benefit of Julia Grant and Horace Porter.[80]

Gould needed Fisk's buying power to carry out the scheme because short sellers had artificially increased the market supply significantly by offering "phantom" gold on the market, which is a characteristic consequence of excessive short selling. Fisk started buying on 15 September. By 22 September gold reached a price of 141. Meanwhile, on 12 September Grant departed on a private railcar owned by Gould for another vacation, this time in western Pennsylvania. Before leaving he wrote additional instructions to Boutwell directing that the secretary make no change in gold sales policy beyond recurring debt-reduction sinking fund requirements "until the present struggle [between bulls and bears] is over." A traveling companion on Grant's trip also noted that the President told him that he had instructed Boutwell "to beware of Wall Street and sell no gold" without Grant's approval.[81]

After Grant arrived at his Pennsylvania vacation spot, Corbin sent him another letter re-urging that the treasury refrain from selling gold. While Julia was writing a letter to Corbin's wife (Grant's sister) the President asked her to tell the couple that they must promptly end all speculations in the gold market. When Julia's letter arrived in New York on 22 September, Corbin asked Jay Gould to pay him $100,000 in unrealized profits from the $1.5 million contract that Gould had bought for him and assume ownership of the underlying gold. Gould declined. Instead he offered to give Corbin a $100,000

[80] William McFeely, *Grant*, 320, 323-24; Ronald White, *American Ulysses* Kindle Location 9549-54; Henry Adams, *Historical Essays*, "The Gold Conspiracy", 344-45; William Hesseltine, *Grant the Politician*, 175; Allan Nevins *Hamilton Fish: The Inner History of the Grant Administration-Volume 1*, (New York: Frederick Ungar Publishing, 1957), 284; John Y. Simon, Ed., *Personal Papers of U. S. Grant: Vol. 27* (Carbondale: Southern Illinois University Press, 2005) 47-48

[81] William Hesseltine, *Grant the Politician*, 174; Henry Adams, *Historical Essays*, "The Gold Conspiracy", 345-46; Joseph Rose, *Grant Under Fire*, 572

check, which Corbin declined because he did not want to retain ownership of the underlying gold.[82]

The next day (Thursday) Fisk and Gould went to the exchange together. While Jim Fisk bought aggressively and drove the price to 144, Gould was secretly selling. On Friday September 24, 1869 Gould and Fisk again went to the exchange together. Gould was promptly informed that bank examiners were heading to investigate the bank that provided most of his credit. He knew they would

Treasury Secretary
George Boutwell

discover that his bank had improperly issued certified checks exceeding the value of all deposits connected with Gould's operation. Essentially, Gould had been using at least some phony money (overstated cashier's checks) to buy gold all along. As a result, he redoubled his furtive selling throughout the day.

Fisk, however, was as an ostentatious a buyer as on Thursday. Trading volume was enormous. As the clock hands approached noon, gold was at 164, when news arrived that the treasury would be putting $4 million on the market. Within fifteen minutes the price was down to 133. Gould was safely divested at the collapse.

Everyone assumed that Fisk was bankrupted, which may have been true. Later, however, he produced a (possibly bogus) document indicating that he had merely been the agent for a brokerage firm owned by William Belden. The Belden firm, he averred, was financially responsible for his purchases. Thus, sellers must go to

---

[82] Henry Adams, *Historical Essays*, "The Gold Conspiracy", 346

Belden to collect their sale proceeds. Since Belden did not have enough money to honor the transactions, he repudiated all but one trade and his firm was bankrupted. But the majority report of a later congressional investigating committee concluded "the conspirators [Fisk and Gould] . . . either before or after the fact . . . bought Belden's consent to this villainy" thereby implying that Belden was paid-off personally even though his firm was ruined.[83]

The comparatively moderate 23% gold price movement (130-to-160) caused by the Gould scheme triggered a financial panic for three reasons. First, speculators normally used margin loans to execute their transactions. Put simply, they commonly bought and sold gold contracts by borrowing most of the money. Since gold was itself a form of money, banks would readily lend ninety percent or so on its market value. Thus, a buyer needed only $100,000 to purchase a $1 million gold contract. If the price went up 10% the buyer doubled his $100,000 equity. But if it went down 10%, his entire investment was wiped out because the banks would sell the underlying gold to recapture its $900,000 (90%) loan.

A second reason it caused a crisis was because all but one of the sellers who sold gold to Belden through Fisk were unable to force Belden to make good on the transactions. The sellers were caught in a position similar to a homeowner who contracted to sell his home at an above-market price only to have the buyer belatedly renege after housing prices had tumbled.

A final reason that the gold price fluctuations damaged the economy is because the market was temporarily dominated by speculators and thereby became dysfunctional to those attempting to conduct routine commercial transactions. As historian Alan Nevins explained, "This meant that the foreign trade of the nation had come to a dead stop; that commodities offered for export could not be sold;

---

[83] Henry Adams, *Historical Essays*, "The Gold Conspiracy", 353-56, 361; House of Representatives, *Gold Panic Investigation*, 41st Congress, 2nd Session, Report Number 31, (March 1, 1870), 17 Available: http://bit.ly/2vEJoTD [Accessed: 8/28/2017]

that goods ready for shipment could not be shipped; that vessels half laden received no more cargo; that clerks, warehousemen, stevedores, sailors and the rest of the great army employed in our export trade were being thrown into idleness."

After the September collapse, Congressman—later President— James A. Garfield headed the investigating committee noted above. The committee's majority report concluded that Mrs. Grant never participated in the conspiracy. Fisk's claim to the contrary was "denied by Corbin and unsupported by Gould." Likewise, the majority report found that General Porter also never participated in the scheme, despite Fisk's contrary statements.[84]

Nonetheless, contemporary observer Henry Adams—grandson and great-grandson of two U. S. Presidents—concluded that Garfield led a whitewashed investigation, perhaps because he and other committee members were also guilty of low ethics. Garfield, it would later be disclosed, participated in the Crédit Mobilier corruption that emerged as the most publicized railroad finance scandal of the era. Years later Adams wrote:

> The mystery that shrouded the famous, classical attempt of Jay Gould to corner gold in September 1869 has never been cleared up . . .

> The Congressional Committee took . . . evidence, which it dared not probe and refused to analyze. Although the fault lay somewhere in the Administration . . . the trail always faded and died out at the point where any member of the Administration became visible.[85]

---

[84] House of Representatives, *Gold Panic Investigation*, 41st Congress, 2nd Session, Report Number 31, (March 1, 1870), 21 Available: http://bit.ly/2vEJoTD [Accessed: 8/28/2017]; Allan Nevins, *Hamilton Fish: The Inner History of the Grant Administration: Volume 1*, 286

[85] Matthew Josephson, *The Robber Barons*, 148; Henry Adams, *The Education of Henry Adams* (Boston: Houghton Mifflin, 1918), 269, 271

At least one modern historian, Joseph Rose, shares Adams's skepticism. In *Grant Under Fire* he notes several problems with the conventional Grant-was-a-naïve-victim interpretation.

First, Grant knowingly permitted the price of gold to rise and did nothing to prevent it until the financial markets were in crisis. Additional increases would have bankrupted the many short sellers and forced even more repudiation of contracts thereby even more severely disrupting commercial activities.

Second, the committee did not permit testimony by a man who signed an Adams Express receipt ledger that he said showed Mrs. Grant had earlier received a $25,000 "money package" at the White House. This might have been the $25,000 check that Corbin said he "sent to Washington." Garfield, writes Rose, "concocted a phony explanation to hush this up."

Third, Grant persuaded Garfield not to subpoena Julia Grant or Virginia Corbin, his wife and sister respectively.

Fourth, given the above circumstances, Grant's post-report expression of his "good many obligations" to Garfield "for the Gold Panic investigation" suggests a whitewash.[86]

While Gould was incubating his gold corner scheme, other men in Grant's circle were working behind-the-scenes on Caribbean adventures involving the region's two biggest islands, Cuba and Hispaniola.

Cuba was in the newspaper headlines when Grant assumed office in March 1869 because indigenous revolutionaries were attempting to overthrow hundreds of years of Spanish rule. Several powerful American groups, including a wealthy expatriate community in New York, the city's *Herald* and *Sun* newspapers, and Illinois Congressman John Logan from Grant's home state, were urging U. S. intervention. Logan had also been a Union Major General during the Civil War. Most significant among the advocates, however, was

---

[86] Joseph Rose, *Grant Under Fire*, 572-73

Secretary of War John Rawlins who had been Grant's most trusted military staff advisor during the war. The island rebels secretly gave Rawlins $28,000 in bonds issued by their conditional Cuban government. The bonds would be worthless if the revolution failed.

Three factors aborted the Cuban adventure. First, Rawlins died of tuberculosis before the end of September. Second, Secretary of State Hamilton Fish correctly observed that intervention would weaken a legal claim for damages against Great Britain for selling warships to the Confederacy during the Civil War. If the USA intervened in Cuba it would be taking a position comparable to that of Great Britain during our Civil War, thereby undermining Fish's legal case against the British. Third, Grant became more enamored with opportunities in Hispaniola than in Cuba.[87]

Hispaniola is east of Cuba and composed of two countries: Haiti and the Dominican Republic, then known as Santo Domingo. In Grant's day it had only about 120,000 residents and appeared as though it might be overrun by Haiti, or domestic revolutionaries. Under the government of Buenaventura Báez, Santo Domingo first asked to be become part of the United States when Andrew Johnson was President, but a hostile Congress would do nothing for Johnson. In April 1869, a month after Grant took office, a New England businessman owning property on the island urged Secretary of State Fish to investigate annexation. When Grant learned that the U. S. Navy wanted to put a coaling station on the island, he took a direct interest. Without telling Fish his full intentions, in July he sent Orville Babcock on a two-month mission to arrange a treaty. During his visit Babcock also ordered a nearby U. S. Navy ship to protect the

---

[87] *The New York Times* "On this Day: September 9, 1869" Available: http://nyti.ms/2ww6xtE [Accessed: September 3, 2017]

President-Elect Grant - 1868

harbor from anti-Báez "pirates." In reality the order meant that the USA was supporting a disputed government.

Fish was dismayed during a September cabinet meeting when Babcock returned to reveal a draft agreement to annex the country and sponsor it for statehood. The other cabinet members were stunned into silence. No doubt Fish would have been even more surprised had he known that sharp interrogation by a minority member of a later Senate investigating committee would reveal that Babcock might have been given property at the island's Samaná Bay that would greatly increase in value upon treaty approval. When Grant asked Fish to draw-up an official agreement to match Babcock's draft, the secretary of state considered resigning. He only agreed to remain after Grant promised to withhold presidential support for Cuban intervention. Fish's formal document agreed to pay $1.5 million to discharge all of Santo Domingo's national debt and pay $150,000 annually for fifty years to rent property at Samaná Bay for a coaling station.[88]

---

[88] *Revolvy*, "Annexation of Santo Domingo", Available: http://bit.ly/2vXuOpa [Accessed: September 3, 2017]; Ulysses S. Grant, "Second Annual Message: December 5, 1870", Available: http://bit.ly/2gvdFNK [Accessed: September 3, 2017]; William McFeeley, *Grant*, 343

Babcock returned to Santo Domingo with Fish's official treaty, which was signed on the island in late November 1869. Rumors of the agreement leaked to the New York press a month later. Meanwhile Grant was compelled to ship firearms to the island and continue using the U. S. Navy to keep Báez in power because of strengthening indigenous opposition in Santo Domingo. Next the treaty would be sent to the U. S. Senate for ratification, which would require a two-thirds majority vote for approval.

On January 2, 1870 Grant visited the Senate's Foreign Relations Committee Chairman, Massachusetts Senator Charles Sumner, to get his support for the treaty. The President arrived at Sumner's Washington home at dinnertime while the senator was dining with two newspapermen. Although Sumner was surprised that any President would take such a personal interest in a treaty, he received Grant cordially.

 Their discussion started at the dinner table and continued in the library afterward until Treasury Secretary Boutwell, an old Bay State friend, arrived for a visit. With Grant standing at the door ready to leave, one of the reporters addressed Sumner, "Of course, Mr. Sumner you will support the treaty." Sumner turned to face Grant and said, "Mr. President, I am an Administration man and whatever you do will always find in me the most careful and candid consideration." Grant left thinking he and Sumner had agreed. One of the reporters would later support Grant on this point.

The treaty arrived at the Senate eight days later but had been widely discussed in the newspapers during the preceding week. Public reaction was generally cautious particularly after the press learned that Administration-supplied weapons and the U. S. Navy were required to keep Báez in power. When an American businessman on the island was thrown in jail for opposing the treaty, newspapers criticized Grant's diplomats for doing nothing to get him out. On 15 March Sumner's Committee released a report advising 5-to-2 against ratifying the treaty.[89]

As a venerable abolitionist, Sumner objected because he wanted the predominantly black countries in the Western Hemisphere to remain independent. He worried that absorption of Santo Domingo into the United States would set a bad precedent against black independence. Grant argued that the treaty would instead benefit blacks because it would strengthen Santo Domingo's economy thereby making the country a haven for runaway slaves from Cuba and Brazil. A stream of such runaways, he suggested, might cause Cuba and Brazil to abandon slavery.

If granted statehood, he added, Santo Domingo would become a favorite destination for African American émigrés wanting to escape Southern violence and discrimination. His motivation, however, is suspect because he could have alternately encouraged Southern blacks to migrate to the North and West. It was, for example, a time when many settlers were given free land as western homesteaders, but the overwhelming majority were whites. Most available evidence indicates that the President, and many other whites outside the South, did not want significant numbers of blacks moving into their regions. Many, perhaps even Grant, thought it best if the country became geographically segregated, with blacks concentrated in the South or completely off the mainland.

Shortly before his death, Grant wrote in his memoirs, "I took it that . . . [America's] . . . colored people would go there [Santo Domingo] in great numbers so as to have independent states governed by their own race. They would still be in the United States . . . but the citizens would be almost wholly colored." Aside from racial prejudice, Northern white workers also feared that their wages would drop should a flood of impoverished blacks, eager for work, arrive

---

[89] William Hesseltine, *Grant the Politician*, 199-202; William McFeeley, *Grant*, 339-341; Ron White, *American Ulysses*, Kindle Location. 10, 149; Allan Nevins, *Hamilton Fish: The Inner History of the Grant Administration: Volume 1*, 311-12

from the South. Before he became Grant's Treasury Secretary, Massachusetts Congressman George Boutwell tried to calm such worries within his state by proposing that the states of South Carolina and Florida be reserved exclusively for blacks.[90]

Even some leading Northern intellectuals, such as Harvard scientist Louis Agassiz, held atavistic racial attitudes. He rejoiced in black emancipation "not only from a philanthropic point of view, but also because . . . [scientists] . . . will be able to . . . advocate a discriminating policy respecting [blacks] without seeming to support legal inequality. Henceforth it will be possible to require for the disowned races a treatment different from that to which the higher races are entitled, just as well as colleges . . . are provided for the more highly gifted individuals and common schools for all." In speaking of his belief that the climate in the South and the tropics fostered immorality, Republican Senator Carl Schurz said, "Our country extends at present to a region which is already in some degree infected by the moral miasma of the tropics . . . Have we not enough with one South? Can we afford to buy another one?"[91]

At least one presidential historian, Thomas Craughwell, reasons that the Santo Domingo episode indicates that Grant had ultimately concluded that American blacks and whites could not live peaceably together; that it was easier to separate the races than to enforce the civil rights of the minority.

> The scheme to ship the former slaves to Santo
> Domingo was in essence a public statement by the
> president of the United States that blacks and whites
> could not live peaceably in the same communities,

---

[90] *Public Broadcasting System*, "A Long History of Racial Preferences – For Whites", Available: http://to.pbs.org/1HMtoBf [Accessed: September 4, 2017]; Nicholas Guyatt, *The Journal of American History,* "America's Conservatory: Race, Reconstruction, and the Santo Domingo Debate", Vol. 97, No. 4, (March 2011), 979-80; Ulysses Grant, *Memoirs*, 588; Allen Guelzo, *Redeeming the Great Emancipator* (Cambridge: Harvard University Press, 2016), 96

[91] Nicholas Guyatt, *The Journal of American History,* "America's Conservatory: Race, Reconstruction, and the Santo Domingo Debate", Vol. 97, No. 4, (March 2011), 984, 987

that the acts of violence committed by the Klan and other vigilante groups like them were regrettable but understandable, and that he, Ulysses S. Grant, would not defend the rights of black Americans nor ensure that they enjoyed the full protection of the law.[92]

Grant biographer William McFeely expressed a more generous interpretation by noting that Grant "cared greatly about the annexation of Santo Domingo . . . on the grounds of highest policy . . . One can doubt not only the practicality but also the wisdom of establishing an all-black American state . . . but one cannot . . . dismiss the effort to achieve it simply as corrupt money grubbing."[93]

Massachusetts Senator
Charles Sumner

The treaty came to a vote in the Senate on June 30, 1870. The final tally of 28-to-28 left it short of the two-thirds needed for ratification. Writing in 1936 historian Allan Nevins concluded that most contemporary Americans disliked the treaty because "all our [prior] territorial expansion had been continental . . . and in districts certain to yield quickly to settlement . . . [submitting] completely to Anglo-Saxon law and tradition . . . The West was still crying out for settlers and capital; while the Reconstruction problem remained unsolved, to annex a new

92 Thomas Craughwell, *Encyclopedia Britannica Blog*, "Top Ten Mistakes by U. S. Presidents: Number Nine", Available: http://bit.ly/2wzNrTL [Accessed: September 4, 2017], January 13, 2009

93 William McFeely, *Grant*, 353

population of ignorant Negroes seemed utter folly. And, finally, many believed that a distant dependency of the kind would prove a fertile field for corruption, of which we had too much already."[94]

Much as Andrew Johnson was angered because General Grant broke his word on their Tenure of Office arrangement, Grant was furious with Sumner because Grant perceived that the senator had failed to keep his word to support the Santo Domingo treaty.[95]

Grant retaliated. Although he aimed to get Sumner dismissed as the Senate's Foreign Affairs Committee Chairman he struck first at Sumner protégée, John Motley who was the American ambassador in London. Sumner and Fish had different viewpoints regarding the settlement of the *Alabama* Claims against Great Britain for providing warships to the Confederacy during the Civil War. (The C.S.S. *Alabama* was the most famous example of such a ship.) During the negotiations, Motley had prioritized Sumner's suggestions over those of Secretary Fish. In November 1870 Grant dismissed Motley and soon replaced him with Major General Robert Schenck. The general would accomplish little in Great Britain beyond introducing the game of poker to English society and selling society members shares of a worthless Nevada silver mine in which he was a stockholder.[96]

Over Sumner's objections, in January 1871 Grant persuaded Congress to fund a three member presidentially appointed commission to visit Santo Domingo in order to evaluate annexation. Among the commission assistants was Frederick Douglass who was America's leading spokesman for the black community. After initial skepticism, Douglass endorsed the scheme. Some of his critics attributed his viewpoint reversal to the enhanced economic and social status he gained from official inclusion in the mission. Esteemed abolitionists William Lloyd Garrison concluded, "Of

---

[94] Allan Nevins, *Hamilton Fish: The Inner History of the Grant Administration*: Volume 1, 320

[95] William Hesseltine, *Grant the Politician*, 205

[96] *Ibid.*, 231

course Frederick Douglass approves the measure, and already has his reward. It is not the first time his ambition and selfishness has led him astray." Underscoring his false assumptions about the endemic geographic distribution of morality, Senator Schurz implied that America's political center of gravity must remain in the North. Grant got his personal revenge in March 1871 when Sumner was deposed as chairman of the Senate's Foreign Relations Committee.[97]

But by the time Grant won his personal revenge against Sumner, Congress had lost interest in Santo Domingo. The government faced more pressing problems concerning Southern Reconstruction, monetary policy, and the *Alabama* Claims.

---

[97] Nicholas Guyatt, *The Journal of American History*, "America's Conservatory: Race, Reconstruction, and the Santo Domingo Debate", Vol. 97, No. 4, (March 2011), 982; William Hesselltine, *Grant the Politician*, 236

CHAPTER 5: BIGGEST ACHIEVEMENT

OVER THE PAST CENTURY-AND-A-HALF historians have differed in their opinions about the Grant Administration's biggest accomplishment. Presently, most praise his civil rights achievements but earlier most cited his diplomatic rapprochement with Great Britain over hostilities triggered by British policies toward the Confederacy. Although the latter may seem less important in retrospect, at the time the dispute threatened the continued existence of Canada, then known as British North America.

In his first annual message in December 1869 Grant announced his intent to obtain monetary compensation from Great Britain for damages caused by the latter's alleged violations of laws governing neutrality during the American Civil War. Commonly known as The *Alabama* Claims, the settlement reached in 1872 would be regarded by most historians prior to the 1960s as the most significant achievement of Grant's presidency.

Less than two months after the outbreak of the war, Great Britain officially declared her neutrality but recognized both the federal union and the Confederacy as belligerents. The Lincoln Administration objected because belligerency standing gave the Confederacy the authority to purchase weapons and borrow money from France, Great Britain and other neutral countries. It would also allow the South to resupply its warships at neutral harbors.

Lincoln argued that the Southern states had never left the Union. Instead, he averred, they merely composed a part of America temporarily experiencing an illegal insurrection. Great Britain responded that Lincoln's blockade declaration against the Southern states was in itself an act of war and proof of the belligerent status for both sides. The British rejected the insurrection argument by explaining that if the United States were a single country, Lincoln should have selectively closed the ports in the rebellious territory as opposed to pronouncing them under blockade, which was a concept governed by international convention.

After the war the chief argument between the two countries centered upon two points. First was a determination of whether three Confederate warships supplied by British builders had complied with Great Britain's own 1819 Foreign Enlistment Act. The act was designed to prevent British subjects from dragging their country into armed conflicts among other nations in which Great Britain was officially neutral. Second was to determine the damage amounts caused by such warships presuming they had been provided illegally.

Although three months before Grant took office President Johnson and the British had a basic agreement in place, congressional Republicans refused to go along. Most significantly, Senator Sumner complained that the scope of President Johnson's claims was too limited because it concentrated on the approximate $15 million in direct damages caused by Confederate commerce raiders such as the C. S. S. *Alabama*. Sumner felt that indirect damages actually totaled about $2.5 billion, which approximated half the cost of the war.

The senator reasoned that Great Britain's award of belligerency status to the Confederacy prolonged the war by two years. In addition to the American merchant ships destroyed by the raiders, he estimated that the U. S. merchant marine lost $110 million in commerce because American hulls were sold to buyers in neutral countries in order to immunize them against Confederate attack. Finally, the senator did not want a cash settlement. Instead, he wanted territories such as Canada, Bermuda, and the British West Indies.[98]

In order to press his interpretation, in May 1869 Sumner had persuaded Grant to appoint John Motley as Ambassador to Great Britain. Motley and Secretary of State Fish soon clashed. Motley pressed Sumner's case for indirect damages based upon the senator's argument that Great Britain erred in recognizing the Confederacy as a belligerent. Fish felt there were stronger legal arguments, such as violations of Britain's Foreign Enlistment Act. Motley minimized Fish's points when discussing America's claims with the British. As noted earlier, Grant sided with Fish and eventually dismissed Motley in November 1870. The dismissal signified a decline in Sumner's influence on the negotiations, even though the Senate would be required to ratify an eventual treaty.[99]

Although America's post-Motley negotiating team did not abandon indirect claims Grant wanted the political boost a settlement might provide before the autumn 1872 elections. First, in May 1871 the two sides agreed to an arbitration procedure with the Treaty of Washington. Next, in June 1872 America conceded that its indirect claims were not "good grounds for an award of damages." Thus, in mid-September the arbitration panel awarded the United States a flat sum of $15.5 million. It was equivalent to about five percent of Great Britain's annual budget at the time, which was a fraction that would approximate $50 billion in 2018. Similarly, the dismissed indirect claims would have totaled about $6 trillion in 2018 dollars, which is six times Britain's present annual budget.[100]

---

[98] Hesseltine, *Grant the Politician*, 163; Chester G. Hearn, *Gray Raiders of the Sea* (Camden, Me.: International Marine Publishing, 1992), 304; Allan Nevins, *Hamilton Fish, Volume Two*, 561

[99] Hesseltine, *Grant the Politician*, 165

[100] Chester G. Hearn, *Gray Raiders of the Sea*, 307-08; Tom Bingham, *International and Comparative Law Journal*, "The Alabama Claims Arbitration", Vol. 54, No. 1 (Jan. 2005), 1

Secretary of State Hamilton Fish

The arbitration panel ruled that British authorities failed to use "due diligence" to ensure that the some of the ships built in their country were not originally intended to become Confederate commerce raiders. Although the Foreign Enlistment Act permitted shipyards to make vessels for a belligerent in a war in which Britain was neutral, the builders were not allowed to deliver armed warships. Confederates circumvented the restriction by taking delivery of the ships in an unarmed condition and arming them beyond British territorial waters. The C.S.S *Alabama,* for example, was delivered as an unarmed ship originally identified as the 290. In late July 1862 the 290 sailed from Liverpool to the Azores where she rendezvoused with a tender loaded with cannons and munitions. Thus, *Alabama* was armed in the neutral waters of the Azores by transferring the tender's cargo to the raider.

Lincoln's ambassador to Great Britain had complained earlier that the 290 appeared to be designed as a fighting vessel. Through bribes to shipyard workers and a network of spies he learned that the 290 was to become a Confederate commerce raider. British authorities responded to his complaint by sending inspectors to board the vessel. Since the inspectors found no evidence of armaments, they did not feel the Foreign Enlistment Act justified detaining the ship. Basically, the arbitration panel ruled that British inspectors were not sufficiently diligent when evaluating the intended use of the 290.

They should have realized from its design, and other evidence, that it was intended to be a Confederate commerce raider.[101]

The Treaty of Washington established a couple of new rules to thereafter govern the conduct of neutrals toward warring nations. First, it obligates a neutral government to use due diligence to prevent any ship built in its jurisdiction to be outfitted as a warship against any nation with which the neutral nation is at peace. Second, a neutral nation my not permit a second country at war with a third country to use any port of the neutral nation as a naval base. The rules were finally incorporated into international law at the Hague Conference in 1907.[102]

Among others, Grant's ambassador to Spain affirmed the settlement's political advantages. "If Grant settles the English question satisfactorily, it will save his foreign policy. And if he wipes out the Ku Klux Klan . . . his record will carry him through safely."[103]

In contrast to earlier historians, modern biographers commonly cite President Grant's achievements on behalf of African Americans as a greater accomplishment than the *Alabama* Claims. Moreover, they generally characterize his civil rights motives—and those of fellow Republicans—as grounded in the morality of racial equality to the near exclusion of any political factors.

Historian Sean Wilentz rates Grant, "as one of the greatest presidents of his era, and possibly one of the greatest in all American history." He adds, "The evidence clearly shows that [Grant] created the most auspicious record on racial equality and civil rights of any president from Lincoln to Lyndon B. Johnson." Similarly, in 2017 biographer Ron Chernow opined, "[Grant's] pursuit of justice for southern blacks was at times imperfect, but his noble desire to protect them never wavered." In 2012 H. W. Brands wrote, "Nearly a century would pass before the country had another president who

---

[101] Chester G. Hearn, *Gray Raiders of the Sea*, 155-56, 308
[102] *Ibid.*, 308-09
[103] Hesseltine, *Grant the Politician*, 251

took civil rights as seriously as Grant did." In his review of Ron White's 2016 Grant biography, author T. J. Stiles remarked, "Reconstruction dominated Grant's presidency. Unlike many, he knew it brought liberation, not occupation, [by] empowering African-Americans in states where they were a majority or large minority. White describes how he pushed Congress and his own administration to essentially invent civil-rights enforcement."[104]

But Reconstruction era Republicans also had a selfish motive for sponsoring Southern blacks. Specifically, when Grant was first elected President in 1868 the Party was only about a dozen years old. Its leaders worried that the Party might be strangled in the cradle if the former Rebel states rejoined the Union without readmission terms that insured the Republicans would keep control of the federal government. Since there were few white Republicans in the South the Party concluded it needed to create a new constituency.

Therefore, as early as 1866 Republicans settled on two objectives. First was mandatory African American suffrage in all former Confederate, but not Northern, states. They expected that such a mostly illiterate and inexperienced electorate could be manipulated to consistently support Republican interests out of gratitude for emancipation and voter suffrage. Second was disfranchisement of the Southern white classes most likely to oppose Republican rule. As a practical matter, both objectives were achieved as a result of the 1867 Reconstruction Acts—passed over President Johnson's vetoes questioning their constitutionality—and the Fourteenth

---

[104] Ron Chernow, *Grant* (New York: Penguin Press, 2017), xxii-xxiii; H. W. Brands, *The Man Who Saved the Union: Ulysses Grant in War and Peace* (New York: Random House, 2012), 636; T. J. Stiles *The New York Times* "Ulysses S. Grant: New Biography of 'A Nobody form Nowhere'" October 19, 2016 Available: http://nyti.ms/2xNTi51 [Accessed: October 18, 2017]; Sean Wilentz, *New Republic* "The Return of Ulysses" (January 25, 2010) Available: http://bit.ly/2ilsgw2 [Accessed: 10/31/2017]

Amendment, which was ratified only a few months before the general election that first put Grant in the White House.[105]

Thus, is revealed the central historical debate about Radical Reconstruction and President Grant's role therein. Specifically, at question is whether Republicans chiefly sought Southern black suffrage in order to promote racial equality or as a political tool for sustaining Republican control of the federal government by creating puppet regimes in the South.

Consensus opinions have fluctuated over the years. Prior to 1970 historians commonly mentioned both factors, with differing emphasis of one over the other. As noted above, however, recent historians usually suggest that racial equality was the prime motivation. The best of them will at least cite examples when political considerations required Republican leaders to compromise. But modern historians commonly narrate such incidents in a manner that suggests they were mere diversions from an overarching altruistic mission of racial equality.

One example of such compromise was the 1872 Amnesty Act, which removed most of the voting and office-holding restrictions imposed on former Confederates by the 1868 Fourteenth Amendment. According to historian Richard White, Republican support for the act was a political maneuver designed to reduce the appeal of amnesty-advocate Horace Greeley who was Grant's opponent in the 1872 presidential election.[106]

Similarly, modern historians normally attribute the failure of Reconstruction almost wholly to violent Southern whites. They seldom fault the federal government for failing to help Southerners of all races rebuild their region. For example, in 1988 Eric Foner wrote, "Events far beyond the control of Southern Republicans

---

[105] J. G. Randall and David Donald, *The Civil War and Reconstruction*, 580-1; Ludwell Johnson, *Division and Reunion*, 200–1, 206; William H. Hesseltine, *Ulysses S. Grant Politician*, 54

[106] Richard White, *The Republic for Which it Stands*, 211

[carpetbaggers] . . . severely limited the prospects for far-reaching economic change. . . . None of these factors, however, would have proved decisive without the campaign of violence that turned the electoral tide in many parts of the South and the weakening of Northern resolve."[107]

In contrast, in 1950 historian Herbert Agar suggested that ex-slaves could have become "truly" free if Republicans had been willing to provide economic aid and fund black education. Instead, impoverished Southern states were required to pay the education bill even though it resulted from emancipation, which was a national—not regional—policy.

> If the Negro had been made a property-owner and if his thirst for learning had been slaked at federal expense, he would have become a truly free man. As professors Morison and Commager say, "[A] government which found it possible to give forty million acres of public land to a single railroad might well have purchased ten million for the freedmen." But neither the Northern capitalist nor the Republican politician would be helped by making the Negro free and independent . . .

> [Instead] Congress provided a South wherein ignorant and destitute freedmen were supported by Northern troops in their "right" to vote the Republican ticket . . .

> It was wicked to force the Negro to rule the disfranchised [Southern] white man, when everyone knew the positions would be reversed as soon as

---

[107] Eric Foner, *Reconstruction: The Unfinished Revolution* (New York: Harper & Row, 1988), 603

Northerners grew sick of governing their fellow Americans with the sword."[108]

In commenting upon the status of Reconstruction in 1871, historian Avery Craven wrote in 1969, "The Republican party . . . could muster the vote to pass sharp legislation for the benefit of the southern Negro, but it could not support the abstract principles behind that legislation." Race consciousness in margin-of-victory states such as Connecticut, Indiana, New York and Ohio sometimes forced that the Party choose between conscience and political expediency. "Regard for the possible political effects in these states," wrote Craven, "had been largely responsible for the failure of the Republican party to come forward at any time with a clear-cut, bold stand on Negro suffrage."[109]

Similarly, in *Ulysses S. Grant the Politician* William B. Hesseltine wrote in 1935, "Fearful the return of the Southern states would result in the overthrow of the Republican Party, the Radical leaders were largely agreed on the necessity of imposing Negro suffrage on the South." Hesseltine later added, "Republican Reconstruction polices were explained on the basis of justice to the Negroes, but frequently the orators admitted that the restoration of white government in the South would endanger their own [Republican] congressional supremacy." In 1963 John Ezell wrote in *The South Since 1865*, "Further rationalization by the Republicans led them to claim that if the war victory were to be insured, the party that produced it had to stay in power . . . by giving votes to the freedmen who would presumably vote Republican from gratitude."

But it was not merely pre-1970 historians who expressed the viewpoint. The chief architect of Republican Reconstruction— Congressman Thaddeus Stevens—argued that the Southern states should never be admitted as "valid states, until the [U.S.] constitution had been so amended . . . as to secure the perpetual

---

[108] Herbert Agar, *The Price of Union* (Boston: Houghton Mifflin, 1950), 452, 454, 466;
[109] Avery Craven, *Reconstruction: The End of the Civil War*, 269-70

ascendency of . . . [the Republican Party."] Nearly four years after he left office and tried for a third Presidential nomination, even Grant implied that his true motivation for backing black suffrage had always been to keep white Southerners out of power in Washington.

Speaking in Syracuse in October 1880 in support of the Garfield Republican ticket he warned that the South would control the Democratic Party and if it came to power, "would sweep down . . . all of your industries and prosperity, all of your banks and your manufactories." At Rochester he added that "Rebel brigadiers" might rule the nation while arguing that only Northern men must be permitted to govern America. In short, Grant suggested that his true aim all along had been to protect Northern economic prosperity and dominance, not to promote racial equality.[110]

---

[110] J. G. Randall and David Donald, *The Civil War and Reconstruction* 581-4; William Hesseltine, *Grant the Politician*, 54, 128, 441-42; John Ezell *The South Since 1865* (New York: Macmillan Publishing, 1963), 72-73

CHAPTER 6: FIRST TERM RECONSTRUCTION

SHORTLY AFTER HIS MARCH 1869 inauguration, Grant extended an olive branch to the whites of the three Southern states that were not allowed to vote in the 1868 election because they had not yet been readmitted to the federal Union. Grant anxiously wanted them to rejoin partly because he assumed they would help ratify the Fifteenth Amendment, as seven of the other eight former Confederate states under carpetbag rule would do by the end of 1869. Unlike the Fourteenth Amendment, which mainly targeted Southern states, the Fifteenth would provide adult male suffrage regardless of race across the country. Significantly, however, it still enabled individual states to deny citizenship to persons of a minority race if they had not been born in the USA. Without citizenship the states could also deny suffrage to such persons. As shall be explained, the Republicans soon addressed the matter with an act that would enable blacks born elsewhere to become naturalized American citizens but simultaneously deny the same privilege to other "non-white" legal immigrants. Among such "non-whites" were Chinese Americans.[111]

Along with Texas and Mississippi, Virginia was one of the three states still seeking readmission. In return for an informal understanding that the Old Dominion would support the Fifteenth Amendment, Grant made a special offer to white Virginians. A year earlier Virginia failed to pass the Radical Republican 1868 state constitution because it contained two clauses that denied the vote to

---

[111] Xi Wang, *The Trial of Democracy: Black Suffrage and Northern Republicans: 1860-1910* (Athens: University of Georgia Press, 1997), 68

many former Confederate soldiers, even while requiring universal black male suffrage. Thus, at Grant's urging, Congress enacted a bill to allow Virginians, Mississippians, and Texans to vote on their new state constitutions and the applicable white disfranchisement clauses separately. Although, none of the three could reject black suffrage, they could vote thumbs-down on white disfranchisement.

Robert E. Lee was among the Virginia leaders who met privately with Grant to pledge support for the Fifteenth Amendment under this *quid pro quo* understanding. Thus, in July 1869 Virginia approved its constitution, but decisively rejected the white disfranchisement clauses. Three months later her legislature voted to ratify the Fifteenth Amendment.[112]

Americans generally approved this conciliatory act toward whites in Virginia, Mississippi and Texas. Horace Greeley's *New York Tribune* endorsed it. He also stated his hope that it would lead to a universal amnesty bill for former Confederates, one that he hoped would wipe away most of the remaining punitive feelings lingering among Northerners.

But it was not to be. The Radicals within the Republican Party remained wedded to the belief that carpetbag regimes must remain in control in the Southern states in order to insure Party control of the federal government. In a July cabinet meeting Treasury Secretary Boutwell outspokenly emphasized that sectional reconciliation could lead the Democrats back to power. Postmaster General John Creswell supported Boutwell's arguments. As a result, it was agreed that Mississippians and Texans would not be permitted to vote on their respective state constitutions until after the autumn general elections. The delay provided time to take actions designed to optimize the probability of installing Radical regimes in the two states.

---

[112] Hesseltine, *Grant the Politician*, 181; J. G. Randall and David Donald, *The Civil War and Reconstruction*, 621

Almost immediately after the cabinet meeting, Radical Republicans aggressively lobbied Grant to keep tight control over the emerging state governments in Texas and Mississippi. Grant began to yield. Even though one of the President's brothers-in-law was running on the conservative ticket in Mississippi, Grant endorsed the opposing Radical ticket in an August magazine interview. Furthermore, he endorsed Radical governments across the South instead of merely the Magnolia State.

Grant and Congress hastily enacted a new bill to delay readmission of the three states until they complied with additional restrictive requirements. Thus, Virginia was not readmitted to the Union until January 1870 even though Congress approved her constitution six months earlier. Despite a pacific beginning, Grant had fully come over to the Radical Republican side before the end of 1869. Once under their influence he showed little respect for the doctrine of states' rights.[113]

In Texas, as in Mississippi, the delayed vote in November would be between two factions of the Republican Party because the Democrats were too weak to offer their own candidate. Each faction claimed to represent the "real" Republican Party. The Texas gubernatorial race was between Republican candidates Alexander Hamilton and E. J. Davis. Hamilton represented the Conservative wing and Davis the Radical one. Both men sought Grant's endorsement, but the President initially tried to be impartial. Davis, however, had better Washington connections. After Davis persuaded the Republican national committee chairman to side with him, Grant increasingly made the necessary changes among local Texas officeholders to insure a Davis victory.

The conservative wing of Mississippi's Republican Party attempted to enable the state to escape Radical rule by nominating the First Lady's brother, Lewis Dent, to be governor. It was a too-obvious attempt to win Grant's favor, especially since the President

---

[113] Allan Nevins, *Hamilton Fish: Vol. 1*, 290-93

wanted to minimize a renewal of nepotism complaints that were common after he took office by assigning family members to enviable posts. Nonetheless, he ultimately appointed about a dozen family members to federal offices including two brothers-in-law who became customs collectors in San Francisco and New Orleans, respectively. Additionally, as shall be explained, Grant's younger brother Orvil evidently used his surname to become a well-compensated silent partner in activities involving frontier trading posts and interior department surveyor contracts.

First Lady Julia Grant

In order to optimize Radical-wing election prospects, Mississippi's military governor increasingly selected Radical-loyal men to replace conservative state officeholders before the election. Thus, a former plantation owner and wartime cotton trader, James Alcorn, won the state's gubernatorial race by a two-to-one margin. Mississippi ratified the Fifteenth Amendment in January 1870. As in Texas, former Mississippi Confederates had little political power. Alcorn was an exception.[114]

Despite having voted for Grant in 1868, Georgia inflamed Radical opinion the following year. Although the state's 1868 constitution permitted black males to vote, by an oversight it failed to explicitly authorize them to hold office. Thus, when the new legislature met, the whites replaced black legislators with additional whites. Black-

---

[114] William Hesseltine, *Grant the Politician*, 183-85; W. E. Woodward, *Meet General Grant* (New York: Literary Guild of America, 1928), 402-03

legislator expulsion on such a flimsy technicality provoked the President to return the state to military rule. The military commander reinstated the black legislators, removed the ex-Confederates and replaced them with runner-up Republicans.

Congress readmitted Georgia representatives in July 1870 after the state ratified the Fifteenth Amendment in February. Grant would only gradually learn thereafter that the South's Radical Republican state governments had only tenuous holds on power. They would increasingly require federal intervention at the point of the bayonet in order to remain intact.[115]

On March 30, 1870 Grant notified Congress that the requisite three-fourths of all states had ratified the Fifteenth Amendment. Since the amendment authorized Congress to adopt laws to enforce it, Congress promptly gave him the Enforcement Act of 1870. Sometimes referred to as the First Ku Klux Klan Act, the 1870 Enforcement Act prohibited state officials from discriminating racially during voter registration. It also empowered the President to appoint elections supervisors who were allowed to bring cases of election fraud, bribery, intimidation or conspiracy into federal—as opposed to state—courts. It established penalties and authorized the President to employ federal marshals, and even the army, to enforce its provisions.[116]

As early as February 1870, however, Grant began to question the Republican Party's ability to hold political power when signs of an incipient Party split first appeared in Missouri. The state's 1865 constitution had tightly restricted former Confederate sympathizers from voting. Consequently, a growing body of Missourians wanted the provisions repealed. Their movement soon gained the support of Carl Schurz, who was a popular Senator and *bona fide* Republican from the much-admired Lincoln era. Schurz was also an early

---

[115] William H. Bragg, *New Georgia Encyclopedia*, "Reconstruction in Georgia", (10/19/2016) Available: http://bit.ly/2xbUwdY [Accessed: September 8, 2017]
[116] Eric Foner, *Reconstruction*, 454

proponent of civil service reform to replace the patronage system that relied upon Party loyalty—sometimes involving salary assessments—in order for applicants to gain, and hold, federal employment.

Grant aggravated the problem with the political appointment of an old army buddy, General John McDonald, as the collector of internal revenue in St. Louis. Immediately upon learning of the assignment, Schurz (then a Missouri congressman), a U. S. Attorney, and the St. Louis federal marshal sent a protest letter to Treasury Secretary Boutwell. "The reputation of this man . . . [is] such that he can bring no moral support to the government," wired the trio. But Grant was more interested in political, than moral, support. As shall be explained, McDonald was given a free hand and would soon be abusing his authority for the benefit of personal and Republican Party interests.[117]

Grant continued to alienate Schurz and other Republican reformers with additional political appointments intended chiefly to benefit the Administration. One example was the customs office at the Port of New York, which collected about three-fourths of America's total tariff duties, making it by far the richest patronage office in the country. Grant replaced the incumbent collector with Thomas Murphy who was one of the contributors to a fund used to purchase Grant's vacation home in Long Branch, New Jersey. Shortly after his appointment Murphy received a note from one of the President's personal secretaries, Horace Porter. It stated that Porter hoped Murphy "will distribute the patronage in such a manner as will help the administration." Over the next eighteen months Murphy assigned about 340 Grant-loyal jobseekers to positions in the office.[118]

During the 1870 congressional elections Democrats promoted civil service reform as a major issue. The even went so far as to criticize Grant's dubious political appointments and his propensity

---

[117] William Hesseltine, *Grant the Politician*, 207-08
[118] *Ibid.*, 213

to accept generous gifts, which led to doubts about his personal honesty. In response, Republicans accused Southern Democrats of violent voter intimidation through organizations like the Ku Klux Klan. After all the votes were counted Republicans lost more than thirty congressional seats, including five states in the South. Grant initially responded superficially by advocating civil service reform in his annual message released in December 1870. [119]

More significantly, however, the 1870 election losses convinced Grant that he needed stronger voter control in order to avoid additional losses in 1872. Since a number of carpetbag regimes had complained that the KKK interfered with the 1870 elections Grant asked that Congress give him the power to forcibly suppress the Klan and gain federal control over the election process in states where he judged that lawless elements intimidated Republican voters.

Congress first responded early in 1871 by launching a yearlong investigation into political conditions in the South that included visits to the six southern-most states from North Carolina to Mississippi. According to historian Hesseltine, the committee was stacked with enough Radical Republicans "to insure a report in accordance with party interests." Consequently, well before the investigation was even completed, Grant signed into law a couple of new enforcement acts in February and April, which are normally conflated under a single moniker as the Second Ku Klux Klan Act. It signified a major shift in legal theory.

The act authorized the federal government for the first time to prosecute and punish individual persons for violating certain laws, chiefly involving voting and civil rights. Such prosecutorial authority had previously been the exclusive domain of the states. Prior to the Second KKK Act the federal government could prevent state and local governments for violating such rights, but the feds could not prosecute individuals. Thus, if a black voter was assaulted on the way

---

[119] William Hesseltine, *Grant the Politician*, 217-19; Richard White, *The Republic For Which it Stands*, 188

to a polling station, it was up to state courts to convict the accused. After the Second KKK Act, however, suspected perpetrators could be prosecuted, convicted, and punished in federal court by treating the crime as a violation of the victim's voting rights.

The act also empowered the President to temporarily suspend the writ of *habeas corpus* thereby enabling federal marshals to jail suspects without charging them with a crime until *habeas corpus* was reinstated. Before Congress adjourned, Congressman Benjamin Butler attached a rider to a funding bill that gave the President authority to use military troops to police state elections in cases when the elections involved federal offices, such as congressman.

Many Americans thought the act's expanded federal jurisdiction was unconstitutional. *The Nation* wrote, "These are momentous changes. They not only increase the power of the federal government, but they arm it with jurisdiction over a class of cases which it had never heretofore had, and never pretended to have, any jurisdiction whatever." One California senator opined, "The Radical laws . . . are unconstitutional clearly so far as they deal with individuals and not with the states." Critics warned that local governments could not survive if the federal government could prosecute crimes within the states. Democrats labeled the new laws as "Force Acts," implying that they represented dire threats to individual liberty. Unsurprisingly, Democrats interpreted the KKK Act as a swindle designed to extend Republican power in the South instead of a measure to defend freedmen from violence.

But it was not merely Democrats and Grant's enemies who voiced such objections. Future Republican President James A. Garfield said, "It seems to me that this [KKK Act] will virtually empower the President to abolish the State Governments. I am in great trouble about the whole matter." Republican Senators Lyman Trumbull and Carl Schurz expressed similar objections. Schurz argued that the crimes of the Klan were exaggerated and caused by Northern interference. General of the Army and wartime Grant buddy, William T. Sherman, told a New Orleans audience "If Ku-klux bills were kept out of Congress and the army kept at their legitimate duties there are enough good and true men in the South to put down all the Ku-klux and other bands of marauders."[120]

After investigating for a year, in February 1872 a congressional KKK Committee released thirteen volumes of hearings and reports documenting Southern white violence during Reconstruction. Like the typical recent Grant biographer who fails to question the veracity of his personal memoirs, so also do modern historians often fail to appreciate similar faults in the reports of the partisan KKK Committee. Ditto the complaints sent by carpetbaggers to Washington.

While specific incidents such as the Colfax massacre—which would come later—are undeniable, historian Ludwell Johnson suggests that general inferences from the committee hearings and the sensational reports from carpetbaggers "... is, in short, the [pre-Civil War] problem of 'bleeding Kansas' all over again: allegations of violence were made a prime weapon of propaganda. The 'facts' were usually produced by a partisan press or by partisan investigations .. . The same problems of evidence are present in Reconstruction."[121]

Historian Johnson's mention of Kansas refers to a pre-Civil War political fight from 1856 to 1859 when the territory sought statehood together with the coupled question of its admission as either a slave state or free state. Since the opposing sides in Kansas each sometimes resorted to violence Horace Greeley's *New York Tribune* sensationalized the situation. His references to "bleeding Kansas," implied that murder and violence had a free hand in the territory. For decades, abolitionist propaganda left the impression that deaths were numerous, and that Northerners were the chief victims. A careful study by Dale Watts in 1995, however, concluded that deaths

---

[120] Eric Foner, *Reconstruction*, 454-56; Kenneth Stampp, *The Era of Reconstruction*, 200; William Hesseltine, *Grant the Politician*, 241, 267; Ron Chernow, *Grant*, 703-04; Richard White, *The Republic For Which it Stands*, 192

[121] Ludwell Johnson, *Disunion and Reunion*, 252-53

totaled fifty-six during the entire four-year conflict and that most victims were pro-slavery.

> Contemporary antislavery accounts and the
> writings of historians generally depict the antislavery
> people as the victims of proslavery attackers.
> Newspaper reporters and other propagandists were
> very adept at creating graphic descriptions of the
> atrocities that the [pro-slavery] Border Ruffians were
> said to be inflicting . . . The data, however, indicate
> that the two sides were nearly equally involved in
> killing their political opponents: thirty proslavery
> people, twenty-four anti- slavery men.[122]

Grant first used his KKK Act authority in October 1871 by suspending *habeas corpus* and declaring martial law in five upland South Carolina counties. In a matter of weeks hundreds of men were arrested and others sought asylum by crossing the state line into Georgia. Partly because of such enforcement and partly because only a minority of lower-class whites remained in the KKK after Nathan Forrest ordered it disbanded in 1869, the "invisible empire" virtually ceased to exist by the end of 1871. Although other paramilitary units would arise to resist Radical Reconstruction in the future, they were typically triggered by political developments isolated in the applicable states, such as Louisiana, Arkansas, Mississippi and South Carolina. The Ku Klux Klan never overthrew a single state government.[123]

During the past half-century historians have extensively researched violent incidents involving white paramilitary units. The results are numerous accusations of voter fraud designed to inflate Southern white votes and deter blacks, carpetbaggers and scalawags

---

[122] Dale Watts, "How Bloody Was Bleeding Kansas?" *Kansas History: A Journal of the Central Plains, Vol. 18, No. 2,* (Summer 1995), 125

[123] William Hesseltine, *Grant the Politician,* 259; J. G. Randall and David Donald *The Civil War and Reconstruction,* 684

from voting. Therefore, most Reconstruction era students are aware of KKK voter suppression, but few recognize that Republican control of the election machinery in carpetbag era Southern states— amplified by the presence of federal troops and the power to use federal soldiers under the KKK Acts—suppressed the Democratic votes. As shall be explained in chapter eight, indirect disfranchisement existed on both sides. As the office-holders, however, carpetbaggers could more often execute dictatorial power without resorting to violence.

A final point on Southern Reconstruction during Grant's first term suggests that he—and fellow Republicans—were primarily interested in the political benefits of black suffrage as opposed to the intrinsic merits of racial equality. Specifically, in July Grant signed the 1870 Naturalization Act. It amended the 1790 Naturalization Act to allow blacks born in other countries to become American citizens through the same naturalization process available to whites. But it limited the permission to "non-whites" who were "aliens of African nativity and to persons of African descent." Thus, it did not permit other "non-white" races to utilize the process, mostly due to anti-Asian prejudice in the Western states. When Grant signed the bill about one fifth of San Francisco's residents were Asian immigrants and one fifth were Irish immigrants. Since the Irish were white, they quickly became one of the city's important voting blocs, whereas the Chinese got no representation, although they were often taxed extra.

As a result, Asian Americans could not vote because they could not become citizens. For decades their rights were significantly more restricted than those of whites, or African Americans. It is, therefore, difficult to avoid concluding that the chief motivation for black suffrage among Reconstruction era Republicans was to enhance political power, instead of providing for racial equality. Since the Asian Americans were not numerous enough to offer a meaningful voting bloc, both Republicans and Democrats were unwilling to pretend—as many Republican leaders did in the case of blacks—that the Chinese should be accepted as racially equal.

Asian Americans also endured discrimination and racially motivated mob violence during the Reconstruction era and for years thereafter. As noted, two-thirds of the lynching victims in California between 1849 and 1902 were Asians and America's biggest lynching involved such victims in Los Angeles during Grant's presidency. Another incident occurred in Eureka, California fourteen years later. After a white man was killed in the crossfire between two quarrelling Chinese in 1885 the city forcibly removed all of its Chinese residents in forty-eight hours. They hurriedly loaded over three hundred onto two ships that happened to be in the harbor and told the Chinese to never return. There can be little doubt that massive bloodshed would have resulted if the Asians had resisted. Five years earlier a mob of three thousand whites gutted Denver's Chinatown as thoroughly as a tornado entered the front door of each dwelling and left by the back door.

Although California had far fewer lynchings than the South, the number of Chinese Americans in the state never topped ten percent and few were permitted to vote until well into the twentieth century. The mob violence against Chinese Americans that might have resulted in California if Asians had been allowed to vote in numbers approximating the forty percent population share that blacks held in the South would undoubtedly have been much more extensive.[124]

Having driven the KKK into near-extinction by the end of 1871, Grant would have had good reelection prospects in 1872 except that his Party was splitting. The defections that began with senators Schurz and Trumbull in 1870 gained momentum. By March 1871 they had evolved into a second wing of the Republican Party, termed the Liberals, while Party members who remained loyal to Grant became known as Stalwarts.

---

[124] Jean Pfaelzer, *Driven Out: The Forgotten War Against Chinese Americans*, (Berkeley: University of California Press, 2008), 45, 52, 59, 119, 123-24; Marian L. Smith, *Prologue Magazine* "Race, Nationality and Reality" (Summer 2002) Available: http://bit.ly/2zF3oJm [Accessed: October 20, 2017]; John Soennichsen, *The Chinese Exclusion Act of 1882* (Santa Barbara, Calif.: Greenwood, 2011), Kindle Loc. 74

Republicans such as former Interior Secretary Cox, Massachusetts Senator Sumner, Chief Justice Salmon P. Chase and former Ambassador to Britain Charles Francis Adams joined the Liberals. In May 1872 the Liberal Republicans nominated *New York Tribune* publisher Horace Greeley as their presidential candidate. He was an early and outspoken advocate of emancipation during Lincoln's Administration. As late as 1870 Grant characterized Greeley as an "honest, firm, and untiring supporter of the republican party."

Greeley's platform mixed Republican and Democratic principles to settle on planks such as civil service reform, sound money, low tariffs and state's rights. He regarded the KKK Act as a usurpation of state's rights. In 1871 he told an Arkansas newspaper, "Not as much violence occurs in Texas as in New York City." Despite his long record championing African Americans, he criticized carpetbag governments. James Pike, who worked for Greeley's *Tribune* and was previously an abolitionist diplomat for Lincoln, wrote an article about Reconstruction in South Carolina after visiting

Horace Greeley

the state in 1872. He concluded, "The men who lead . . . the State Government are thieves and miscreants, ignorant and corrupt." He found new sympathy for white Southerners and characterized the black legislators as a "mass of ignorance and barbarism." Shortly before the Stalwart Republican convention in June, Charles Sumner assailed Grant from the Senate floor as "first in nepotism, first in gift-taking repaid by official patronage, first in presidential pretentions and first in quarrel with his countrymen."[125]

A month after the Liberal wing of the Republican Party nominated Greeley, the Stalwart wing re-nominated Grant. Conventioneers chose, however, to replace Vice President Schuyler Colfax of Indiana because they questioned his loyalty to Grant after he disclosed months earlier an ambition to be President. Massachusetts Senator Henry Wilson replaced Colfax in order to geographically balance the ticket. Ironically both VPs would fall into disrepute after first denying—and later admitting—that they accepted bargain-priced stock in Crédit Mobilier, which was an affiliate of the Union Pacific Railroad and a tool for siphoning-off federal subsidies used to build the eastern half of the first transcontinental railroad.

Democrats met in July and endorsed the Liberal Republican ticket. Thus, Greeley could become President if he could capture a significant share of the Republican vote to combine with the Democratic voters. Senator Sumner's support held promise to corral black votes because the Senator had consistently been a high-profile advocate for African Americans. Although Greeley conducted a whistle-stop campaign, Grant was mostly stationary. The latter had evolved into a shrewd political powerbroker. His political machine included a "correspondents association" that wrote articles and editorials for newspapers across the country. Powerful businessmen such as Jay Cooke donated generously to his campaign because of his support for high tariffs and gold-backed money.

In the end Greeley lost by a humiliating margin and died before the Electoral College report, which gave Grant an 80% majority. The President also won a decisive 56% of the popular vote and captured thirty-one states compared to Greeley's six. Blacks voted overwhelmingly for Grant, helping him win eight of the eleven former Confederate states. Republicans also gained congressional seats. The

---

[125] Ron Chernow, *Grant,* 740-42; Richard White, *The Republic For Which it Stands,* 192

Party once again would control the Senate and House with commanding majorities.[126]

---

[126] Ron Chernow, *Grant,* 743-45, 748-51

CHAPTER 7: TURNING POINT

IN THE MIDST OF THE AUTUMN elections, on September 4, 1872, the *New York Sun* published an article headlined "King of Frauds: How the Crédit Mobilier Bought its Way into Congress," which referred to the Union Pacific's construction company discussed in chapter three. The article listed a number of politicians suspected of participating in the scandal including James G. Blaine who was Speaker of the House. Blaine, and others among the accused, were dismayed that the chatter would not die down. Even the *Springfield Republican* added to the story by implicating Massachusetts Congressman Henry Dawes, preventing him from getting elected to the Senate as he expected. The ensuing revelations would shake public confidence in the integrity of the nation's railroads and its federal government, laying the foundation for an economic debacle.[127]

After the general election, the House and Senate each responded by forming investigative committees thereby providing a steady stream of gossip for newspapers. But most times when evidence pointed toward officeholders, committee interrogators became reticent and the trails typically faded, or the excuses provided by the pertinent politicians were routinely accepted. Congressman John Bingham, for example, admitted that he owned stock but denied that it influenced his votes. He justified his ownership by explaining that it was not explicitly illegal.

Others, like Congressman Dawes and vice-presidential candidate Henry Wilson, testified that they had initially accepted bargained-

---

[127] Richard White, *Railroaded* (New York: W. W. Norton, 2011), 63

priced Crédit Mobilier stock but later returned it without profit. Dawes said he initially gave Congressman Oakes Ames, who distributed Crédit Mobilier stock to politicians, $1,035 for ten shares. Over the next six months Dawes's shares paid dividends composed of $600 in cash, $800 in Union Pacific bonds and $1,000 in Union Pacific stock. The congressman later returned the dividends in exchange for his original $1,035 investment. Wilson said he lost money on his transaction. Similarly, Pennsylvania Congressman Glenni Scofield held the stock only five months, although he profited by a total of about $1,000.[128]

In his defense, Ames argued that Crédit Mobilier shares could not be bribes because they were distributed under terms that were below the market rate for a congressional vote. They were merely a *quid pro quo* for influential "friends" of the Union Pacific. "If you want to bribe a man," testified Ames, "you want to bribe a man who is opposed to you, not . . . one who is your friend." Like John Bingham, he also argued that, "There is no law and no reason legal or moral why a member of congress should not own stock in a road any more than he should not own sheep when the price of wool is to be affected by tariff." But it was a bad analogy because a congressman would obviously be compromised if he accepted an offer to buy a flock of sheep at a discount price shortly before voting in favor of a wool tariff. Similarly, legislation affecting the interests of the UP repeatedly came before Congress.[129]

Congressmen James Garfield and William "Pig Iron" Kelley accepted dividends from shares purchased with prior dividends but the two were spared official reprimand. Blaine, Senators Roscoe Conkling and John Logan as well as former Treasury Secretary

[128] Edward Martin, *A Complete and Graphic Account of the Credit Mobilier Investigations: Chapter 7* Available: http://bit.ly/2nzA57q [Accessed: December 6, 2017]

[129] Richard White, *Railroaded*, 63-65; Richard White, *The Republic for Which it Stands*, 256-60; John Ford Rhodes, *History of the United States: 1850 – 1877 Vol. VII*, (New York: Macmillan Company, 1904) Available: http://bit.ly/2DML3NK [Accessed: December 3, 2017]

George Boutwell, were found to have never received any stock, although Ames's records suggest that he intended to include them. Former Vice President Schuyler Colfax and Senator James Patterson were seriously compromised but not officially reproved. Most of the other congressmen and senators accused of complicity confessed that while they had been approached by Ames, they either rejected his proposal or only temporarily accepted Crédit Mobilier stock, which they returned along with all dividends received. Congressional criticism was generally reserved for those who had accepted stock but denied it.

Senators Patterson and James Harlan were basically permitted to serve out their lame-duck terms without reprimand. Although Harlan had not accepted stock, in 1865 he took a $10,000 campaign contribution from a Union Pacific officer. Colfax flatly denied receiving stock from Ames, but the public never believed him. Not only did Ames's contemporaneous memorandum book record a $1,200 dividend paid to Colfax but Colfax stumbled badly before the investigating committee when he tried to explain away a $1,200 cancelled check written by Ames and payable to Colfax. Historian James Ford Rhodes concludes, "It is impossible to believe he [Colfax] told the truth."

In the end, only New York Senator James Brooks and Congressman Ames were censured. Each died in disgrace within a few months. Although Brooks was the only Democrat implicated, he was an official government representative on the Union Pacific board of directors. The whitewashed investigations appalled the public. Of his censure for gifting the shares, Ames commented to a reporter, "It is just like the man in Massachusetts who committed adultery and the jury brought in a verdict that he was as guilty as the devil but that the woman was as innocent as an angel. [The uncensored recipients] are like that woman."[130]

-----

[130] Jack Beatty, *Age of Betrayal* (New York: Alfred A. Knopf, 2007), 230; John Ford Rhodes, *History of the United States: 1850 – 1877 Vol. VII*, 9, 13-14 Available: http://bit.ly/2kfLWGm

Ames died two months later convinced of his own martyrdom. Historian Matthew Josephson writes, "Ames . . . felt sincerely that public esteem and profit was owing to him for having carried out the daring transcontinental railway enterprise from which . . . 'the capital of the world shrank.'" Given the tens-of-millions of dollars in profits paid to the Central Pacific's Big Four and the major shareholders of Crédit Mobilier, he was dismayed that the comparatively trivial amounts connected with his scheme to reward congressional friends created such uproar. Only about $65,000 of profit was traced to the politicians connected with his conspiracy.[131]

Immediately after the Crédit Mobilier hearings Congress gave the public another reason to doubt the integrity of the national government when they voted a significant pay raise for all three federal branches. Grant's annual salary was increased from $25,000 to $50,000, while the salaries of his cabinet members grew from $8,000 to $10,000, as did the salaries of the Supreme Court justices. Yearly pay for senators and congressmen climbed from $5,000 to $7,500 and was augmented by a one-time bonus of $5,000.

Moreover, Massachusetts Republican Congressman Benjamin Butler had arranged for the salary provisions to be buried as a rider in a general appropriations bill in order to minimize publicity. But when a New York newspaper disclosed the rider, the public became outraged. Consequently, Congress repealed the law less than a year later but paid a price. Of the 102 incumbents who took backpay, only 24 were re-nominated and only half of the 24 were reelected. Although Grant did not initiate the scheme he hungered for a salary

---

[Accessed: December 3, 2017]; *United States Senate*, "James Patterson Expulsion Case" Available: http://bit.ly/2nmEwlK [Accessed: December 3, 2917]; Matthew Josephson, *The Politicos* (New York: Harcourt, Brace, 1958), 171

131 Matthew Josephson, *The Politicos*, 170

increase and made no effort to oppose the bill as a matter of public interest.[132]

Even before the Crédit Mobilier machinations first became public, Americans were generally suspicious of rampant corruption between business and government. Nearly a year earlier, one newspaper correspondent famously suggested that notices be nailed to the congressional doors when a new session of the Forty-Second Congress opened in December 1871 stating, "The business of this establishment will be done hereafter in the offices of the Pennsylvania Railroad," which was then America's biggest corporation.[133]

Vice President Schuyler Colfax

Despite Grant's present-day reputation for civil rights activism, his treatment of Attorney General Amos Akerman suggests insincerity. Specifically, notorious business moguls may have led Grant to subvert the interests of Southern blacks to those of railroad industry tycoons.

Akerman was the second of President Grant's five attorneys general. He served a little over a year from November 1870 to December 1871. Although born in New Hampshire, at the age of twenty-one in 1842 he moved to Georgia where he first worked as a

---

[132] Charles Calhoun, *The Presidency of Ulysses S. Grant* (Lawrence: University Press of Kansas, 2017), 402 – 03; Mark Summers, *The Era of Good Stealings* (Oxford: Oxford University Press, 1993), 255

[133] Claude Bowers, *The Tragic Era* (Cambridge, Ma.: Riverside Press, 1929), 371

tutor but later became a lawyer. Despite initially opposing secession he remained loyal to the South and served as a Confederate quartermaster during the Civil War. He moved to a combat brigade after Union Major General William T. Sherman invaded Georgia in 1864.[134]

Akerman was the most vigorous of Grant's attorneys general in prosecuting the Ku Klux Klan. In order to expedite prosecutions, he expanded the powers of the then newly created federal Justice Department. About six hundred Klan members were convicted. Although most received light sentences, sixty-five were imprisoned for up to five years at a federal penitentiary in Albany, New York.[135]

Grant, however, may have revealed his secondary interest in racial justice when he abruptly asked Akerman to resign in December 1871. Partly at the prompting of Secretary of State Hamilton Fish, Grant had misgivings about Akerman's "obsession" with the Klan. Perhaps more importantly, Akerman also frustrated important Northern capitalists. He was, for example, critical of the dubious terms under which railroads often qualified for federal subsidies. In June 1871 Akerman had denied land and bond grants to the Union Pacific Railroad, which had given Crédit Mobilier lucrative contracts to build the line.[136]

Shortly before resigning Akerman confronted the previous attorney general, Ebenezer Hoar, when the latter was representing a railroad client's land grant claims. Akerman told Hoar that the client had not completed the work required to qualify for the grants. Nearly simultaneously Interior Secretary Columbus Delano complained to President Grant that Akerman had annoyed railroad moguls Collis Huntington and Jay Gould with rulings unfavorable to their interests. Whether at the urging of Fish, Delano, or Hoar, Grant

---

[134] William McFeely *Grant*, 367

[135] Jean Edward Smith *Grant* (New York: Simon & Schuster, 2001), 542, 547

[136] John Y. Simon, Editor *The Papers of Ulysses S. Grant, 31 volumes, 1988 ed.*, (Carbondale: Southern Illinois University Press, 1967), 22:188; Claude Bowers, *The Tragic Era*, 396, 398; William McFeely *Grant*, 373

replaced Akerman with Oregon's George Williams who later resigned under bribery accusations, as did Delano. The *New York Sun* reported in January 1872 that Williams's appointment was essentially a triumph for the Pacific Railroads.[137]

Grant biographer William McFeely concluded: "[After Akerman's resignation] the finest champion of human rights in the Grant administration went home to Cartersville, Georgia where he practiced law privately for only eight more years. He had given up on his native North and Northerners."[138]

Attorney General Amos Akerman

Aside from the 1869 Gould-Fisk attempt to corner the gold market with the help of Grant family members and others connected to the President, little was generally known about the scandals directly involving Administration officials until they came to light after his 1872 re-election. Americans would grow increasingly disgusted with the lies, evasions, whitewashing and mere knuckle-rapping punishments that materialized during Grant's second presidential term.[139]

---

[137] William McFeely, *Grant* 372-3; Jean Edward Smith, *Grant*, 584; Claude Bowers, *The Tragic Era*, 371

[138] William McFeely, *Grant* 373

[139] Claude Bowers, *The Tragic Era,* 371

CHAPTER 8: SECOND TERM RECONSTRUCTION

A LTHOUGH THE PRESIDENT'S DECISIVE win over Greeley and the coupled Republican congressional gains in the 1872 elections suggest that Grant might further advance civil rights in his second term, the disputed results in Arkansas and Louisiana threw a monkey wrench into such plans, if any ever existed. When combined with increasing corruption scandals in Washington, the tragic dramas of Republican opportunism in the Razorback and Pelican states would provide plenty of reasons to doubt honesty in the federal government.

Arkansas carpetbagger Powell Clayton was the center of political power during much of the state's Reconstruction period. He became her first Republican governor in 1868 and later became one of her U. S. Senators in 1871, holding the seat until 1877. Immediately upon moving into the governor's office in 1868 he consolidated his power by strictly enforcing the disfranchisement of most former Confederates. Unlike the Gulf States, which were typically populated by a majority—or near majority—of blacks, only 25% of Arkansans were African American. Clayton, therefore, felt it necessary to minimize the number of whites who could vote in order to ensure that the Republican-loyal blacks were the dominant electorate.[140]

In order to enforce his authority, he promptly formed a state militia. It barred former Confederates as members since only voters were permitted to join. As in other Southern states it was, therefore, commonly labeled a Black Militia, even though it also included whites that had not supported the Confederacy. Clayton

---

[140] James Randall and David Donald, *The Civil War and Reconstruction*, 5

unhesitatingly used his militia to suppress any genuine, or suspected, civilian resistance to his policies.

After he moved to the Senate in 1871, he informally anointed Elisha Baxter as his heir apparent to be the Republican gubernatorial candidate in 1872. As noted earlier, however, 1872 was also the year when the national Republican Party split into two wings: Liberal and Stalwart. Clayton and Baxter were Stalwarts, who supported President Grant as the leader of their wing nationally. Locally, Arkansas's Republican Liberal wing advocated an end to corruption, more economical government, less power in the governor's office, and a renewal of voting privileges to former Confederates. They

Powell Clayton

nominated Joseph Brooks to challenge Baxter who gradually began to echo some of the national Liberal wing's planks, including the return of voting rights to former Rebels.

Due to Clayton's original disfranchisement of ex-Rebels, however, the Democratic Party was too weak to offer its own gubernatorial candidate. As a result, the governor's race was a contest between two Republicans. Since Clayton still controlled the state's political machinery Baxter won the 1872 election and took office early in 1873. Brooks, nonetheless, filed a couple of lawsuits charging fraud. He quickly lost the higher-profile suit while the second one languished in a lower county court.

A year after Baxter took office, however, he angered Powell and Stephen Dorsey, who was the state's junior senator. Both Clayton and Dorsey had become wealthy in Reconstruction era Arkansas. Dorsey's path to prosperity had been railroad finance manipulation. He would later become secretary of the national Republican committee. But he would also get implicated in a nation-wide U. S.

Post Office scandal for rigged bidding of rural delivery routes, which were allocated to private companies at the time under lucrative contracts. Although one of the senator's clerks, who had fingered Dorsey as a co-conspirator, was convicted in the corruption, Dorsey escaped conviction.

Clayton also profited from taxpayer-funded railroads but additionally owned 40,000 acres in cotton lands. After the Civil War many impoverished Arkansas farmers lost their lands due to inability to pay property taxes. They resented that the buyers were often politically connected to Powell's regime and that the sales were at the bargain prices typical of tax deficiency liquidations.

Baxter attacked rail promoters for recklessly issuing too many state-guaranteed bonds to finance the construction of their railroads. Attempts by the companies to force the state to accept stock, instead of cash, for repayment of the bonds triggered Baxter's opposition. Ultimately every Reconstruction era railroad in Arkansas financed in this manner defaulted on its interest payments. Construction costs were unaccountably high as were the bond sales commissions. There can be little doubt that much of the excess went into the pockets of the promoters, such as Clayton and Dorsey.

Baxter further alienated the two senators by urging that Arkansas hold a new constitutional convention to reverse some provisions of the 1868 constitution, which launched the state's carpetbag era. Chief among the desired changes was voter enfranchisement of former Confederates but a more economical state government as well as more localism in government were two other goals. Thus, the resultant 1874 state constitution significantly reduced the power of the governor's office, limited his term to two years and only permitted the Arkansas legislature to assemble every other year. The salaries of elected officials were also cut sharply.

Consequently, the two senators quickly switched sides in the governor dispute. They got the obscure county court to declare Brooks the true winner of the 1872 election. Accompanied by ten armed men on April 15, 1874, Brooks physically ousted Baxter from the governor's office in a *coup d'état*.

From a nearby Little Rock hotel, Baxter put out a call for militia to return him to office. Brooks sent out a separate call to defend his occupation of the state house. Thousands of white and black men showed up to support their candidate. Federal troops from a nearby arsenal temporarily kept them apart but inevitably the opponents collided in an adventure termed the Brooks-Baxter War. Forces clashed at four sites. Eventually the two sides suffered as many as a combined two hundred casualties. Ironically, armed black men fought on opposing sides in one skirmish at the now-vanished town of New Gascony.

Meanwhile Baxter and Brooks each maneuvered for support from the expected surge of whites that would be permitted to vote in the next election. (This was due to a March 1873 amendment to the 1868 state constitution that re-enfranchised former Confederates.) In the end, white leaders lobbied President Grant to simply choose a winner. They merely wanted a temporary placeholder in the governor's office until their restored voting rights could put the Democrats back in power. Grant chose Baxter on May 15, 1874 but appointed Brooks as the Little Rock postmaster. As expected, Democrats regained power in the autumn 1874 elections. Since Arkansans replaced its 1868 carpetbag constitution with a new one in 1874, Grant later regretted his choice of Baxter, but curiously blamed Congress for failing to retroactively correct his mistake. [141]

Specifically, Grant soured on Baxter when the latter supported calls for a new Arkansas constitutional convention in the summer of 1874 to replace the 1868 constitution. The October elections ratified

---

[141] Brooks Simpson, *The Reconstruction Presidents,* 180; Thomas A. DeBlack, *With Fire and Sword: Arkansas, 1861-1874* (Fayetteville: University of Arkansas Press, 2003), 210-224; Carl H. Moneyhon, *The Impact of the Civil War and Reconstruction in Arkansas* (Baton Rouge: LSU Press, 1994), 250-53, 256-262; James A. Pierce, "From McMath to Rockefeller: Arkansas Governors and Illegal Gambling in Postwar Hot Springs, 1945 – 1970" *Thesis for Master's Degree* (University of Arkansas, 2008), 8; Thomas DeBlack, *Lecture* "The End of Reconstruction in Arkansas" Available: http://bit.ly/2AHsVUq [Accessed: November 29, 2017]; John Mooney, *Lecture* "The Brooks-Baxter War" Available: http://bit.ly/2zOU6MX [Accessed: November 29, 2017]; *Harper's Weekly,* "A Fable—With a Modern Application" (March 25, 1882) Available: http://nyti.ms/2jhTaXj [Accessed: December 5, 2017]; William Gillette, *Retreat from Reconstruction* (Baton Rouge: LSU Press, 1979), 141

the new constitution and chose Democrat Augustus Garland to replace Baxter as governor.

Not only did Grant oppose the new Garland regime, he objected to the 1874 constitution by citing a technicality in the 1868 constitution that he believed invalidated the new constitution. Moreover, during his 1874 annual message in December, Grant flip-flopped on his own intervention the previous May that had made Baxter governor. Retrospectively, he claimed that Baxter had no authority to call for a new constitutional convention because Brooks— not Baxter—was Arkansas's legitimate governor! Grant's true objection to the new constitution was its shift toward localism, which would hinder the Republican Party's ability to hold power by controlling all of the state's election machinery remotely from Little Rock.

Although Grant threatened to use federal troops to force his will in Arkansas, he was prepared to first await the recommendations of a House investigating committee headed by Vermont Republican Luke Poland. Early in February 1875 the Committee rejected Grant's interpretation. It concluded that there was "no just reason" for the federal government to interfere in Arkansas's state elections. The House of Representatives accepted the Committee's majority report in a vote of 150-to-81. Even among Republicans, support for Grant was disappointing. While eighty Republicans voted to support the minority report, sixty-five voted against it, as did eighty-five Democrats. The Senate followed suit by failing to adopt its own resolution for federal intervention. Reconstruction in Arkansas was finished, as was the state's Republican Party for the next one hundred years.[142]

No doubt the inability to keep Arkansas's Republican Party united sank black hopes for racial equality in the state but it probably

---

[142] Ulysses S. Grant, Sixth Annual Message, December 7, 1874 Available: http://bit.ly/2yXRVBA [Accessed: December 19, 2017]; Charles Calhoun, *The Presidency of Ulysses S. Grant*, 474-76; Thomas DeBlack, *With Fire and Sword*, 218; William Gillette, *Retreat From Reconstruction*, 144, 148

reduced the propensity for racial violence. Without ex-Confederate disfranchisement, which Baxter eliminated, there were not enough black voters to prevent a Democratic victory in the fall of 1874. Consequently, whites had little reason to let resentments of the carpetbag era linger. In contrast, the consequences of a falling-out among Republican thieves in Louisiana would be more tragic.

After losing support of the Stalwart wing of the Republican Party and becoming isolated in the Liberal wing by default, Louisiana's carpetbag incumbent governor, Henry Warmoth, declined to run for re-election in 1872. The thirty-year-old had never enjoyed a good relationship with Grant anyway. The two men originally became acquainted when Warmoth was a foot soldier under Grant's commanded at Vicksburg in May 1863. When the first Union army assault on the Confederate fortress failed, Warmoth was wounded and criticized Grant to a Chicago newspaper reporter. Thereafter, Grant despised Warmoth.

Unfortunately for Warmoth, Grant had a powerfully connected brother-in-law in New Orleans. Specifically, one of Julia's sisters had married Kentuckian James F. Casey who had been appointed as tariff collector at the Port of New Orleans in 1869. It was an important tax collection post where duties, and ancillary fees such as temporary storage, might be diverted to businesses connected with the ruling political Party as well as to collection's officials individually. Thus, Casey quickly became a potential king maker in Louisiana's Republican Party due to the patronage he commanded by reason of his office.[143]

According to historian Hesselstine, "Casey interpreted his position to involve the control of local politics in the interests of the national Administration." Casey cooperated with Warmoth for a time, but in 1870 they had a falling-out when Warmoth declined to support Casey's bid to become a U. S. Senator. Among Casey's allies was U. S. Marshall Stephen Packard who controlled the federal troops in New Orleans, which was then the state capital. Thus,

[143] Ted Tunnell *Crucible of Reconstruction* (Baton Rouge: LSU Press, 1984), Kindle Location 2234

Packard used the soldiers to block Warmoth delegates from an August 1871 state Republican convention held to choose a new state central committee. Although Warmoth attempted to complain to Grant, the President refused to hear him.

Without support from the President, Warmoth made overtures to Louisiana Democrats and attended the 1872 Liberal Republican Convention in Cincinnati that nominated Horace Greeley for President. He thereby became a political enemy to Grant as well as Casey. As a result, in the autumn elections Warmoth backed Greeley for President and former Confederate officer John McEnery for governor. McEnery ran on a fusion ticket composed of Democrats and Liberal Republicans. Casey backed brother-in-law Grant for President and carpetbagger William Kellogg for governor. Kellogg, who was one of Louisiana's U. S senators at the time, ran as a Stalwart Republican.

The elections were "remarkably quiet and orderly," according to Washington's *National Republican* newspaper. According to Louisiana historian Ted Tunnell, McEnery probably won the majority of votes cast but also benefitted from Warmoth's control of the Returning Board responsible for compiling and validating the votes. Warmoth's board officially tallied a 10,000-vote majority for McEnery. In response, Kellogg created his own Returning Board, which manufactured an 18,000-vote majority for Kellogg even though it had no ballots to count. According to historian Robert Henry, since Kellogg's board had no ballots, its "returns" were derived from "affidavits, newspaper estimates, and even their own calculations . . . from what the vote in a given parish might, or should, have been."

Since Warmoth had the legal ballots, his board could fill the state legislature with his supporters. They were, therefore, on the verge of getting McEnery installed in the governor's office when Kellogg hurriedly persuaded federal Judge Edward Durell to arbitrarily rule on 6 December that Kellogg's board was the only legitimate Returning Board. Kellogg thereby blocked Warmoth's legislature, which was scheduled to assemble in three days. As a result, on 9 December Marshall Stephen Packard used federal troops to forcibly prevent Warmoth legislators from assembling. Packard admitted only Kellogg lawmakers into the legislature. Warmouth supporters were outraged at Grant because, as historian William Gillette put it, "By having involved federal authority in civil law and having employed federal force in state politics, [Grant] had mounted a successful *coup d'état*.[144]

Although mostly criticized in Louisiana and the South, interference by a federal judge in a state election was questioned all over America. The *New York Herald* accused Grant of keeping political allies in power "regardless of the will of the people, the right of self-government or the forms of state law."

Judge Durell's action had little basis in law except for the 1870 Enforcement Act passed two years earlier. In practice, the act enabled the federal government to step-in anytime a carpetbag regime complained that Southern whites had intimidated black voters. Carpetbaggers could submit dubious evidence, as had Kellogg who presented questionable affidavits from citizens who claimed to have been denied the right to vote. According to historian Henry, "These affidavits were printed in blank by the thousands, before the election, and signed in bulk by obliging officers. The special marshals obliged to complete them had only to dig up names, from any convenient source, and fill in the blanks."

Two years later, in January 1874, the House Judiciary Committee in Washington under the chairmanship of Massachusetts Representative Benjamin Butler began investigating Durell. Butler, it should be noted, had few native Louisiana friends because of his confiscatory policies as commander of the city's Union occupation army during the Civil War.

Butler's committee voted six-to-five to impeach Judge Durell for systematic bribery in bankruptcy cases and for exceeding his authority in the 1872 elections. After the autumn 1874 elections increased the Democratic majority in the House and because he felt

---

[144] William Hesseltine, *Grant the Politician*, 342-43; Charles Lane, *The Day Freedom Died* (New York: Henry Holt, 2009), 52, 65; John Ezell, *The South Since 1865*, 92; Robert Selph Henry, *The Story of Reconstruction*, 460, 478, 482, 485; William Gillette, *Retreat from Reconstruction*, 112

the Senate would convict him, Durell resigned. In sum, Kellogg did not become governor in 1872 because he won at the polls. He was artificially made governor because a possibly corrupt federal judge that Congress appeared likely to impeach only two years later had unilaterally selected Kellogg the winner.[145]

To return to the 1872 narrative, it may be seen that Louisiana's governance situation was intolerable. The state was left with two governors, two legislatures, and potentially two sets of tax collectors, each collecting for rival state governments. Since Kellogg had to resign as senator in order to become governor, and one of Louisiana's Kellogg-faction congressman was elected "at-large," it fell to Congress to indirectly select the proper state government. Washington's House of Representatives decided that the Kellogg regime was illegal and "not much better than a successful conspiracy." A Senate investigation concluded that the election had "so many frauds and forgeries as to make it doubtful what candidates received a majority of the votes actually cast." Thus, Congress recommended new elections.

President Grant would not have it. Instead, he criticized Congress for failing to choose one of the two "available" candidates and relied upon Judge Durell's ruling as a legal fig leaf to settle on Kellogg. But Grant's verdict also became a widely controversial decision. Historian Hesseltine concluded, "That Grant's support of Kellogg was simply the partisan support of a Republican admits no doubt." In March 1873 Grant amplified suspicions about his motives by reappointing brother-in-law Casey to the New Orleans customs post for another four years even though a congressional investigating committee had condemned Casey for corruption and gross misconduct only months earlier.[146]

---

[145] Charles Lane, *13 Green Bag 2D* "Edward Henry Durell: A Study in Reputation", (Winter, 2010), 153, 161-62, 166-68 Available: http://bit.ly/2A5syzA [Accessed: 10/31/2017]; Robert Selph Henry, *The Story of Reconstruction*, 479; William Gillette, *Retreat from Reconstruction*, 112

[146] William Hesseltine, *Grant the Politician,* 344-46; Robert Selph Henry, *The Story of Reconstruction,* 488; *Tulane University: Media Nola,* "1872 Gubernatorial Election" Available: http://bit.ly/2xIJj1V [Accessed: October 31, 2017]; C. Vann Woodward, *American*

Louisiana's Fraudulently Elected
Governor William Kellogg

The unsettled gubernatorial dispute had dreadful consequences. Although Kellogg was able to gain control in New Orleans while being protected by a well-equipped state militia and nearby federal troops, he had difficulty exercising authority in the hinterland. Since remote parishes were often beyond the reach of his military forces, he sometimes compromised with McEnery supporters by appointing some of them to local government posts. A parish named for President Grant where the local seat of government was in a hamlet named for Vice President Colfax provided a tragic example.

Grant Parish and Colfax were located about 220 miles up the Red River from New Orleans. Before Grant's decision to support Kellogg, McEnery supporters had already occupied the flimsy Colfax courthouse and took over the local political offices. After Grant chose to back Kellogg over McEnery the former met with Grant Parish McEnery backers in mid-March 1873. As a conciliatory gesture he promised to appoint local McEnery supporters to the posts of sheriff, tax collector, clerk, and recorder, among other positions, in Grant Parish. After Kellogg loyalists in the parish complained, however, on 20 March Kellogg rescinded his promises to the McEnery group. Instead he designated two of his own followers as parish sheriff and judge. On the night of 25 March local Kellogg supporters clandestinely occupied the Colfax courthouse. The next day Kellogg's

Heritage, "The Lowest Ebb" Volume 8, Number 3 (April, 1957) Available: http://bit.ly/2ydpIdA [Accessed: October 11, 2017]

sheriff and judge designees took their oaths of offices thereby claiming to be the official legal authorities in Grant parish.[147]

On 28 March McEnery's men resolved to retake the courthouse, by force if necessary. Skirmishing around the parish increased during the next two weeks as whites gradually abandoned it and the blacks at Colfax would not permit any whites to enter the town. In early April the freedmen attacked the home of one white. He was among the McEnery supporters that originally negotiated in New Orleans with Kellogg for a Grant Parish post. Although nobody was killed, the blacks recklessly shot into his home at night. They also attacked and ransacked other white-owned homes, forcing more McEnery leaders to leave the parish.

The first death came on 8 April, to a black man. Local armistice attempts had flopped. Kellogg's failure to intervene left McEnery supporters suspicious that he was hoping for a race riot in order to provide an excuse to get President Grant to supply federal soldiers. Such troops would enable Kellogg to flex his authority well into the state's distant parishes without having to make compromising political appointments to Liberal Republicans and Democrats—he could limit such appointments as spoils to Stalwart (Grant-Kellogg) Republicans.

On 10 April, instead of troops, Kellogg proposed to send militia commander James Longstreet to Colfax. Since Longstreet was formerly a top Confederate general the governor hoped the emissary could bridge the two sides into a settlement. But Longstreet never departed. The next day, Good Friday, a delegation of Colfax freedmen arrived in New Orleans. They picked up about five law enforcement officers to accompany them on their return in hopes of enforcing a peace. But they did not arrive in time.[148]

At around noon on Easter April 13, 1873 about a hundred and fifty armed whites stood before the Colfax courthouse to demand that the freedmen disband. Chris Nash, who had been elected sheriff on the

---

[147] Charles Lane, *The Day Freedom Died*, 68-70; Hodding Carter, *The Angry Scar* (New York: Doubleday, 1959), 203

[148] Charles Lane, *The Day Freedom Died*, 85-89; Hodding Carter, *The Angry Scar*, 204-05

Grant Parish McEnery ticket, was their unofficial leader. Before withdrawing his original conciliatory offer to Grant Parish McEnery representatives, Governor Kellogg had promised Nash that he would appoint Nash as sheriff. Better armed than their opponents, the whites also had a small artillery piece, which would enable them to destroy the protecting walls of the flimsy structure protecting the blacks inside.

Sporadic negotiations continued between the two sides until the black men were given two hours to evacuate women and children. According to black accounts, Nash's cannon began firing about two o'clock in the afternoon, causing all black men to retreat inside the courthouse, which the whites promptly set on fire. When two whites approached the burning structure under a truce flag in order to arrange a surrender that would allow the blacks to evacuate, both were shot and mortally wounded.

According to historian Hodding Carter, "What followed was indiscriminate butchery. Many Negroes were shot down as they ran from the burning courthouse; others were ridden down in the open fields. Those who fell wounded in the courthouse square were bayoneted." When the fighting stopped about four o'clock approximately forty blacks remained alive as prisoners. Nash ordered that they remain unharmed. During the ensuing hours most whites left the scene, including Nash who departed about ten o'clock that night. Bill Cruikshank was among those who remained. By agitating that the prisoners be executed, Cruikshank transformed the remaining whites into a vengeful mob. Thirty-seven blacks were shot—massacred.[149]

Cruikshank and eight cohorts were tried in federal court under the authority of the 1870 Enforcement Act. Instead of murder, however, the defendants were charged with violating the civil rights of the freedmen. After an initial mistrial, all nine were convicted in a second trial. They appealed the ruling.

---

[149] Robert Selph Henry, *The Story of Reconstruction*, 491-92; Charles Lane, *The Day Freedom Died*, 95, 98, 102-103, 105; Hodding Carter, *The Angry Scar*, 207

Almost three years after the massacre, the U. S. Supreme Court reversed the conviction in *United States v. Cruikshank* in a March 1876 ruling. The Court decided that the Fourteenth Amendment only protected freedmen against illegal actions by state and local governments, not individuals. Since the Colfax murders had been committed by private citizens it was Louisiana's responsibility to prosecute Cruikshank and his co-defendants. They had never been—or would be—convicted in state court. Four of the five majority-opinion Supreme Court justices were Republicans and one was a Democrat. Lincoln appointed three of the five and Grant had selected the other two.[150]

Readers should note that Grant had an almost unique opportunity among post-bellum Presidents to influence the civil rights profile of the Supreme Court. Less than a year after the midpoint of his two terms he had nominated four of the Court's nine justices. As suggested in the Cruikshank case, however, his appointees compiled a spotty civil rights record. In contrast to herd-following modern historians who overly praise Grant, Richard White admits, "The Supreme Court was Grant's to remake, but his appointments were odd . . . Without any clear method or intent, he created a court that would help eviscerate the legislative base of Reconstruction. He mostly elevated mediocrities to the bench . . ."[151]

White anger against the Stalwart Republican state government grew bigger as a result of Kellogg's ensuing corruption, high taxation and tyrannical control. A nationwide economic downturn triggered by the collapse of Jay Cooke & Company in September 1873, six months after the Colfax incident, further amplified resentment. New Orleans property values dropped by two-thirds compared to 1868. Despite the lower tax base, the local sheriff paid himself a $60,000 annual salary, which amounts to $700,000 in 2018 inflated dollars.

---

[150] Carol Gelderman "Cruikshank Case." In *knowlouisiana.org Encyclopedia of Louisiana*, edited by David Johnson. Louisiana Endowment for the Humanities, 2010 Article published September 4, 2013. Available: http://bit.ly/2AMzgOm [Accessed: November 30, 2017]

[151] Richard White, *The Republic for Which it Stands*, 255

In 1874 Kellogg's legislature passed a bill giving him even greater control over voting returns than Warmoth had in 1872.

Blacks represented about half of Louisiana voters. Since they routinely voted Republican, even national personalities such as Horace Greeley and Carl Schurz as well as Northern writers such as Charles Nordhoff, Edward King and James Pike described the Deep South states as existing under the thumb of "Negro Rule." National reconciliation, they concluded, could not happen until white Southerners were granted "home rule." The editor of *The Nation* criticized Republicans for their "insane task of making newly emancipated field hands, led by barbers and barkeepers, . . . [believe that] they knew as much about government . . . as . . . whites."

Louisianans who felt victimized by "Negro Rule" increasingly rallied to the contra-concept of "White Supremacy." To them, "White Supremacy" was not merely a term meaning white racial superiority *per se*. It was also metaphorically an antidote to the perceived poison of "Negro Rule." Even though Northerners also believed in the intrinsic superiority of the white race almost as universally as did Southerners, there were not enough Northern blacks to gain control of any Northern state government through a democratic process. In the antebellum "free" states, for example, blacks represented only one percent of the population. There can be little doubt that contemporary Northerners would likely have objected just as strongly if their own state governments were abruptly turned over to "Negro Rule" as Pike portrayed the term.

As a result, in 1874 Louisiana Democrats organized White Leagues, which they avowed were "peaceable bodies formed for . . . protection against 'Republican Alliances' . . . organized among the Negroes." Unlike the KKK, the White Leagues were not secret. They regarded their birth to be an inevitable reaction to the secretive "oath bound" black leagues (Union Leagues) that "voted like a body of soldiers" obeying commands from carpetbagger leaders "known to be unworthy and dishonest."

In some parishes the White Leagues were nothing more than an alliance of white voters committed to overthrowing "Negro Rule" whereas in other parishes they were capable of suddenly transforming into paramilitary groups willing to use force. In the latter context, however, White League members considered their violence to be no more unlawful than that of the black militia defending the illicitly elected Governor Kellogg.

One of the first examples of White League violence emerged in the northwest part of the state. It followed Governor Kellogg's enactment of a bill in July 1874 that gave him even greater dictatorial control over election Returning Boards in the approaching fall elections than Warmoth. Thus, Kellogg's new authority virtually assured another crooked Republican-controlled election, but this time for Kellogg's benefit. In August, White Leaguers in Red River Parish responded by forcibly removing six Republican officeholders whom they regarded as tyrannical. As the officials were being escorted out of the state, a lynch mob intercepted the entourage and executed the six prisoners.[152]

An even bigger confrontation—known as the Battle of Liberty Place—happened a month later in New Orleans. On Saturday September 12, 1874 rumors ran through the city suggesting that Kellogg had ordered a river steamer suspected of carrying a commercial cargo of repeating rifles be prevented from unloading. Whites had been angry for months that the governor's militia and police had been disarming them. They considered it a violation of the Second Amendment. The order to block the replenishing arms shipment was the last straw.

In response, three thousand men gathered on Monday at a Canal Street statue where they resolved to ask Kellogg to abdicate. The governor was ensconced behind the granite walls of the customs house, which was protected by his militia under the command of the previously mentioned former Confederate leader James Longstreet. Longstreet, however, was also a prewar friend and relation by marriage of President Grant's and a willing recipient of the

---

[152] Adam-Max Tuchinsky, *Horace Greeley's New York Tribune*, (Ithaca, N.Y.: Cornell University Press, 2009), 227; Edward Blum, *Reforging the White Republic* (Baton Rouge: LSU Press, 2005), 126; Robert Selph Henry, *The Story of Reconstruction*, 516-17; Charles Lane, *The Day Freedom Died*, 227

President's patronage, much to the resentment of most ex-Confederates.

To formalize the abdication request, D. B. Penn proclaimed himself acting governor since he had been McEnery's running mate in the disputed 1872 election and McEnery—Kellogg's opposing gubernatorial candidate—was not present. From the White League's perspective, the proclamation transformed the pending conflict into a contest between two militias, instead of a fight between a renegade paramilitary group and a legitimate militia.

Fighting started when Longstreet led his men forward to force the "Penn Militia" to disperse. It was over quickly. Longstreet was captured after his men sustained seventy-six casualties, while the "Penn Militia" suffered forty. On Tuesday, Penn was inaugurated governor and New Orleans was orderly. While Kellogg remained bunkered in the customs house, McEnery arrived to replace Penn as governor.

But President Grant continued to insist on backing Kellogg. On Thursday 17 September, U. S. military forces under General William H. Emory demanded that McEnery abandon the state capitol and return all state government facilities to Kellogg. McEnery complied, satisfied that the White League had demonstrated that Kellogg's government had no power beyond that which could be sustained under the glitter of federal bayonets. Many Northerners agreed with McEnery's assessment. New York Congressman Samuel Cox, for example, commented that the episode demonstrated Kellogg's "humiliating . . . incapacity to govern" without the constant presence of federal troops.[153]

Although Louisianans did not vote for a governor in 1874 they did elect a new legislature. Kellogg's control of the ballot counting predictably resulted in a majority of Republican legislators. When Democrats challenged disputed seats during the swearing-in process, Kellogg called forth the U. S. Army again, this time to seat only those

---

[153] Robert Selph Henry, *The Story of Reconstruction*, 518-20; Claude Bowers, *The Tragic Era*, 439; Charles Lane, *The Day Freedom Died*, 220; Ted Tunnell, *Crucible of Reconstruction*, Kindle Location 3174

candidates that his Returning Board had authorized and to forcibly remove any challengers. In short, Louisiana's 1874 elections were another Republican-controlled fraud that created a phony Republican majority in the legislature.

This time, however, many more Northerners—and even some Republicans—criticized the situation. Not only was it increasingly evident that the Republican Returning Boards would never permit honest elections, but discipline over dissenting Southerners was becoming increasingly tyrannical. After a hurried and secret summons to New Orleans, Lieutenant General Philip Sheridan suggested that the federal government classify any Southerners suspected of physically resisting carpetbagger governments as bandits, making them subject to arrest and trial under military regulations as opposed to civil standards.

In response, the *New York Tribune* pointed out that if Grant could use the army to select his preferred legislators in Louisiana, he might one day use it to select those he would allow Congress to seat. Republican Senator Carl Schurz explained that many political leaders were asking, "If this can be done in Louisiana, and . . . sustained by Congress, how long will it be before it is done in Massachusetts and Ohio?" Republican Congressman and future President James A. Garfield observed, "This is the darkest day for the future of the Republican party that I have ever seen." Public mass meetings against Republican totalitarianism in Louisiana were held in such cities as New York, Cincinnati and even Boston. The legislatures of Ohio and Pennsylvania officially condemned the federal military "invasion" of Louisiana. Even the President's cabinet was divided. Those siding with Kellogg, such as War Secretary Belknap and Navy Secretary Robeson as well as Attorney General Williams, would all later resign under the clouds of other scandals.

Future President
James A. Garfield

Eventually a House investigating subcommittee composed of two Republicans and one Democrat concluded that Louisiana's fall 1874 elections were peaceable and fair; that what fraud did take place was predominantly on the Republican side due to their control of the election machinery. It even concluded that the Democrats had won a majority of the seats in the legislature but had been denied the majority by "arbitrary, unjust, and illegal" methods exercised by the Returning Board. The subcommittee characterized the Kellogg government as a usurpation.

Similarly, Northern journalist Charles Nordhoff added that by 1874 "all white men and many blacks" detested Kellogg's government. He added that such distrust of government had driven business in the state into depression. Even the New Orleans federal District Attorney, James Beckwith—who was prosecuting the Colfax White Leaguers—was fed up with Kellogg. He wrote Grant's attorney general to request legislation that would permit the Kellogg regime to be replaced by a provisional government until new elections could be held in 1876.[154]

Modern historians, such as Ron Chernow, Charles Lane, Ronald White, Eric Foner, David Blight and Charles Calhoun, generally fail to provide logical explanations for the rise of Louisiana's White League. They falsely imply that it resulted from a virulent form of racism mysteriously endemic to white Southerners. While

---

[154] Robert Selph Henry, *The Story of Reconstruction*, 532-36; Charles Lane, *The Day Freedom Died*, 227-28; William Hesseltine, *Grant the Politician*, 350; Brooks Simpson, *The Reconstruction Presidents*, 176, 178

organizations such as Louisiana's White Leagues and South Carolina's Red Shirts where often racially hostile to blacks, they may never have been organized but for the corruption and tyranny of the carpetbag regimes in their states. Years later, South Carolina's last carpetbag governor, Daniel Chamberlain, condemned the violence of such organizations but added that "It flourished where corruption . . . had climbed into power and withered where the reverse was the case."

In contrast to modern writers, earlier historians and era-specific contemporaries connect Kellogg's usurpation and tyrannical rule to the public reactions that provoked the formation of the White Leagues. Hesseltine, for example, explains how Kellogg's Returning Board transformed a 72% Democratic majority in the lower house of the legislature into a modest Republican majority. Claude Bowers described how Kellogg's police routinely disarmed white citizens and his tax collectors drove many whites into poverty. Except for extraordinary events such as the Colfax Massacre, Charles Nordhoff concluded that white-on-black violence in Louisiana was exaggerated in the Northern press. Historian Robert Henry cited the Republican-majority U. S. House subcommittee findings against Kellogg.[155]

In short, Kellogg's government was bad regency, certain to ignite resentments among its subjects. Grant should have at least removed his brother-in-law from Kellogg's machine, if only to reduce suspicions that the President might have been profiting personally from Casey's tariff and fee collections. Instead Grant put political interests ahead of good government. Consequently, Republicans stole the 1876 presidential election for their Party's candidate when Louisiana's disputed electoral votes—controlled again by Kellogg's Returning Board—were the deciding factor, as shall be explained in chapter fourteen.

---

[155] Claude Bowers, *The Tragic Era*, 438-39, William Hesseltine, *Grant the Politician*, 350; Robert Selph Henry, *The Story of Reconstruction*, 536; Daniel Chamberlain, *Atlantic Monthly* "Reconstruction in South Carolina" (April, 1901) Available: http://bit.ly/2DnK6b4 [Accessed: January 20, 2018]

In neighboring Mississippi, Republicans first encountered a Democratic challenge only months before Kellogg used his augmented control of Louisiana's Returning Board to fraudulently win the state's 1874 autumn elections. Specifically, the Republicans controlling the town of Vicksburg, Mississippi were ousted in a peaceable August 1874 election due to excessive corruption in the municipal government.

During the preceding five years debts for the town of 11,000 grew from nearly zero to $1.4 million under Republican rule. The increase essentially burdened each family of four with a debt of over $500, equivalent to nearly $10,000 in 2018. Since few African Americans owned real estate the tax burden fell chiefly on white families. The long-delayed voter revolt began in the spring when the Republicans announced their nominees. The mayoral choice had twenty-three indictments against him while the eight candidates for alderman included one illiterate white and seven poorly educated African Americans. The Republican ticket was so objectionable that even about five hundred local blacks voted against it, as did the Republican U. S. Congressman representing the district that included Vicksburg.

White Vicksburg-area leaders next turned their attention to the county government, which was possibly even more corrupt. A black-majority grand jury, for example, had indicted three existing and former county court clerks for embezzlement. Unfortunately, all records regarding the indictments were lost before the defendants could be brought to trial. (They were later found under the house of one of the indicted clerks.)

Two days before the County Sheriff and Tax Collector, Peter Crosby, was scheduled to collect taxes in December 1874 protestors assembled in Vicksburg to ask for his resignation. They explained that they could not afford to pay the taxes, which had increased 1,400% in the last five years. When Crosby refused to resign, five hundred men escorted him out of town. A few days later Crosby, who was African American, returned to regain his office with an armed force of blacks. During one of the parleys on the roads leading to Vicksburg, fighting broke out that caused the deaths of more than twenty blacks and two whites. Crosby, who had temporarily disappeared, was not among the casualties.[156]

At this point carpetbag governor Adelbert Ames requested that federal troops intervene. Ames was Benjamin Butler's former subordinate as a Brigadier General in the Union army during the Petersburg Campaign and had also married Butler's daughter, Blanche, in 1870. Ames only lived part-time in Mississippi because his wife refused to move there from Massachusetts with the couple's children. Grant, who was oddly popular among Mississippi Democrats, had hoped to rely on the state's electoral votes for a possible third-term presidential bid in 1876. He was, therefore, disappointed to be confronted with an apparent necessity to act. Nonetheless, he ordered his commanders "to comply with the request of Govr. Ames as far as practicable."[157]

Since the 1874 elections yielded a Democratic majority in the U. S. House for the first time since before the Civil War, white Mississippians sensed an opportunity to rid the state of carpetbagger rule in their 1875 elections. Northerners, they reasoned, were now more likely to acquiesce if Mississippi and other Southern states regained "home rule." As in Arkansas and Louisiana, the state's Republican Party began to weaken when two GOP gubernatorial candidates opposed one another. It would completely fracture later. Unlike the 1872 splits in her two neighboring states, the first cracks in Mississippi's Republican Party appeared in 1873.

By 1875 Mississippi's Democratic leader, Congressman Lucius Lamar, felt that his Party was ready to regain control. First, he successfully urged it to adopt a progressive platform that would appease Washington Republicans. It recognized the civil and political equality of all men and endorsed public education. Second, the Democrats selected former Confederate General James George to run the campaign. Although George opposed outright violence, he encouraged paramilitary organizations to march as a "show of force." Throughout the state such organizations drilled conspicuously and

---

[156] Robert Selph Henry, *The Story of Reconstruction*, 530
[157] Ron Chernow, *Grant*, 788, 790

often. As they became increasingly organized, they even intruded upon Republican campaign meetings. Although George's men were generally well disciplined, some confrontations inevitably evolved into violence. Examples include meetings at Clinton, Yazoo City, Friars Point, and Rolling City.

In early September 1875 Ames again appealed to Grant for federal troops. Instead, Attorney General Edwards Pierrepont suggested that Ames enforce peace with state militia. After the militia was called into active duty, Ames and George worked out a truce. George agreed that there would be no disturbances by whites on Election Day in exchange for Ames's agreement to disband the militia. Unfortunately for Ames, George's men were able to continue breaking up Republican campaign meetings without provoking race riots. They were also able to discourage African American voter turnout with continued parading and threats of economic sanctions. Nonetheless, the November Election Day was generally peaceful.

Carpetbag Mississippi Governor Adelbert Ames

As a result, Mississippi Democrats won overwhelmingly. But it was not merely a white man's victory. A number of the state's black leaders, including Hiram Revels who was the first black senator from Mississippi, applauded the outcome as a win over "corruption, theft, and embezzlement." Rather than face impeachment charges and try to serve out his term until 1877, Ames resigned in March 1876 after the legislature agreed to drop all charges. Mississippi's lieutenant governor, however, was impeached and convicted on a vote of thirty-two to four. Six Republicans voted for conviction including one black.

A bitter Ames later claimed that the true purpose of Southern whites was to restore the Confederacy as a separate nation and put the black man in a state of serfdom, if not slavery. He also resented Grant's failure to send federal troops as Ames requested in early September, forcing the governor to broker the ineffective disarmament with General George.

Grant's true reasons for declining to send federal bayonets would not be known by the public for nearly forty years when former Republican Mississippi Congressman John Lynch revealed that Grant confessed to him in November 1875 that Ohio politicians told the President that such intervention would likely cause Republicans to lose the autumn Ohio elections. As evidenced by the Ohio and Pennsylvania legislative resolutions noted earlier, Ohio voters worried that federal intervention in state elections might ultimately be applied in Northern states if the practice continued in the South. Basically, Grant traded a Republican victory in Mississippi for one in Ohio. Thus, the President abandoned Mississippi's mostly black Republicans in favor of the mostly white Ohio Republicans.[158]

By the end of 1875 carpetbag regimes ruled in only Louisiana, South Carolina, and Florida, where they were artificially sustained by the presence of federal troops. Carpetbag rule had collapsed in six of the nine remaining former Confederate states less dramatically than it did in Mississippi and Arkansas. Nationally, the Democratic Party's gains in the 1874 congressional elections signified that Northerners were retreating from Reconstruction. They increasingly focused on economic issues such as tariffs, monetary policy, military pensions, and subsidies along with the stunning increase in public revelations about scandals inside the Grant administration after he won his second term in 1872.[159]

---

[158] Ron Chernow, *Grant*, 816-817; Hodding Carter, *The Angry Scar*, 219-222
[159] Brooks Simpson, *The Reconstruction Presidents*, 184

CHAPTER 9: ECONOMIC COLLAPSE

THE PUBLIC'S LOSS OF CONFIDENCE in good government after the Crédit Mobilier hearings ended in March 1873 provoked a coupled cynicism with the railroad industry. In combination, the two factors triggered an economic depression. During the preceding eight years railroad expansion had fueled an era of economic prosperity that gave cover to a host of political sins that an economic downturn might force into the light of day. Capitalists who could accept political extortion as a mere cost of doing business in affluent times might complain bitterly—even tattle—when vanishing profits made it difficult to sustain the campaign contributions and outright bribes otherwise tolerated.

After the Central Pacific and Union Pacific lines met in Utah in 1869, other roads such as the Southern Pacific, Santa Fe, and Texas & Pacific augmented the industry's continued transcontinental expansion. None, however, were more publicized than the Northern Pacific (NP). It was backed by Philadelphia's Jay Cooke & Company, which had risen to become America's most distinguished investment bank as the leading underwriter of the nation's bond sales during the Civil War. When the end of the war slashed Cooke's government bond business, he looked to the railroad industry to replace it and propel his bank's future growth.

Originally chartered by Congress in 1864, the Northern Pacific was to connect Lake Superior with Puget Sound. Yet by 1870 it had not built a mile of track. Cook reasoned that he could buy the company at a bargain price if he could get Congress to extend the life of its charter and provide him other concessions.

After paying consulting fees to one of President Grant's personal secretaries, Horace Porter, he learned that Grant was as "firm as a rock" on an 1870 bill tailor-made to Cooke's needs. He decided to raise $100 million directly from investors by selling new issues of Northern Pacific securities in the United States and Europe. In order to stimulate demand among public investors he persuaded several prominent men to become shareholders. Examples included Horace Greeley, Henry Ward Beecher, future President Rutherford Hayes, and the Grant's first Vice President, Schuyler Colfax.

The 1870 act gave the company more time to complete construction without losing rights to its land subsidies, which were unusually generous. It also permitted Cooke to collect a $200 fee in stock for each $1,000 bond sold as well as a 12% cash commission. As the railroad stretched westward from Minnesota rumors of corruption filtered back east. Civic leaders in the towns along the route competed to have their sites included on the line and contractors seemed to be inflating construction costs. Still, Cooke was selling about a million dollars in bonds every month. Overseas investors arrived on junkets to ride the rails to the ever-lengthening end of the line. By late summer 1873 it had reached Bismarck in present-day North Dakota.

But the railroad was generating little revenue. Debt funded nearly all its operations and construction. Anything that prevented Cooke from selling more bonds and stock would cause the Northern Pacific to coast to a halt. The Crédit Mobilier scandal was just such a factor.[160]

On the morning of September 18, 1873 Grant shared breakfast with Jay Cooke at the latter's estate outside of Philadelphia where the President was a houseguest. By noon of the same day Jay Cooke & Company closed its doors. There could hardly have been a bigger surprise to the public confidence. One Philadelphia newspaper reported, "No one could have been more surprised if snow had fallen during a summer noon." Without new sales of Northern Pacific

---

[160] Matthew Josephson, *The Robber Barons*, 95-7; Allan Nevins, *The Emergence of Modern America* (New York, Macmillan, 1927), 294-9

securities, Cooke & Company soon ran out of cash. Hinterland banks triggered the debacle when they tried to draw down deposits at Cooke's bank in order to pay farmers for their harvests.[161]

Cooke's failure initiated a panic and then a depression. The total bonded indebtedness of the railroad industry was over $2.2 billion. That was equal to the entire debt of the federal government, which had been inflated by massive deficit spending during the Civil War. Huge blocks of railroad securities were quickly put on the market, but there were few buyers. Price declines of 50% were common among the leading rail stocks. Brokers called customers for more securities margin but too many did not have enough cash or liquid collateral to meet the calls. Their brokers failed. The New York Stock Exchange closed for ten days, amplifying the panic.

Business failures in 1873 climbed to 5,000, from 4,000 in 1872 and 3,000 in 1871. Cooke's failure was a tocsin for five ensuing years of depression. Twenty-five railroads defaulted on their debts during the first few months following the Cooke collapse. Seventy-one more followed in 1874 and another twenty-five in 1875. By 1876 almost half of America's railroads were in receivership.[162]

Railroads had overbuilt. There wasn't enough traffic to support the available capacity. In 1860 America had about 1,000 residents for each mile of track but in 1873 the density had dropped to about 600 per mile. About half of the nation's railroads would be bankrupted during the resulting depression. No geographical region would be untouched. Municipal and state government bonds issued to build the roads remained taxpayer obligations even if the applicable railroad was never built. Towns that gave bonds or cash to roads that failed typically lost all they gave. By the end of 1876 the industry had defaulted on more than $800 million in debt. Railroad operating revenues dropped by a third.

---

[161] Jack Beatty, *The Age of Betrayal*, 232-3; Matthew Josephson, *The Robber Barons*, 169-70; Ron Chernow, *Grant*, 777

[162] Richard White, *The Republic for Which it Stands*, 261, 266

Panic Begins at Jay Cooke & Company Office

Track construction also declined by a third in 1874, causing 500,000 layoffs within the railroad ecosystem including the iron and steel industry. Prices fell. Philadelphia pig iron dropped from $56 a ton in 1872 to $17 five years later. Wages fell by about 50% between 1873 and 1877. When the poverty income line was a dollar a day, 10,000 Massachusetts textile workers and 60,000 Pennsylvania miners fell under the threshold. The country seemed to be overrun with hoboes and vagrants.[163]

Although the economic downturn started to uncover mischief in the Grant Administration as early as 1873, Republican losses during the off-year 1874 elections prompted investigations that disclosed even more. Despite holding onto a Senate majority, Republicans lost control of the House of Representatives. When a special session of the Forty-Fourth Congress convened in March 1875, Democrats held a 62% majority in the House as compared to a 35% minority in the Forty-Third Congress.

Since they controlled the chamber for the first time in fourteen years, Democrats readily opened House committee investigations—previously blocked by a Republican majority—into Grant Administration scandals. While some Grant-partisan historians suggest that the investigations of the Forty-Fourth Congress were

---

[163] Jack Beatty, *The Age of Betrayal*, 233-4; Matthew Josephson, *The Robber Barons*, 168; H. W. Brands, *American Colossus*, 89 Matthew Josephson, *The Politicos*, 235; Allan Nevins, *The Emergence of Modern America*, 294-9; Treasury.gov *Historical Debt Outstanding* Available: http://bit.ly/2BoLqmv [Accessed: December 7, 2017]

politically motivated, there can be little doubt that the collapse of the railroad economy combined with the Crédit Mobilier whitewash and the 1873 Salary Grab produced an angry and suspicious electorate. Moreover, the worsening economy alone disclosed several corruptions in the Administration before the new Congress took their seats in 1875.

George Boutwell initiated a chain reaction that led to the first disclosure when he resigned as treasury secretary in March 1873 to take his seat as a new Massachusetts Senator. Boutwell recommended his First Assistant Treasury Secretary, William Richardson, as a replacement. Grant agreed. Previous to joining Boutwell at the treasury, Richardson had been a Massachusetts probate judge. During the war he was subordinate to Major General Benjamin Butler who commanded the Union occupation troops in New Orleans and later in Norfolk, Virginia. In both cities Butler was suspected of profiting from commercial transactions with Confederates.

The same month that Richardson succeeded Boutwell, the apparently ubiquitous Benjamin Butler—then a congressman—sneaked a rider into an appropriations bill that re-authorized the treasury secretary to designate private individuals as tax collectors for the internal revenue bureau. Unlike the customs houses at America's port cities that collected tariffs, the bureau collected duties pertinent to the domestic economy, such as excise taxes. Butler's rider allowed collection designees to keep half of the taxes gathered as a fee under a policy known as the moiety system.

Butler persuaded Secretary Richardson to appoint John D. Sanborn to the collections post in Massachusetts. Next, Sanborn presented his contract to the U. S. Treasury's regional Boston office where he obtained a list of delinquent taxpayers. Sanborn ultimately collected about $430,000 in taxes and kept nearly $215,000 for himself as moiety. Of the latter amount, Sanborn claimed he paid "probably $160,000" to others who helped him make the collections. Experienced political observers suspected that Butler was among those who shared in the $160,000. They also suspected that the arrangement was a quid pro quo to Butler for his behind-the-scenes help in getting Richardson appointed as Boutwell's replacement.

Sanborn might have escaped scrutiny except for three factors. First, the economic depression left taxpayers more than normally resentful of tax collectors. They were especially appalled to learn that the collector earned a fee proportional to the tax collected. Second, some taxpayers complained that both Sanborn and regular treasury employees were independently demanding payment for the same tax. Third, Sanborn made powerful enemies when he gained authority to add railroads to his delinquency list. As historian Matthew Josephson put it, "[Among Sanborn's victims] were prominent corporations, including large railroads, who promptly made public their knowledge of the corrupt practices they suffered from."

Like other taxpayers, however, the railroads were justifiably offended by Sanborn's collection technique. He obtained much of their taxes by sending demand letters to almost six hundred railroads listed in Appleton's Railway Guide. Nearly all the letters contained a false oath that Sanborn had received information suggesting the applicable railroad was attempting tax evasion. Sanborn's approach seemed indistinguishable from extortion to the letter recipients.

Consequently, the House Ways and Means Committee began an investigation in January 1874. Although Richardson claimed that he had no knowledge of the affair, Sanborn testified that he met with Richardson a half dozen times. Richardson next tried to shift responsibility to the treasury department's legal counsel, who countered that he was merely following Richardson's instruction. When the Committee released its report in May 1874 it concluded that all of the taxes that Sanborn had collected would have been taken in by internal revenue officials "in the ordinary discharge of their duty" as salaried employees.

Although the Committee criticized the conduct of both Richardson and Sanborn, it did not penalize either. It could not direct Sanborn to return any of the fees because they were not strictly illegal.

However, Congress soon put an end the moiety system that legitimized the Butler-Sanborn-Richardson scheme.[164]

While not officially penalized, after release of the May 1874 report Grant realized that Richardson would have to go. Some congressmen were even preparing a resolution calling for Richardson to personally refund the treasury for the fees paid to Sanborn. After Richardson resigned Grant appointed him as a judge in the U. S. Court of Claims where suits against the federal government were adjudicated. Historian Allan Nevins dismayingly wrote of Grant's decision, "The judicial bench was obviously the place for an officer found guilty of misconduct."

In June 1874 Grant replaced Secretary Richardson with Benjamin Bristow who had been Amos Akerman's chief solicitor when Attorney General Akerman used the KKK Act and the newly formed federal justice department to prosecute Klan members in 1871. Bristow continued in that role after George Williams replaced Akerman as attorney general late in 1871. As the new treasury secretary, Bristow moved almost immediately to combat corruption when he discovered widespread tax evasion that both Boutwell and Richardson had missed. Before Bristow's investigation was over it would lead many

Benjamin Bristow, Treasury

---

[164] Charles Calhoun, *The Presidency of Ulysses S. Grant*, 446-47; Matthew Josephson, *The Politicos*, 183-84; Allan Nevins, *Hamilton Fish: Volume Two*, 708-09

to question President Grant's personal honesty as shall be explained in chapter twelve.[165]

Another scandal unearthed by the economic depression that started in 1873 culminated with the collapse of the Freedman's Savings Bank in February 1874. Congress created the bank, along with the Freedman's Bureau, in March 1865. It was designed to help former slaves concentrate their savings into a putatively trustworthy bank instead of distributing their deposits among a variety of often inexperienced and sometimes fraudulent banks. Depositors, which were limited to ex-slaves or their descendants, were actively sought. Although the federal government did not guarantee the deposits of any financial institution, the bank's advertisements included images of Abraham Lincoln, Ulysses Grant and William T. Sherman, which suggested otherwise to the inexperienced freedmen. At its peak the bank had thirty-four branches in seventeen states as well as the District of Columbia. It was one of America's first multistate banks. By 1870, blacks managed nearly all of the branches.

Since the federal government failed to give free homesteads to former slaves, the freedmen were encouraged to deposit their savings at the Freedman's Bank where they might one day accumulate enough savings to buy farms. Given such a mission the bank initially made only conservative investments such as U. S. Treasury notes. Like other working Americans, the freedmen conscientiously saved their nickels and dimes. Unlike the present, during the Gilded Age American savings rates averaged almost one-quarter of the Gross National Product.

Unfortunately, after the bank's headquarters moved from New York to Washington in 1868, its mostly white board of trustees increasingly came under the influence of politically connected connivers. In 1870 Washington City alderman Alexander Shepherd led a movement to combine his city, Georgetown, and the remaining areas of the District into a unified Territorial Government. He

---

[165] Allan Nevins, *Hamilton Fish: Volume Two*, 714, 716

succeeded in January 1871. The next month Grant appointed Henry Cooke—Washington branch manager of brother Jay's investment bank—as the territorial governor. As a close Henry Cooke associate, Shepherd won a coveted post on a territorial government board from which he could control the District's multimillion-dollar public works projects.[166]

In 1870 Freedman's Bank trustees persuaded Congress to amend its charter in order to permit commercial loans. Henry Cooke and other Shepherd colleagues soon controlled the bank's lending portfolio. Among Shepherd's 1873 initiatives popular with voters who paid little in direct taxes was an ambitious spending program to modernize the capital city. Partly because of strong support among black voters, Shepherd was able to get a bond referendum approved to finance the expenditures. The District's mostly white taxpayers and property owners, however, were horrified by the implications of the ballooning debt.

A year later the $6 million initiative had already exceeded $9 million. When local taxpayers complained of losing properties for tax deficiencies caused by the unsustainable spending, the House of Representatives formed a bi-partisan investigative committee. It learned that the program's chief beneficiary was a ring of Shepherd business associates and real estate developers.

The District went into bankruptcy after an audit revealed its bills were $13 million in arrears in 1874. The Freedman's Bank was among the casualties. It had invested heavily in Washington real estate in response to the temporary boom triggered by Shepherd's unsustainable spending.

One of the bad loans was to the Seneca Sandstone Company, which Henry Cooke had organized in 1866. Much like Congressman

---

[166] Richard White, *The Republic for Which it* Stands, 265-68; BlackPast.org, "Freedman's Savings Bank & Trust: 1865 – 1874" Available: http://bit.ly/2ALzCSC [Accessed: December 11, 2017]; John C. Rodrigue, *Encyclopedia.biz*, "Freedman's Savings & Trust Company" Available: http://bit.ly/2koHd1p [Accessed: December 11, 2017]

Ames would later do for Crédit Mobilier, Cooke sold shares to influential Republican politicians at half price. Among the buyers was General Ulysses Grant whose stock was valued at $20,000. Grant purchased the shares a year before he was elected President and sold them four years later, six months after appointing Henry Cooke as D.C.'s Territorial Governor. Like the discounted stock sales of Crédit Mobilier by Congressman Ames, the Seneca transaction was not strictly illegal. Unlike the disgrace piled upon Vice President Schuyler Colfax's for dealing with Ames, however, criticism of the Cooke-Grant transaction was almost inaudible.

Under Henry Cooke's authority, the bank also started lending money directly to Jay Cooke & Company, which offered worthless Northern Pacific bonds as collateral. Only months before the Freedman's Bank collapsed, Jay Cooke had been Grant's leading financial donor during the President's 1872 reelection campaign.

Upon closing its doors in 1874 the bank had nominal deposits of about $3 million. In reality, however, it had only $31,000 to return to 61,000 depositors. Boss Shepherd moved his family to Mexico in 1876 after declaring personal bankruptcy. The District did not completely repay the Shepherd era debts until 1916.[167]

When the House Ways and Means Committee started its Sanborn investigation the month before the Freedman's Bank folded, Grant was unrelatedly forced to withdraw his request that the Senate permit Attorney General George H. Williams to replace Supreme

---

[167] Garrett Peck, *Boundary Stones: WETA's Local Blog* "The Seneca Stone Ring Scandal" Available: http://bit.ly/2Bdo5hG [Accessed: December 11, 2017];

William B. Hesseltine, "Economic Factors in the Abandonment of Reconstruction," *The Mississippi Valley Historical Review 22, no.4* (Sep. 1935), 206; William B. Hesseltine, *Grant the Politician*, 280; Robert Selph Henry *The Story of Reconstruction*, 522-23; Eric Foner, *Reconstruction*, 533; Francis Simkins and Charles Roland, *A History of the South* (New York: Alfred A. Knopf, 1973), 282; John Richardson, "Alexander R. Shepherd and the Race Issue in Washington." *Washington History 22* (2010): 17-35 Available: http://bit.ly/2APksfc [Accessed: December 12, 2017]; Mark David Richards, "Touring Hidden Washington: Living in the Shadow of Congress" Available: http://bit.ly/2kqkjXQ [Accessed: December 11, 2017]; Richard White, *The Republic For Which it Stands*, 266

Court Chief Justice Salmon P. Chase who had died the previous May. Prior to becoming attorney general, Williams had been an Oregon Senator with close to ties to the Pacific railroads. The railroads, it will be recalled, applauded Grant's 1871 choice of Williams to replace Attorney General Amos Akerman who had annoyed railroad tycoons by denying land grant awards on the grounds of incomplete construction work.

Williams's nomination stood for only a month when it became obvious that the Senate would block it for three reasons. First, many informed observers questioned his ability. Second, he never convincingly rebutted allegations of financial improprieties and corruption. Third, and most tantalizingly in gossip-prone Washington, his beautiful second wife's reputation had provoked revengeful enmity among the city's political wives. Kate George Williams was on her third marriage even though she was more than ten years younger than her forty-nine-year-old husband. Among the most vicious rumors about her was that she had "'screwed' her husband into the Attorney Generalship."[168]

Williams's December 1873 nomination was not even initially well received. The press generally felt that he lacked ability and experience. One assistant attorney general admitted that his boss's nomination met "general disapprobation" and was "a bitter pill to the lawyers of the Senate." Evidently a number of senators felt that Grant should have chosen them instead of Williams.

The Senate's Judiciary Committee soon discovered problems with the nominee. One witness testified that Williams fired an Oregon federal prosecutor who was building a fraud case against Oregon Republican Senator John Mitchell. Since the incident happened only a week after Williams was nominated, it left an impression that the nominee was trying to win Mitchell's approving vote. Years later,

---

[168] Charles Calhoun, *The Presidency of Ulysses S. Grant*, 434

along with others in the Oregon delegation, Mitchell would be convicted of land fraud that benefited timber companies.[169]

Even worse were discoveries of financial irregularities at the Williams justice department. Most damaging was evidence that he used department funds to buy an expensive carriage and team of horses that his wife wanted and to pay the salaries of two personal servants. In another instance he used department funds to temporarily pay other household bills. He explained that the second instance coincided with the financial panic caused by Jay Cooke's collapse in September 1873 when, Williams claimed, banks were not paying personal checks. His avowals that he eventually replaced the government money were not well documented. A detailed explanation for all of the financial irregularities sent to the Committee raised more questions than it answered.[170]

In truth, his wife's ostentatious and scheming lifestyle may have unfairly poisoned attitudes against him, particularly among the spouses of many senators. Nearly everyone described Kate as a then strikingly gorgeous and intelligent lady. After her husband left the Senate to become attorney general, she alienated the wives of the other senators by presuming that her status as the wife of a cabinet member was superior. Her attitude conveyed the notion that a senator's wife was obliged to first call upon her socially before she would visit them. Rumors circulated that she would accept "presents" from those with cases under adjudication by the justice department during regal receptions at the couple's mansion.

The ladies of Washington concluded that they could not tolerate Kate as the wife of the Supreme Court's chief justice. Their behind-the-scenes posturing may explain why the Judiciary Committee

---

[169] Cain Allen, *The Oregon History Project*, "Land Fraud Trial of Senator John Mitchell" Available: http://bit.ly/2BmTnCZ [Accessed: December 9, 2017]; Charles Calhoun, *The Presidency of Ulysses S. Grant*, 434; Ron Chernow, *Grant*, 765

[170] Charles Calhoun, *The Presidency of Ulysses S. Grant*, 434-35; Ron Chernow, *Grant*, 766

switched from unanimous endorsement for Williams on its first vote to a later majority of disapproval.

Kate's response to the weakening support for Williams was characteristic and politically fatal. She threatened to ruin the reputations of opponents if George's appointment failed. For starters she told Secretary of State Hamilton Fish's wife that secret service funds had been used to win New York Senator Conkling's reelection. Her claim is not easily dismissed even though Grant explained flippantly to Fish that the funds were used in compliance with the 1871 KKK

Attorney General George Williams

Act to supervise voter registrations. It seems doubtful, for example, that the funds were used to register voters who favored Conkling's Democratic opponent. Predictably, Kate's accusation helped turn Grant against Williams and led him to ask the attorney general to "voluntarily" withdraw his name.[171]

Despite Williams's damaged reputation, Grant permitted him to hold onto his attorney general post. The President characteristically urged subordinates caught in controversies to remain in place until news coverage had died down. But a resentful Kate continued to foment mischief. She defended herself by sending anonymous letters accusing other political leaders of wrongdoing, including sexual

---

[171] Charles Calhoun, *The Presidency of Ulysses S. Grant*, 435; Finn J. D. John, *Offbeat Oregon History*, "Oregon Man's Supreme Court Confirmation Scotched by His Wife" (April 16, 2012) Available: http://bit.ly/2nJAaW1 [Accessed: December 9, 2012]

misconduct. Letter recipients interpreted them as blackmail. Among such people were the wives of cabinet members and even First Lady Julia Grant. Julia had already been among those who disapproved of Kate. During a formal reception in December 1874, the First Lady received Kate in "a cold and distant manner" and tried to exclude her from the approaching New Year's Day White House reception.

About the same time as the anonymous letters fueled Washington gossip, Treasury Secretary Bristow told Grant that he learned about "very alarming" transactions in New York involving Williams. Similarly, Roscoe Conkling informed Grant that a politically motivated justice department employee was passing along compromising information about Williams to Democratic Party leaders. Finally, Secretary Fish told Grant that while in New York he heard a compromising story involving a justice department case against the import-export firm of Pratt & Boyd. Apparently, Kate had asked Pratt & Boyd to pay a $30,000 bribe in order to ensure that the justice department would not pursue a case against the firm. Fish further stated that his source not only reported that the $30,000 had been paid, but that Grant's brother-in-law, James Casey, pocketed a share of it.

When Williams finally resigned in April 1875 Kate took to her bed for "a long-long time." Eventually the couple returned to Portland where Williams was elected mayor early in the twentieth century. Even though in his eighties, he did not escape controversy. Mayor Williams was indicted for failing to enforce antigambling laws. Although the charges were eventually dropped, some residents continued to complain of gambling, prostitution and crooked contracting during his tenure as mayor. One observer who later became an Oregon senator summed up the era by remarking that Williams "has not been a bad mayor. He has been no mayor at all."[172]

---

[172] Charles Calhoun, *The Presidency of Ulysses S. Grant*, 489-90; Finn J. D. John, *Offbeat Oregon History*, "Oregon Man's Supreme Court Confirmation Scotched by His Wife" (April 16, 2012) Available: http://bit.ly/2nJAaW1 [Accessed: December 9, 2012]; John Terry, *The*

Williams's failed attempt to become Supreme Court chief justice led indirectly into another scandal. When Grant nominated Williams for the Court he simultaneously announced that Treasury Secretary Benjamin Bristow would succeed Williams as attorney general. The Bristow announcement was greeted warmly, except by a few members of the Administration. The exceptions were revealing. One example was Grant's closest personal secretary, Orville Babcock. As shall be explained, he was in danger of becoming ensnared in a tax evasion case involving the distilled spirits industry. Another example was Interior Secretary Columbus Delano, who was allied with Babcock.

Delano had replaced Jacob Cox in October 1870 because Cox's commitment to civil service reform alienated traditional Republican Party bosses who were still wedded to political patronage. For example, he rejected demands that political appointees in his department make mandatory Party contributions. He also rebuffed lawmakers who tried to meddle with Indian agent appointments. Much like army sutler posts, Indian trading posts were lucrative local monopolies coveted by politicians as patronage awards. Finally, it will be recalled that Delano was among those who complained to Grant that Attorney General Akerman had irritated railroad moguls. During the next four years Delano's interior department became rife with misconduct.[173]

Thus, the very month (December 1874) when Grant nominated Williams for the Supreme Court, an interior department assistant secretary privately told Bristow that Delano was secretly opposing Grant's plan to have Bristow replace Williams as attorney general. The interior department confidant also told Bristow that Delano's son, John, was involved in dubious land office schemes out West. A

Oregonian "Portland Mayor George Williams Faced Charges in Court" Available: http://bit.ly/2BQl6bm [Accessed: December 9, 2017]; Allan Nevins, *Hamilton Fish: Volume 2*, 771

[173] Ron Chernow, *Grant*, 730, 819

few months later Bristow asked an old army friend to informally investigate John Delano.

The friend's inquiry revealed questionable surveying contracts in Wyoming Territory. The territory's surveyor general had been awarding work to contractors who would agree to share their fees with silent partners, even though such partners did no work. John Delano was not only involved as such a partner, but Secretary Delano was fully aware of the agreements. Among the evidence sent to Bristow was a cancelled bank draft payable to John Delano for one such contract.

The whistleblower would later disclose that President Grant's younger brother, Orvil, also participated in the arrangements even though Orvil had never set foot in Wyoming and had no survey work experience. Nonetheless, like Grant's purchase of Seneca Sandstone stock, the dubious contracts were not technically illegal. Therefore, Delano fired the whistleblower with impunity. But in April 1875 Grant decided that Delano should ultimately resign. He did not, however, want Delano to resign "under the fire" of adverse publicity because that might lead the public to believe exaggerated accusations in the press. Hence, Delano remained in office until September 30, 1875.[174]

---

[174] William McFeely, *Grant*, 430; Charles Calhoun, *The Presidency of Ulysses S. Grant*, 492-93

CHAPTER 10: INDIAN POLICY

ALTHOUGH GRANT'S FIRST ANNUAL MESSAGE in December 1869 promised to expand a new, protective policy toward Indians, the economic depression that followed Jay Cooke's 1873 bankruptcy would prompt the President to implement an exploitive plan.[175]

In his first annual message Grant said, "The building of railroads . . . is rapidly bringing civilized settlements into contact with all the tribes of Indians. No matter what ought to be the relations between such settlements and the aborigines, the fact is they do not harmonize well, and one or the other has to give way . . . I see no substitute . . . except in placing all the Indians on large reservations . . . and giving them absolute protection there." The Indians, Grant concluded, can be nothing other than "wards of the nation" until they might ultimately be integrated into the white man's society, earn a living in the manner of whites and worship as whites instead of as pagans. Although Grant felt that prior treaty terms should be honored, he also believed that America could no longer pretend that the tribes were sovereign nations capable of enforcing treaty terms on all of their members.[176]

The policy had a promising start shortly after Grant took office when he appointed General Ely Parker as Commissioner of Indian

---

[175] "Native-Americans" will hereafter be referred to as "Indians."

[176] Ulysses S. Grant, *First Annual Message: December 6, 1869*; Ulysses S. Grant, *First Inaugural Address: March 6, 1869* Available: http://bit.ly/2wQtXH4 [Accessed: September 24, 2017]

Affairs. Parker not only had served on General Grant's staff as an engineer during the Civil War he was a full-blooded Seneca Indian. In the prime of life at age forty-one, Parker brought energy and an understanding for both whites and Indians to his new office. Under Grant's aegis he established a system of Indian agent appointments that relied upon pacific-minded civilians such as Quakers to teach the aborigines how to adopt the white man's culture. So many Quakers volunteered that the plan became known as Grant's "Quaker Policy" or "Peace Policy."

Nonetheless, Parker had made enemies among congressmen that resented losing the power to make political appointments under the "Peace Policy" in the Indian regions. In 1870 they delayed approval for funds required to provision the reservations. Soon the agents reported that the reservations were desperately short of food and other necessities. Consequently, Parker purchased supplies on credit without advertising for bids. He also shipped the supplies to the reservations at slightly above normal freight rates, which he deemed necessary in order to ensure that they arrived before hunger might provoke the Indians to violence. [177]

The Indians would face bigger problems after October 1869 when William Belknap replaced the recently deceased James Rawlins as secretary of war. Belknap had been recommended to Grant by General-in-Chief William T. Sherman, whom the appointee had served under as a division commander during the Civil War. Belknap, nonetheless, would become an irritant to Sherman because the new war secretary excluded the General-in-Chief in matters Sherman regarded as his prerogative. One such category was Indian affairs where Belknap increasingly bypassed Sherman when sending directives into the field. His reasons for bypassing Sherman would not become public until after the Democrats took control of the House of Representatives in the 1874 elections. Since the election

---

[177] Dee Brown, *Bury My Heart at Wounded Knee* (New York: Holt Reinhardt & Winston, 1971), 175-176

empowered Democrats to select House committee chairmen, the Party was finally able to initiate investigations into persistent rumors of corruption in the Grant Administration during the 1875-76 sessions of the Forty-Fourth Congress[178]

During his two-term presidency from 1869 to 1877, most of Grant's focus on Indians concerned western tribes, particularly those in the Great Plains. When he moved into the White House, Andrew Johnson's Administration had already set the stage for Indian relations in the region with two treaties arranged in 1867-68. The first was with the southern Plains tribes (Arapaho, Cheyenne, Comanche and Kiowa) at Medicine Lodge Creek, Kansas in October 1867. It led to the formation of many reservations in an area then officially known as the "Indian Territory," but which ultimately would become the present state of Oklahoma. It aimed to assimilate the Indians into white culture via agency schools, farming instruction and Christian teachings. The treaty was largely successful in maintaining peace north of Texas and south of the northern plains.

Six months later the northern tribes (various Sioux and the Crow) signed the Fort Laramie Treaty. They did not, however, endorse it until after the Bozeman Trail from eastern Wyoming Territory to Virginia City, Montana Territory was closed to whites and the U. S. Army destroyed its three forts along the trail. After the trail closure a Great Sioux Reservation was set aside west of the Missouri River in Dakota Territory. "Un-ceded" lands west of the Reservation in Montana and Wyoming were available to the Indians for hunting "so long as the buffalo may range thereon in such numbers to justify the chase."[179]

---

[178] James Lee McDonough, *William Tecumseh Sherman: In the Service of My Country* (New York: W. W. Norton, 2016), 667-68

[179] James Donovan, *A Terrible Glory* (Boston: Little Brown & Company, 2008), 27-28; S. Lyman Tyler, *A History of Indian Policy* (Washington, D. C.: Bureau of Indian Affairs, 1979), 79

When Belknap became secretary of war, the Plains Indians were at peace everywhere. In January 1870, however, a Montana Indian village was massacred either without cause, or by mistake. Only about 50 of its 220 inhabitants survived. In order to reassure the northern tribes that the massacre did not signify the army's overall intent, Ely Parker invited several chiefs from the northern tribes to Washington to meet with President Grant and other officials.

They first met with Interior Secretary Jacob Cox who promised to provide rifles for hunting as long as the Indians remained peaceful. Unfortunately, the Indians learned that when Congress ratified the Fort Laramie Treaty it changed the reservation location from the western part of the Dakota Territory to the eastern part where the chiefs did not want to live, far away from the hunting grounds. After days of brinksmanship, Secretary Cox relented. He told the Indians that they could hunt in the un-ceded lands and that the Great Sioux Reservation would remain in western Dakota Territory, which would include the Black Hills. The meetings concluded in a spirit of friendliness all around.

Chief Red Cloud was reluctantly persuaded to visit New York City before returning home. He was astonished at his favorable welcome in the Cooper Union auditorium. It was the first time he had a chance to make his case to ordinary white citizens instead of government officials. "We want to keep the peace," he said. "Will you help us? In 1868 men came out and brought papers. We could not read them and they did not tell us truly what was in them . . . When I reached Washington, the Great Father explained to me what the treaty was, and showed me that the interpreters had deceived me. All I want is right and just . . . I have not altogether succeeded."[180]

Red Cloud and the other regional chiefs kept the peace for a time, but by 1873 a rising tide of white immigrants had illegally moved onto some of the Indian lands. Military forts were constructed. Meanwhile, Ely Parker lost the influence needed to successfully

---

[180] Dee Brown, *Bury My Heart at Wounded Knee*, 173-4, 177-83

represent the tribes by mid-1871. Toward the end of 1870 Parker's initiative, noted earlier, to ship supplies on credit to reservations prior to an official congressional appropriation led to accusations that he violated regulations for personal gain. His prime accuser charged him with "fraud and improvidence in the conduct of Indian affairs" and blamed Grant for appointing a man to office "who is but a remove from barbarism." The House Committee on Appropriations launched an investigation into thirteen charges. Although Parker was eventually exonerated the experience provoked him to resign in the summer of 1871.[181]

Coincident with the 1873 flood of white immigrants into the northern Great Plains, a collapse in railroad speculation sent the American economy into a tailspin in September as explained in chapter nine. As the economy deteriorated in the months following the crash, President Grant reflected on how earlier gold discoveries in California and the Rocky Mountains had reenergized America's economy. Thus, in the summer of 1874 he sent a military expedition into the Black Hills of present-day South Dakota to investigate rumors of gold. Since the Hills were part of a Lakota Sioux reservation— officially off limits to white civilians—the expedition's goal was falsely represented as a site-search for a new military fort.

Lieutenant-Colonel George Custer led the thousand-man expedition that included

Chief Red Cloud

---

[181] *Ibid.,* 184-186

President Grant's eldest son as well as three newspaper reporters, a photographer and two gold prospectors. Although the group saw few Indians they discovered modest, but tempting, quantities of gold. Soon the first rush of prospectors began tearing through the Hills. Within two years the largest deposit in the Continental United States, ultimately to become the Homestake Mine, was discovered. A year after discovery, George Hearst and two partners purchased the mine for $70,000. Before ending production in 2001, Homestake yielded over one billion dollars in gold and helped finance the businesses of George's legendary son, William Randolph Hearst, as well as modern Hearst publications such as *Women's Wear Daily*, *Elle*, and *Cosmopolitan*.

Initially Grant made little effort to control the prospecting, but within a year there were so many prospectors that the he decided the government must acquire the Black Hills from the Sioux. When chief Red Cloud learned of Grant's intent in May 1875 he again travelled with several other chiefs to Washington to meet with the President. The Indian leaders reminded Grant that the 1868 Treaty of Fort Laramie granted their tribes perpetual ownership of the Black Hills.

Grant told Red Cloud that the chiefs must confront two unpleasant truths. First, the government's obligation under the treaty to supply rations to the Sioux reservation had expired. They continued only because of the President's kind feelings toward the tribes. Second, Grant could not prevent miners from swarming over the Black Hills. He ended the meeting by informing his visitors that they must either agree to cede the Black Hills or risk losing their rations. Red Cloud returned to the Great Plains without an agreement.

In response Grant organized a civilian commission that travelled to the Dakota Territory in September 1875 to negotiate the purchase of the Black Hills. The Indians demanded more than ten times the amount the commission was authorized to pay. When the commission leader returned to Washington, he recommended that the Sioux be starved until they agreed to give up the Hills at a price to be set by Congress.

But Grant settled on a more radical solution. He contrived a reason to start a war in order to justify seizing the Hills by force. His plan was to provoke the small minority of Lakota living off their reservation in un-ceded lands where the Fort Laramie Treaty granted them hunting privileges. Historian John Gray explained that, "A punishing terrifying campaign against these wild bands would certainly subdue them and at the same time so intimidate their . . . relatives [remaining on the reservation so] that a legal three-fourths might sign away the Black Hills. And failing that, the nation could seize the Black Hills as spoils of war without legal hindrance."[182]

In November 1875 Grant summoned the general commanding the region and the commissioner of Indian affairs to a White House meeting. Although the general and the commissioner were both on record as reporting that the Lakota had been peaceful in recent years, an inspector of the Indian Affairs Bureau issued a contrary report nine days later. According to historian James Donovan the report "cited various trumped-up accusations and smoothly worded falsehoods regarding Indian violations." Accordingly, the "wild" Indians in the hunting territories were told that they must return to the reservation by January 31, 1876 or be declared hostile, which would authorize the army to force their return.

It was an impossible demand. The weather-weakened Indian ponies were unable to move entire villages that included women and children. One warrior later said, "It was very cold and many of our people and ponies would have died in the snow. We were in our own country and doing no harm." Even the departmental military commander, Phil Sheridan, said the ultimatum "will in all probability be regarded as a good joke by the Indians."[183]

---

[182] Nathaniel Philbrick, *The Last Stand* (New York: Viking, 2010), 3-4; Peter Cozzens, *The Earth is Weeping: The Epic Story of the Indian Wars for the American West* (New York: Alfred Knopf, 2016), Kindle Location, 4087-4092, 4143, 4159, 4179-4184; John S. Gray, *Centennial Campaign: The 1876 Sioux War* (Norman: University of Oklahoma Press, 1988), 23

[183] James Donovan, *A Terrible Glory*, 34-35

In March 1876 cavalry attacked and burned an isolated Montana Indian village but could not successfully make off with the pony herd, which the Indians recaptured. Chief Crazy Horse could not understand why the soldiers attacked since the Indians had been peaceful. He could only conclude that the "white grandfather" in Washington—meaning Grant—could not always control all of his soldiers just as chiefs could not always control all of their warriors. "The sad truth," according to historian Nathaniel Philbrick, "was that the white soldiers were acting under the explicit, if evasively delivered, orders of the grandfather."[184]

After the solitary winter village attack, the army launched a three-pronged coordinated offensive against the off-reservation Lakota in June 1876. They converged on the Powder River country in the southeastern part of Montana. One column approached from the south out of Wyoming and a second approached downstream along the Yellowstone River from western Montana. A third column under General Alfred Terry marched upstream along the Yellowstone from the column's starting point at Bismarck, Dakota Territory. Terry's force included the seventh cavalry regiment under Custer's command.

In response, the scattered Indian settlements concentrated into a single village along a tributary of the Big Horn River blandly named the Little Big Horn. The army's Wyoming column was quickly turned back at the Battle of Rosebud creek. As Terry continued marching westward along the Yellowstone with his infantry, he sent the seventh cavalry on a reconnaissance in force, south of the river, to find the Indian village, or villages. Custer located the Little Big Horn village on 25 June. He divided his command into four components and attacked it with two of them. The third went on a fruitless reconnaissance before joining the fourth that guarded the slower moving pack train.

---

[184] Nathaniel Philbrick, *The Last Stand*, 67

The village had about 1,800 warriors as compared to about 500 troopers in the entire seventh cavalry. Custer's fraction of the regiment totaled 225 men. He allocated another 140 of the regiment's men to Major Marcus Reno with orders to attack the village from the south, while Custer apparently intended to attack the village from either the east or the north. The third and fourth components that included the pack train totaled a combined 125 troopers under Captain Frederick Benteen.

After the Indians repulsed Reno's attack his command was thrown into a panicked retreat to a defensive position on the east side of the Little Big Horn on a bluff overlooking the stream. Benteen's force joined him there. The Indians annihilated Custer's troopers, also east of the river but at points about four-to-five miles north of the Reno-Benteen hill. Reno and Benteen suffered 53 killed and 60 wounded. The Lakota moved their village beyond sight of the enemy the evening before General Terry's infantry arrived on 27 June.[185]

The Indian victory was merely temporary and only intensified white hostility. A new Indian commission led by George Manypenny arrived in Dakota Territory in September 1876 to annex the Black Hills from those Sioux who had remained on the reservation. When the Indians replied that the Fort Laramie Treaty required a three-quarter supermajority vote by their adult males, the commissioners replied that the treaty had been abrogated when the Indians attacked Custer. The claim was hard for the Sioux who had remained on the reservation to understand since none of them had participated in the fighting. To compel acceptance, some commissioners implied that unless the Indians signed-over the Black Hills they would be moved to present day Oklahoma, forfeit their firearms and horses and no longer be supplied rations. Congress approved the resulting Manypenny Agreement in February 1877.[186]

---

[185] Robert Utley, *Custer Battlefield: Official National Park Handbook* (Washington, D. C.: U. S. Government Printing Office, 1988), 52, 53, 55-57, 67-68, 72

[186] Dee Brown, *Bury My Heart at Wounded Knee*, 286

Sioux descendants litigated the settlement well into the twentieth century. In 1980 the U. S Supreme Court awarded eight Sioux tribes $106 million in compensation for "a taking of tribal property," but the tribes refused it. The money has remained in escrow and by 2011 grew to $1.3 billion due to accumulated interest. Prior to the Supreme Court ruling, a lower court judge wrote in 1975 of "President Grant's duplicity" and the Manypenny Agreement: "A more ripe and rank case of dishonorable dealing will never, in all probability, be found in our history."[187]

Four months before Custer and his men were killed along the Little Big Horn, a drama began to unfold in Washington that helped explain why the Indians had been in a rebellious mood. On March 2, 1876 War Secretary Belknap urgently arranged an audience with President Grant. In it, he tearfully confessed that for some years he had been the beneficiary of financial kickbacks from frontier sutler posts.

During the Civil War, Union soldiers purchased supplies from private vendors, termed sutlers, who followed the armies as they advanced into the Confederacy. After the war, sutlers set up trading posts at frontier forts where regimental commanders selected them. But in 1870 Belknap convinced Congress that the secretary of war should have exclusive authority to choose all army sutlers. In addition to soldiers, army civilian employees such as white and Indian scouts bought most of their supplies from such shops. Since every post was basically a local monopoly the shops enjoyed high profit margins. The *New York Times* estimated that a $15,000 investment in a post would return $40,000.

Belknap's first wife, Carrie, originated the plan shortly before she died of tuberculosis in December a few months after her husband

---

[187] Frederic Frommer, *The Los Angeles Times*, "Black Hills Are Beyond Price to Sioux" Available: http://lat.ms/2yo096M [Accessed: September 19, 2017] (August 19, 2001); Francine Uenuma and Mike Fritz, *PBS News Hour*, "Why the Sioux are Refusing $1.3 Billion." Available: http://to.pbs.org/1GECxYi [Accessed: September 19, 2017] (August 24, 2011); Bryan Wildenthal, *North American Sovereignty on Trial* (Santa Barbara, Ca.: ABC-CLIO, 2003), 163

took office in 1870. She suggested that her New York friend Caleb P. Marsh be awarded the Fort Sill trading post in present day Oklahoma. But, as is often the case in shady dealings, the existing post operator, John Evans, demanded to be included in exchange for his silence. In the end, Evans operated the post but paid $1,000 monthly to Marsh for the privilege, who in turn paid Carrie Belknap $500 every month. After Carrie's death, Marsh told Carrie's sister that he would continue to pay the sister the monthly $500 kickback for the benefit of Carrie's child.

Even though the child soon also died, Carrie's sister, Amanda, continued to take Marsh's kickbacks. Two years later in December 1873, William Belknap married Amanda, a gorgeous socialite. Since William and Amanda enjoyed the social status bestowed on a cabinet member, they were living beyond the means of his $8,000 annual salary. As is often the case with corruption, once started it inevitably grew until the culprits were exposed.

By mid-morning on March 2, 1876 Belknap anticipated that the House would soon indict him on impeachment charges. In order to avoid prosecution, he requested that Grant immediately accept his one sentence resignation so that his official position would revert to that of an army officer. His legal counsel suggested that such a change would immunize him from civil prosecution by placing him under the authority of military law. After the brief explanation Grant accepted the secretary's resignation note.

By eleven o'clock that same morning the investigating House committee received

War Secretary
William Belknap

copies of the letters of resignation and acceptance. Committee members were furious at Belknap's obvious attempt to avoid justice. They were also angry with Grant for permitting the dodge. At the next cabinet meeting Grant could see that Treasury Secretary Bristow and State Secretary Fish were dismayed by the President's complicity. The House committee promptly voted an impeachment resolution. The Senate trial acquitted Belknap, however, partly because twenty-three of the Senators who thought him guilty refused to vote for conviction on the technical excuse that he was no longer in civilian office but was instead a military officer.[188]

*   *   *

Although not mentioned among his goals in his December 1869 annual message, Grant would appoint a new customs collector at the Port of New York in the summer of 1870. Since he narrowly lost the state in the 1868 election Grant was eager to build an effective political organization there. But he first had to await a settlement between the state's two Republican Senators, Roscoe Conkling and Reuben Fenton, who feuded for political control of the state. The chief factor that would enable one of them to hold such power was behind-the-scenes control of New York City's customs house. Eventually, Grant sided with Conkling after the latter discovered, and threatened to disclose, court records that suggested Fenton had once been involved in a large theft.[189]

Thus, on July 1, 1870 Grant chose Thomas Murphy, a well-known Conkling ally. Murphy, it will be recalled, was among the businessmen who contributed money to buy Grant a 27-room vacation "cottage" in Long Branch, New Jersey the previous year. The appointment enabled Conkling to put dozens of men on the customs house payroll where they reliably devoted their time and energy to the senator's ambitions. Among the loyalties expected of Conkling in

---

[188] William McFeely *Grant*, 428-29, 432-3, 435, 436
[189] Charles Calhoun, *The Presidency of Ulysses S. Grant*, 290

return would be political donations from customs house employees and its favored patrons to the Republican Party.

Shortly after Murphy's appointment George Leet, who had formerly been a minor member on General Grant's staff during the war, asked that Murphy designate Leet's warehouse as the solitary depository for "general order" freight. Under this arrangement, imported freight that could not be immediately shipped to its consignees was stored temporarily in Leet's warehouses where Leet charged excessive fees. Importers that resisted the procedure would often encounter mysterious delays in receiving their shipments. Newspaperman Horace Greeley accused Grant's personal secretaries, Porter and Babcock, of being involved, although he had no proof. Both secretaries denied the accusations.

Nonetheless, the arrangement led to complaints from importers and Leet competitors, which prompted a congressional investigation. Among those complaining was A. T. Stewart who had been Grant's first— but ill-fated—choice for treasury secretary. The investigation led to Murphy's resignation in the fall of 1871, which Grant accepted by ironically complimenting Murphy on his "efficiency, honesty and zeal." Since it was among the earliest of Grant Administration scandals, the public initially credited the President for conscientiously punishing malfeasance when he accepted Murphy's resignation.

Grant replaced him with future President Chester A. Arthur. Unfortunately, other forms of mischief continued under Arthur. In one instance metal importer Phelps-Dodge & Company (PD) was caught apparently trying to evade several thousand dollars in tariff duties. The rather small violation permitted Arthur to hold the entire PD shipment of almost $2 million subject to forfeiture. As a result, Dodge agreed to pay a $270,000 settlement to the customs house. As regulations at the time permitted, half of the settlement went to the top three New York customs officers, including Arthur, as well as an agent they had engaged. The customs house also paid New York Senator Roscoe Conkling and Massachusetts Congressman Ben Butler a combined $50,000 fee for legal advice. Starting with

Murphy's appointment, Grant had essentially given Conkling behind-the-scenes control of the post as political patronage.[190]

The 1870-71 off year elections that followed Murphy's appointment resulted in Republican setbacks. Although the infant GOP retained majorities in both the Senate and House, it lost thirty-two seats in the House and four in the Senate. Consequently, Grant turned his attention to new legislation, which might generate better Republican results in the South where he was convinced many black voters had been violently and otherwise kept away from the polls.

---

[190] Matthew Josephson, *Politicos*, 89-90, 117; Charles Calhoun, *The Presidency of Ulysses S. Grant*, 368-69; William Hesseltine, *Grant the Politician*, 264-65; Claude Bowers, *The Tragic Era*, 317

CHAPTER 11: THE NEW REPUBLICAN

THE SCANDALS EXPOSED in the wake of Jay Cooke's 1873 collapse were partly symptomatic of a greater truth. Specifically, the slump led Grant and his fellow Republicans to reveal that the humanitarian idealism—presumably foremost among the original anti-slavery Republicans—had become secondary. It was replaced by an economic ideology that put the interests of wealth and capital over laborers. After Republicans clarified their post-1873 priorities Southern blacks were increasingly cast aside.

In reality, Grant's pandering to the aristocracy was evident no later than his first annual message in December 1869 when he criticized the "evil" of "irredeemable currency," meaning greenbacks. As his inaugural address nine months earlier demonstrated, Eastern bankers had already convinced Grant that paper money should eventually be made redeemable at face value for specie. Their "sound money" goal was to have greenbacks accepted at par on international markets, particularly in financial centers like London.

But the President realized that it would take time to achieve the goal for two reasons. First, the U. S. Treasury's specie reserves were not then big enough to redeem all the greenbacks. Second, an attempt to abruptly withdraw greenbacks from circulation would likely trigger a depression by contracting the money supply. Two months after his speech, the Supreme Court complicated the situation with its 4-to-3 *Hepburn v. Griswold* decision.

In that case the Court ruled that an 1860 borrower of $1,000 in specie could not require her creditor to accept an 1862 repayment of the loan in greenbacks. Since the financing requirements of the Civil

War led the treasury to suspend specie redemption of paper currency in December 1861, the ruling threatened to throw American finance into anarchy. As long as greenbacks could not be redeemed at face value for gold, it called into question the forms of money that might properly be used to repay debts incurred during the nine years preceding the 1870 court ruling.

The great irony is that Chief Justice Salmon P. Chase sided with the majority in the decision even though as treasury secretary in 1862 he was the main proponent of the Legal Tender Act passed that year, which authorized greenbacks as fiat money. As chief justice, however, Chase reasoned that the act was a wartime necessity and that its authority to require that greenbacks be accepted as legal tender expired at the end of the war. He pointed out that the constitution did not permit the government to issue paper currency as legal tender. It was only allowed to "coin money" as specie. The distinction was no mere oversight. The failure of the earlier Continental dollar left the constitutional authors acutely aware of the dangers of fiat currency.

Grant felt that the only acceptable solution would require two conditions. First, greenbacks must be accepted as a way to repay debts incurred prior to *Hepburn v. Griswold*. He would have to get the ruling overturned. Second, the only way that lenders accepting greenbacks could be made whole in all cases was to eventually require that greenbacks be made redeemable for specie at face value.

Fortunately for Grant, two vacancies soon developed on the Court, which he filled with new justices that shared the President's viewpoint. In two 1871 cases the Court reversed *Hepburn v. Griswold*. It ruled that the Legal Tender Act was both constitutional and generally applied to prospective and retroactive debts. Grant planned that the rulings would give him time to stock the treasury with enough gold so that greenbacks might be exchanged for specie without exhausting the department's inventories. This partly explains how his Indian policy discussed in the previous chapter was influenced by gold in the Black Hills.[191]

Specie redemption would remain Grant's main economic policy throughout his presidency, but the aftermath of Jay Cooke's September 1873 bankruptcy would require the President to consider other factors and alternative viewpoints. Less than three months after Cooke's failure, Grant first spoke about the economic decline during his annual December message. Since the panic was still in progress he mused that "The full effect of this disaster . . . [might] 'prove a blessing in disguise.'" Nonetheless, he offered two recommendations.

First was to cut federal spending because of the depression-induced drop in taxes collected was already obvious. Second was to double-down on specie resumption. Specifically, he wanted Congress to give him a bill that would erase any lingering public doubts that greenbacks might fail to be redeemed by the treasury for gold at face value in the not-too-distant future.[192]

While Keynesian time-travelers would likely have been repelled by the spending cut, the greater contemporary controversy was the monetary policy. Grain farmers in the Midwest and cotton growers in the South sold much of their output as exports. Since overseas buyers paid in gold, the farmers received more in paper money when greenbacks traded at a discount to gold. Given a 20% discount, for example, an export farmer would receive $1.25 in domestically spendable paper money for each dollar in gold the overseas buyer paid. Thus, face value redemption of greenbacks for gold was contrary to the interests of such farmers.

---

[191] *The Lehrman Information Institute: The Gold Standard Now,* "The Legal Tender Cases," (February 7, 2012) Available: http://bit.ly/2vNiRaw [Accessed: 9/6/2017]; H. W. Brands, *Greenback Planet,* Kindle Location 182-89; Ulysses S. Grant, *First Annual Message: December 6, 1869* Available: http://bit.ly/2w7XdZz [Accessed: 9/6/2017]

[192] Ulysses S. Grant, The American Presidency Project, "Fifth Annual Message" (12-1-1873) Available: http://bit.ly/2AIBqeh [Accessed: December 16 2017]

As the 1869 Gould-Fisk Gold Corner attempt discussed in chapter four explained, railroads also favored the greenback discount precisely because it made farm exports more competitive abroad. As a result, it stimulated autumnal railroad freight traffic from the hinterlands to export centers, especially New York. Additionally, some domestic manufacturers favored the discount because it made competing brands produced overseas more expensive for domestic buyers in terms of American paper currency. In such instances the discount functioned as a surrogate tariff that boosted a protected industry's tariff wall even taller.[193]

The banking sector, which was concentrated in the Northeast by reason of the wartime National Banking Acts, was among the chief supporters of the gold standard. Creditors' loans made as greenbacks when the currency traded at a discount to gold would gain a windfall profit when the loans got repaid with greenbacks redeemable at face value for gold. Other financial conservatives also favored greenback redemption. They argued that the United States could not stand equal among the world's leading economic nations until American currency was accepted at face value everywhere, without hesitation. They also believed that face value conversion would combat inflation. Some even suggested that the 1873 Panic might never have happened if the United States had been on the gold standard.

Soon after his December 1873 annual address Grant was flooded with pleas to do something more than merely suggest that the depression might be a blessing in disguise. Thus, in April 1874 Congress gave him a bill designed to stimulate the economy. In terms of modern economic theory, it was ahead of its time. The bill was designed to inject flexibility into a monetary system that was regularly characterized by seasonal demand variations as well as irregular economic fluctuations. Pejoratively known by its

---

[193] Murray Rothbard, *A History of Money and Banking in the United States* (Auburn, Ala.: Ludwig von Mises Institute, 2002), 147-49; Michael F. Holt, *By One Vote: The Disputed Presidential Election of 1876* (Lawrence: University Press of Kansas, 2008), 14

opponents as the Inflation Bill it would expand the money supply instead of shrinking it, which would be the alternative result if greenbacks were taken out of circulation.

To be sure, the bill only authorized a modest $64 million increase in a combination of greenbacks and banknotes, but passage would likely prove to be pivotal in terms of future monetary policy. Instead of a step toward a fixed gold standard, the bill was an implied endorsement of fiat currency, which might enable the treasury to expand the money supply when judged to be advantageous.

The Grant of his younger civilian years in Missouri might appreciate the benefits of a larger and better geographically distributed money supply. During the post-war era, for example, Connecticut had more paper banknotes in circulation than Michigan, Wisconsin, Iowa, Minnesota, Kansas, Kentucky, Missouri and Tennessee combined. But the Grant of 1874 had fallen under the influence of America's financiers who were among his chief campaign contributors. They argued against the bill with emotion-packed terms and phrases, claiming that it would "debase" America's currency, compromise "the good faith of the nation," repudiate "national obligations to creditors," and was contrary to a "sound" money policy.[194]

On April 22, 1874 Grant made his choice on the side of the wealthy and vetoed the bill. As a result, according to biographer McFeely, "Grant's veto made the stand of the Republican party official. From this date it was the party not of the working class but of those who were or aspired to be the capitalists."[195]

The aristocracy applauded the President. Secretary of State Fish who had resolved to resign if Grant approved the bill, shelved his drafted resignation letter. He wrote a like-mined friend, "You must give the President undivided credit for what he did. Never did a man

---

[194] William McFeely, *Grant*, 393-96; Jeffrey Hummel, *Emancipating Slaves, Enslaving Free Men*, 330; Charles Calhoun, *The Presidency of Ulysses S. Grant*, 440-43

[195] William McFeely *Grant*, 397; Richard White, *The Republic for Which it Stands*, 261, 266

more conscientiously reach his conclusions . . . in spite of the strongest and most persistent [opposing] influences brought to bear upon him." A Connecticut congressman's note to Grant waxed, "So long as we have a history, you will be remembered as having saved the nation [during the Civil War] but in the coming centuries there will be historians who will claim that in saving our national honor [by his veto of the Inflation Bill] you have done the cause of republican government an even greater service."[196]

Inflation Bill supporters, including some Republicans, predictably vented their anger. Illinois Senator John Logan who had expected the President to sign the bill told reporters, "Grant . . . is being flattered all the time by the aristocrats of the country until no one can tell what he contemplates. I begin to feel that our country will not last long under Republican rule of this kind." Most other bill supporters concurred with Logan's election prediction. One newspaperman who talked with many of them wrote, "The inflationists all assert that Grant has committed political suicide and stabbed the party to death." Consequently, the approaching 1874 off year elections would result in a Democratic sweep.[197]

When given a chance to clarify his stance, he doubled-down on the side of "sound" money. In a letter to Nevada Senator John P. Jones, Grant went so far as to recommend that a key provision of the 1862 Legal Tender Act be repealed. Specifically, he suggested that it no longer be mandatory to accept greenbacks as legal money, which was opposite to his earlier stance when appointing Supreme Court justices to overrule *Hepburn v. Griswold*. Instead, he would have debts, wages, and purchases of any kind paid only in specie. Greenbacks and banknotes might only be accepted in transactions when all participating parties agree. Not only would modern economists shake their heads at a suggestion to reduce the nation's

---

[196] Ulysses Grant, *The Papers of U. S. Grant*, Vol. 25, 76
[197] Charles Calhoun, *The Presidency of Ulysses S. Grant*, 443

money supply during a depression, it's also likely that attempts to implement the repeal would have caused chaos in financial system.

But Grant's next suggestion would confound today's economists even more. Specifically, he added that all greenbacks should be retired in only two years, by July 1, 1876. The treasury, he wrote, could get the gold required for greenback redemption in two ways: higher taxes and government bond sales. In contrast, modern economists would almost universally advise against increasing taxes when the economy is weakening.

Grant's Party was fortunate that Republican House Speaker James G. Blaine recognized that Grant's suggestions "would be ruinous to the Republican Party and the country." As a result, Congress passed a compromise bill in June 1874. It did little except reduce reserve requirements on banknotes and endorse a redistribution of $55 million in such banknotes from the northeast to other parts of the country. The endorsement was a toothless plea that had no effect on banknote redistribution.[198]

James G. Blaine

After Democrats won the 1874 elections, the Republicans shoved through economic legislation in the early months of 1875 before the new Democrats could be seated. Foremost among such measures was the Specie Resumption Act. Most importantly it stipulated that beginning January 1, 1879 any holder of greenbacks could present his bills to the U. S. Treasury and demand that they be redeemed in gold at face value. It was a decisive victory for Grant's plan to put

---

[198] *Ibid.,* 444-45

America on a strict gold standard. In terms of a then-popular expression among his opponents, Grant had sided with the bondholders over the plough holders.

As a compromise nod to soft money advocates the act also authorized national banks to issue more banknotes if they desired. There was, however, a devil in the details of the compromise. Specifically, the act required that greenbacks in circulation be reduced by an amount equal to 80% of new banknotes issued. Thus, if $100 million in new banknotes are issued and $50 million are retired the net increase of $50 million in banknotes would require a $40 million (80%) reduction of greenbacks. Consequently, there would be only a modest $10 million increase in all types of paper money circulating (greenbacks + banknotes). But President Grant interpreted the wording for the banknote-greenback formulation in a manner that put a second devil in the details. He declared that the greenback-reduction requirement applied to the *gross* value of new banknotes issued instead of merely the net amount.

Thus, if $100 million of new banknotes are issued and $50 million are retired, Grant's interpretation stipulated that greenbacks must be reduced by $80 million—80% of $100 million—thereby exceeding the $50 million net increase in banknotes by a total $30 million. In short, Grant's interpretation virtually assured that greenbacks in circulation would drop, even if the banknotes in circulation also declined. Thus, the combined greenback-banknote money supply would almost certainly shrink even as the economy continued to weaken. Nonetheless, Grant and his fellow Republicans were anxious to reduce the face value of greenbacks outstanding because they feared that the U. S. Treasury might otherwise be overwhelmed with requests to redeem greenbacks for gold on the January 1, 1879 deadline.[199]

The persistent economic depression compelled Northern businessmen, the heart of Republican Party campaign support, to

---

[199] *Ibid.,* 485

enlarge their search for ways to reverse the economic decline. When they looked Southward many concluded that the carpetbag governments were partly to blame for continued weakness. The regimes, they reasoned, stifled the region's economy and were therefore an obstacle to America's overall economic recovery.

They noticed, for example, that Virginia's economy was the most rapidly recovering of all former Confederate states and that it had never been under carpetbag rule. Similarly, after visiting New Orleans during the initial slowdown a few months before Jay Cooke's bankruptcy, Wisconsin Senator Matt Carpenter concluded that Louisiana's carpetbaggers unnecessarily constrained the state's economy. A month later a Maine congressman addressed his state's Republican convention to say that he was "tired and sick of some of the carpet-bag governments."

According to historian William B. Hesseltine, Northerners "were coming to the belief that the poverty of the southern states was due to the villainies of the carpetbaggers and they were coming to perceive that this had a national significance." The *New York Tribune* argued that removing carpetbagger impediments in the South would lift the region's economy and enable it to pay a higher share of federal taxes thereby reducing the tax burden on Northerners.

Even Grant's first attorney general, George Hoar of Massachusetts, admitted that no Northern state would tolerate governments that were as corrupt as the Southern carpetbag regimes. Northern capitalists were reluctant to invest in the capital-starved South as long as such governments were in power. Similarly, in December 1874 Grant's postmaster general, Marshall Jewell of Connecticut, said he did "not blame" Southerners for rejecting carpetbag rule. Surveying the lot, he added that there was "not one really first class man" among such regimes.

The focus shift to the economy increasingly led Northern Republicans to question the steady mantra of anti-black atrocities cited by the Party's Southern wing. They increasingly interpreted carpetbagger chants as a disreputable technique to enlist their support for federal intervention to keep the corrupt regimes in power. During the 1874 elections in Alabama, for example, the *New York Tribune* investigated a long list of atrocities cited by a campaigning Republican congressman but found no substantial basis for the charges. When Southern Republicans gathered at a Chattanooga convention during the election season they appointed a "Facts and Statistics Committee" to provide a statistical summary of such atrocities. The committee never made a report. After the onset of the Jay Cooke depression and the 1874 elections, Northerners were more often doubtful of, or little concerned with, atrocity stories.[200]

Northern Republicans also recognized that geographic population growth and migration patterns favored states with small numbers of blacks where their Party already had a stronger presence, or prospects, than did the Democrats. From 1860 to 1876 the electoral votes for the eleven states of the former Confederacy where blacks composed forty percent of the population increased from 88 to 95. By comparison, over the same period the electoral votes from the twenty-two states that remained Union-loyal during the Civil War where blacks composed less than three percent of the population increased from 215 to 260. Additionally, the Republican-dominated states of Kansas, Nebraska, Nevada, and Colorado, which had not voted in 1860, but had later been admitted to the Union provided an additional 14 electoral votes to the Republican presidential candidate in 1876.

In short, the states of the former Confederacy represented only 29% of the total electoral votes cast in 1876 as compared to 35% in 1860. Moreover, few blacks lived in the Northern and Western states holding 71% of the total electoral votes in the centennial year. Finally, the next seven states to join the union after 1876—North Dakota, South Dakota, Montana, Washington, Idaho, Wyoming, and

---

[200] William Hesseltine, "Economic Factors in the Abandonment of Reconstruction," *Mississippi Valley Historical Review* Vol. 2, No. 2 (September 1935), 206-09

Utah—were overwhelmingly white and generally Republican. Although some, particularly with mining interests, backed Democrat William Jennings Bryan in the 1896 presidential election due to his "Free Silver" platform, each of the seven sent two more Republicans to the United States Senate when they were admitted as states.

Oklahoma would be the first decidedly Democratic state to initially join the union after the Civil War. That would not happen until 1907, which was thirty years after Grant left office. Thus, the pragmatic Republican politician of 1875 realized that Southern black votes would increasingly become an unnecessary way of retaining the Party's control in Washington.[201]

While Grant and the aristocracy were busy in 1875 elevating capitalism and the gold standard as the signature Republican tenets over the Party's original humanitarianism, two converging political factors would strengthen the trend toward scandal disclosure during the last two years of Grant's presidency. One was the Democratic success in the 1874 elections, although the Party would be unable to exercise its power until the first session of the Forty-Fourth Congress convened in December 1875. The second factor was the crusading influence of politically ambitious Republicans, who were given appointments due to their credentials as reformers, in response to the corruption exposed in their Party following the 1872 elections.

---

[201] Encyclopedia Britannica, "United States Presidential Election of 1860" Available: http://bit.ly/2zh2Ab6 [Accessed: December 27, 2017]; Encyclopedia Britannica, "United States Presidential Election of 1876" Available: http://bit.ly/2lhQpoV [Accessed: December 27, 2017]

CHAPTER 12: CRUSADING INVESTIGATORS

ALTHOUGH THE JAY COOKE DEPRESSION indirectly disclosed some improprieties such as Sanford's unearned tax-collection fees, political motivations would also induce investigations during Grant's final two years as President that would unearth even more scandals. When the first ordinary session of the Forty-Fourth Congress opened in December 1875 the Democrats finally controlled the U. S. House of Representatives for the first time in almost twenty years. As a result, they eagerly sought to investigate a number of matters that the Republicans had refused to examine when the GOP dominated the chamber. Additionally, after the indignities disclosed earlier in his second term, Grant was forced to appoint a few Republican reformers to key positions. Such men were eager to root-out corruption. At least one also wanted to succeed Grant as President.

Among the offenses the Democrats exposed was misconduct by Grant's ambassador to Great Britain since 1871, Robert Schenck. Like Grant, Schenck was from Ohio and had been a Major General in the Union army during the Civil War. But unlike Grant he left the army in the middle of the war to become a congressman after being wounded at Second Bull Run. He remained in office until shortly before being designated minster to Great Britain.

Soon after arriving in London, Schenck introduced poker to English aristocrats. The game became sufficiently popular that he was persuaded to write a book describing its rules. Although Schenck enjoyed his popularity among the English gentry, he was living beyond his means. As a result, he permitted his name to be used in a promotional investment scheme involving a Utah-based silver mining company. Since Jay Cooke & Company had promised

Schenck a job upon his return from London, little credibility can be given to any claim that the ambassador was unaware that the stock promotion compromised his reputation. At the time, Jay Cooke & Company was as well-known as any American investment bank.

In October 1871 he became a paid director of the Emma Silver Mine Company and allowed his name to be used in advertisements for the company's shares in London. When American newspapers disclosed the linkage, Secretary of State Fish and President Grant ordered Schenck to part ways with the mining company. Although he complied, he kept his resignation private for over a month thereby maintaining the impression that he was still endorsing the company's stock as the English continued to buy shares.

When the company stopped paying dividends at the end of 1872, the stock price dropped from $165 to $20 per share. Soon rumors circulated that English investors had lost 85% of their $5 million investment. By the summer of 1873 Grant suspected that the Emma Mine was a Ponzi scheme from which "no returns came to the investors except a few dividends from funds they had paid in." He also believed that Schenk may have profited by as much as $500,000 from stock subscriptions sold to the English.

He ordered Secretary Fish to draft a letter to Schenck detailing the accusations that might be levied against the ambassador. But after consulting his cabinet Grant decided not to send it. If sent, the message would require Schenck to either admit, or deny, the allegations. If he denied them the Administration would be forced to defend the ambassador's conduct, which Grant evidently did not want to do. If Schenck instead responded with an explanation, the Administration would be compelled to launch an investigation "and become a prosecutor." If an investigation was necessary, reasoned Grant, let someone else initiate it.[202]

---

[202] Charles Calhoun, *The Presidency of Ulysses S. Grant*, 527-28; William Hesseltine, *Ulysses S. Grant Politician*, 231-32; Allan Nevins, *Hamilton Fish* Vol. 2, 651-54; Michael Holt, *By One Vote: The Disputed Presidential Election of 1876*, 17

After the Democrats swept to victory in the 1874 elections, the new congressmen waited until they took office during the Forty-Fourth Congress of 1875-76 to conduct the inquiry that Grant declined to begin. The resulting House committee investigation concluded that Schenck did nothing technically illegal under American law. But to avoid prosecution in England, Schenck invoked diplomatic immunity before resigning his ambassadorship in March of 1876. Nonetheless, the discoveries about Schenck's conduct by the House committee were shameful.

Ambassador Robert Schenck

First, Schenck's directorship included an annual $2,500 salary. Second, it also contained an arrangement to carry $50,000 worth of stock with guaranteed dividends in his name. Third, if the stock price dropped the ambassador could return his shares for no loss. If the stock price increased, he was free to sell it and keep the profit. Fourth, when he learned in advance that the company would soon suspend its dividends, Schenck sold his stock at high prices. Fifth, in addition to liquidating his personal holdings of the stock before the dividend cut, he attempted to profit further by selling the stock short. Such insider trading later became explicitly illegal in the United States after the 1929 stock market crash.[203]

Democrats were also eager to investigate George Robeson who had been navy secretary since Grant had appointed him three months after moving into the White House back in 1869. Previously

---

[203] Allan Nevins, *Hamilton Fish* Vol. 2, 814

Robeson had been New Jersey's attorney general. After seven years of steady rumors about dishonesty in the navy department, an 1876 investigation by the House Naval Affairs Committee confirmed a number of incriminating facts.

First, when Grant appointed Robeson the latter's accumulated wealth totalled less than $20,000 and had been earned mostly through a small law practice. Second, soon after his appointment he formed a relationship with Philadelphia-based A. G. Cattell & Company, which was connected to former New Jersey Senator Alexander Cattell. It was a small commission agent for grain, flour and feed supplies that had no prior relationship with the navy. But soon after Robeson's appointment Cattell & Company started collecting generous fees as a middleman between the U. S. Navy and its contract suppliers of grain and related products. According to historian Allan Nevins, "it was evident that the contractors paid these sums simply because of [Cattell's] influence with the Secretary." Third, for each of the four years prior to the investigation Robeson deposited an average of $80,000 a year into his personal bank accounts although his annual salary was only $8,000.[204]

When ordered to produce accounting records, Cattell & Company presented papers that were too confusing to follow. Payments as large as $180,000 were noted with a single entry and no itemization. Although the firm denied that Robeson shared in its commission, Robeson conducted large transactions with the firm of an ill-defined nature. Moreover, about eighteen months before the investigation Robeson tried to interfere in the affairs of the treasury department on behalf of Alexander Cattell. Specifically, he urged that Cattell be designated the government's financial agent to market an issue of federal bonds that were to be sold in London. Instead, Treasury Secretary Benjamin Bristow selected a venerable department employee, John Bigelow, to negotiate the arrangements and choose the marketing agent.

---

[204] *Ibid.*, 815-16

The Committee released its report in July 1876. The investigation concluded that Robeson was guilty of carelessness and extravagance but found no direct evidence of corruption. Without such evidence Grant stood by his subordinate and did not request his resignation. Nonetheless, Robeson lost in the court of public opinion. The *Nation* wrote, "No man can read the evidence taken and doubt that a secret partnership existed between the Secretary and the Cattells by virtue of which they levied toll on contracts and he levied tolls on them." After about a decade of refection, Thomas Nast of *Harper's Weekly* wrote in 1885, "The Cattells had clearly furnished Robeson with favors, including substantial loans, repayment of large debts, and real estate." The Naval Affairs Committee suggested that the House refer the matter to its Judiciary Committee to consider impeachment in the next session. By that time, however, the incident was ignored because Congress was preoccupied with resolving the disputed 1876 presidential election.[205]

After Benjamin Bristow replaced the disgraced William Richardson as treasury secretary in June 1874, the newcomer soon detected a sizeable fraud that Richardson and several predecessors had overlooked, ignored, or possibly even had joined as participants. Bristow's discovery would evolve into the biggest scandal of the Grant Administration since the failed attempt by Gould and Fisk to corner the gold market in 1869. The problem was indirectly a consequence of one of the financial legacies of the Civil War.

As explained earlier, the federal government needed large new revenue sources to fund the war. Therefore, preexisting tax rates were raised, and new taxes levied on previously untaxed items. Among those with the highest rates were excise taxes on distilled spirits, which continued after the war. As a result, evading such taxes became a parlor game. Distillers were almost compelled to join the

---

[205] Allan Nevins, *Hamilton Fish, Volume 2*, 816; Charles Calhoun, *The Presidency of Ulysses S. Grant*, 448; Thomas Nast, *Harper's Weekly,* "Preserved Lumber," (June 20, 1885) Available: http://bit.ly/2lkAWVU [Accessed: December 29, 2017]

fraud because the evaded taxes were so large that an honest distiller could not compete with the lower retail prices that corrupted distillers could afford to charge consumers by reason of avoiding the evaded taxes.

When measured by the original humanitarian ideals of the Republican Party, Bristow was a man of impeccable credentials. It may be recalled that he was a leading prosecutor of the KKK in North and South Carolina in 1871-72. Even though he was from Kentucky, he remained Union-loyal during the Civil War and raised a cavalry regiment. He was badly wounded at the Battle of Shiloh and eventually offered a promotion to major general, which he turned down out of modesty. After the war he returned to Kentucky to serve as a federal prosecuting attorney. In three-and-a-half years he won thirty convictions against whites that had perpetuated racial violence, including one against a Klansman for murder.

Grant was aware of the tax evasion as early as his 1868 presidential race when a campaign aide told him, "the whisky ring alone can raise . . . a million [dollars] a day." Although a new staff of internal revenue agents had been appointed to clean up the muddle in the last year of Andrew Johnson's presidency, the Internal Revenue Department remained a refuge for dishonest agents. In exchange for bribes they would validate deliberately understated production figures submitted by the distillers to the treasury. By the time Bristow completed his investigation it was obvious that the industry had been evading millions of dollars in taxes annually for years.[206]

In October 1869 President Grant had appointed an old army buddy, General John McDonald, as supervisor of internal revenue for Missouri and Arkansas. Several members of First Lady Julia Grant's St. Louis family had recommended McDonald. Rochester-born McDonald was orphaned before he turned ten years old in 1842 and

---

[206] Ron Chernow, *Grant*, 797; Thomas J. Craughwell, *Presidential Payola* (Vancouver, British Columbia: Fair Winds Press, 2011), 34

worked his way to St. Louis by 1847. Before the Civil War started, when he was still under age 30, he operated a steamer carrying freight and passengers on the Missouri River. After the war began, he raised a Missouri regiment and ultimately became a brigadier general even though he was illiterate. After the war he became an agent for plaintiffs pursing claims against the federal government.

In February 1870 Grant instructed McDonald to move to St. Louis in order to support Stalwart Republican interests against an incipient rebellion from Liberal Republicans then led by Missouri Senator Carl Schurz. McDonald soon began channeling funds to Grant-friendly Republicans with money he obtained from bribes collected from area distillers. In exchange he allowed the distillers to evade taxes by underreporting their production. At the time, liquor excises taxes were second only to customs duties as a source of federal tax revenue. Ultimately, McDonald's operation became the center of a vast Whiskey Ring throughout the Midwest and Mississippi Valley, although the scam also spread to other parts of the country.[207]

Grant maintained a dubious relationship with McDonald even as Bristow's investigation progressed. For example, when Grant visited St. Louis in October 1874, McDonald provided the President an entire floor of a hotel at no charge. Similarly, when Grant entered two horses into a local competition during the visit, McDonald arranged for one of Grant's animals to win a blue ribbon. But that went too far. Grant knew horseflesh too well. When he got a look at the competitors Grant knew his horses were far outclassed and was embarrassed that everyone present could see that the award was an obvious fraud. "This is an outrage," he said, perhaps indicating that he preferred that McDonald stick to less public forms of gratuitous tribute, such as free hotel rooms.

---

[207] William Hesseltine, *Grant the Politician*, 207-08; Max Skidmore, "General Grant, General Babcock, and Journalist Colony: A Study in Scandal & Friendship." *History? Because its Here.* Available: http://bit.ly/2EsU5wV [Accessed: January 1, 2018]; Thomas J. Craughwell, *Presidential Payola*, 33; Nicolas Barreyre, *Gold and Freedom: The Political Economy of Reconstruction* (Charlottesville: University of Virginia Press, 2015), 83

The same month as Grant's visit, Secretary Bristow sent revenue inspectors to St. Louis from Washington. But somebody from the capital tipped off McDonald's cabal in a telegram stating, "Put your house in order. Your friends will visit you." The warning enabled the conspirators to disguise their affairs and avoid detection.

Although Bristow could not then identify the Washington informant, by December 1874 he got a clue when he became suspicious that both Orville Babcock and Interior Secretary Delano wanted him removed from the cabinet, as noted in chapter nine. Bristow reasoned that Babcock might be the more powerful enemy of the two because he was gatekeeper to the President's office. According to General of the Army, William T. Sherman, " . . . those who go to see the President see Babcock first. He is a kind of intermediator between the people and the President."

Nonetheless, Bristow's investigation persisted. He hired Bluford Wilson as the treasury department's solicitor general. Wilson was a U. S. Attorney in Illinois and had been a Union major during the Civil War. His brother, General James H. (Harry) Wilson, had been a distinguished Union cavalry commander during the war and a favorite of General Grant's at the time.

Among the men reporting to Bristow was J. W. Douglass, commissioner of internal revenue. In December 1874 he suggested that many of the collection officers in the field be rotated to other locations. He planned, for example, to send the trusted Philadelphia collector to St. Louis under instructions to search for evidence of taxpayer non-compliance. When Bristow ordered the rotation in January 1875, Babcock learned about it and urged Grant to block it, which the President did in February 1875.

Nonetheless, Bristow and Wilson got a break that same month when a St. Louis newspaper publisher discovered evidence of the fraud. He also volunteered to supply reporter Myron Colony as an undercover informant. Colony was ideally situated to gather evidence. He was widely known among the city's business community where he regularly collected statistical information. It only took about a month for the reporter and his assistants to gather the information Bristow needed to make arrests. Wilson and Bristow also sent a secret service agent to snoop around in Chicago and Milwaukee. Soon Bristow had evidence that the distilleries in St. Louis, Chicago, Milwaukee and Louisville should have been paying about three times the amount of taxes they habitually remitted.

Bristow met with Grant in mid-April 1875 and sketched out the investigation's methods and initial findings. A few days later he summoned McDonald to Washington. When Bristow presented the evidence against McDonald, the latter confessed. But McDonald also requested that he be granted immunity in exchange for collecting the $1.7 million in taxes evaded during preceding eleven months—the evidence period—and for assisting to enlarge the investigation. Bristow rejected the offer.[208]

On 7 May Bristow and Wilson met with Grant to explain their plans for a surprise raid on distillers at multiple locations. Bristow would later recall that Grant seemed to fully support the investigation at the time. But Babcock somehow also learned about the raids that same day and further learned that they were scheduled for 10 May. As a result, Babcock sent two cautionary messages to McDonald, one in his name and the other in a pseudonym. He implied that McDonald would be protected.

Specifically, he wired, "Your friend is doing the best he can. You can, I believe, rely on him." McDonald would later state that Babcock's reference to "your friend" meant President Grant. Babcock also advised that participants in the lower strata of the corruption fraud "will not be allowed to turn informers and then go free themselves." That was welcome news to McDonald who was one of the biggest wheels in the machine. It would discourage underlings

---

[208] Ron Chernow, *Grant,* 798-99; Allan Nevins, *Hamilton Fish, Volume 2,* 764, 768; Charles Calhoun *The Presidency of Ulysses S. Grant,* 495; William McFeely, *Grant,* 406; Max Skidmore, *History? Because its Here* "General Grant, General Babcock, and Journalist Colony: A Study in Scandal & Friendship" Available: http://bit.ly/2EsU5wV [Accessed: January 1, 2018]; Timothy Rives, "Grant, Babcock & the Whiskey Ring; Part 1" *Prologue Magazine: Part 1* Vol. 32, No. 3 (Fall 2000) Available: http://bit.ly/2CAJpvr [Accessed: January 1, 2018]

from tattling on him. Another telegram said, "The plague is moving west. Advise our friends to leave the city."

Despite Babcock's warnings, the raids succeeded. In the first two days thirty-two companies were caught at tax evasion. Soon hundreds of Ring members were arrested. Some, apparently close to Chicago, did "leave the city" by escaping to Canada. Given the centrality of McDonald's operation within the overall scheme, Grant selected a new federal prosecutor, David Dyer, for St. Louis. As Dyer prepared his case he found telegrams between Ring members in St. Louis and Washington. One from Washington in December 1874 said, "I succeeded. They will not go." It was mysteriously signed by, "Sylph." In August 1875 Babcock admitted to Bristow that he wrote the telegram but claimed that it was unrelated to the Whisky Ring. Bristow, nonetheless, told Babcock that he was likely to be indicted after the St. Louis grand jury convened in November 1875.[209]

Unfortunately, when Bristow laid the case against Babcock before Grant in September 1875, the President rejected it. Grant claimed that Babcock's December 1874 telegram merely referred to the President's decision to block the geographic reassignments of field collectors proposed earlier by Internal Revenue Commissioner Douglass. Bristow explained that such an explanation was impossible because Grant rejected Douglass's musical chairs suggestion in February 1875—two months *after* the "Sylph" telegram. It is hard to avoid concluding that the telegram referred to Babcock's success in blocking Commissioner Douglass's attempt to send investigators to St. Louis in December 1874. Nonetheless, Grant refused to change his mind and continued to avow that Babcock was innocent.[210]

Consequently, Bluford Wilson asked brother Harry for help. As noted, Grant respected Harry, with whom he was well acquainted.

---

[209] Charles Calhoun, *The Presidency of Ulysses S. Grant*, 497-98; Allan Nevins, *Hamilton Fish*, Volume 2, 768

[210] Allan Nevins, *Hamilton Fish*, Volume 2, 788-89; Charles Calhoun, *The Presidency of Ulysses S. Grant*, 498

When General Harry Wilson arrived at the White House he was told that the President was out for a walk with Alexander "Boss" Shepherd, the notoriously corrupt District of Columbia political honcho. Wilson also realized that Shepherd was allied with Babcock since the latter was superintendent of public buildings in the District, where he could help allocate lucrative public works construction contracts.

Nonplussed at Grant's friendship with "Boss" Shepherd, Wilson returned the next day determined to alert the President to Babcock's complicity in the Whiskey Ring. But Grant would not believe Harry Wilson either. The former cavalryman then asked if the President would believe Dr. Alexander Sharp, who was the First Lady's brother-in-law. How Dr. Sharp had such information has never been explained. Nonetheless, the doctor soon visited the White House to confirm the Bristow-Wilson accusations against Babcock, but Grant continued to remain outwardly incredulous. Thereafter, Harry Wilson was not welcome around the Grant household despite their wartime friendship.[211]

A few weeks later Grant and Babcock visited St. Louis where McDonald and Babcock repeatedly conferred in meetings that at least once included Grant. McDonald was convicted on November 25, 1874. Two weeks later Babcock would be indicted for conspiring to defraud the government of tax revenue. McDonald would be sentenced to three years in jail and fined $5,000. Grant pardoned McDonald after the prisoner had served about half his term in January 1877 when Grant was a lame-duck President.

The nearly simultaneous trials of McDonald and Treasury Department Clerk William Avery revealed additional evidence against Babcock. More telegrams from December 1874 showed that Babcock had repeatedly used cryptic language to notify St. Louis that he had blocked Commissioner Douglass's plan to send investigators to the city that same month. When alluding to Grant's obstruction of

---

[211] William McFeely, *Grant*, 408-09

Bristow's January 1875 order for collections officers to rotate to different geographic locations as a means of breaking the collusion chain, one assistant prosecutor remarked during a summation to Avery's jury, "What right does the President have to interfere with the of the honest discharge of the duties of the Treasury Secretary? None whatsoever."

When news of the statement reached the White House, Grant went ballistic and succumbed to paranoia. He became convinced that Bristow was out to get him personally. He told Attorney General Edwards Pierrepont to fire the offending assistant prosecutor, John Henderson, who happened to be a former U. S. senator. Pierrepont complied and told lead prosecutor Dyer to choose another assistant. But Grant did not like Dyer's replacement either. He wanted to fire the second man as well, but Pierrepont explained that such dictatorial action would undermine public confidence in the Administration.

Instead Grant directed Pierrepont to forbid any more plea-bargaining. Such a directive meant that the time-proven technique of providing lighter sentences for low-level offenders in exchange for testimony against higher-status criminals would be unavailable. Consider, for example, how the American public would have reacted if John Dean had been forbidden to plea bargain in exchange for testimony against Nixon, Haldeman and Ehrlichman.

The House Judiciary Committee later condemned Grant's action exclaiming that, "The testimony of accomplices has been used against their associates from the earliest ages of jurisprudence." Unfortunately, Pierrepont's directive got results. When thirteen Chicago distillers pled guilty in January 1876, the prosecutors had hoped that at least one would implicate Illinois Republican Senator John Logan and two congressmen for accepting campaign donations from the Ring, but Pierrepont's circular dashed such hopes.

Finally, Grant put an undercover operative named C. S. Bell on the public payroll and sent him to St. Louis to penetrate prosecutor Dyer's office. "I want to know all that is going on," he told Bell. But after beginning his mission Bell concluded that Babcock was guilty when the latter urged him to destroy all the evidence he could get. The President also tried to get Babcock's case switched to a military tribunal in Chicago since Babcock was still an army officer as well as a personal secretary to the President. He even appointed three friendly generals to head the inquiry along with a Grant-loyal judge advocate (military prosecutor). Federal prosecutor Dyer correctly replied that it was illegal to send the evidence out of St. Louis, which was the location of the civilian court having jurisdiction.[212]

Babcock's trial began in St. Louis on February 7, 1876. Up to that point all the leading indicted Whisky Ring participants had been convicted. St. Louis was America's fourth largest city at the time. During the preceding forty years the town's population had increased almost tenfold from 37,000 to 350,000. It had evolved from a fur-trading village to a steamboat and railroad center. General of the Army William T. Sherman located his headquarters in the city, which counted President Grant among its former residents.

The trial was big news. Leading newspapers from across the country arrived to cover it. The courtroom had to be enlarged to accommodate their reporters. Controversy over jury selection began even before the trial started when prosecutor Dyer accused federal marshals of stacking the jury selection pool with Republicans. A *New York Times* reporter confirmed that the stacking excluded "the rebel element," which he implied would be prone to convict anyone connected with Grant.[213]

---

[212] Charles Calhoun *The Presidency of Ulysses S. Grant*, 515-21; Allan Nevins, *Hamilton Fish,* Volume 2, 786-87, 795-96

[213] Timothy Rives, "Grant, Babcock & the Whiskey Ring: Part 1" *Prologue Magazine* Vol. 32, No. 3 (Fall 2000) Available: http://bit.ly/2CAJpvr [Accessed: January 1, 2018]

Whiskey Ring Trial

Most newsworthy of all, however, was the arrival of a voluntary deposition from Grant presented by the defense. Basically, the President provided written testimony to defend Babcock notwithstanding that his own justice department had accused the subordinate of defrauding the federal government. No President had voluntarily taken such action before, nor has one done so since. Grant's solitary exception provoked speculation that he may have been trying to protect himself as much as Babcock. Put bluntly, he might have been guilty of participating in the Ring himself. But despite Grant's paranoid belief that Bristow was targeting him, the treasury secretary deliberately tried to avoid implicating the President.

Grant made his deposition at the White House on February 12, 1876. That very morning prosecutor Dyer in St. Louis wired his representative at the White House with instructions to cross-examine the President in a manner that would enable Grant to show that he was unaware of Babcock's alleged activities. Specifically, Dyer told his representative that he "must show on cross-examination that the President had no knowledge of the secret correspondence of

Babcock with Joyce and McDonald." (John Joyce was McDonald's St. Louis subordinate.) The kid-glove treatment toward Grant was duplicated in St. Louis. A *New York Times* reporter wrote that the prosecutors "emphasized the fact that if Gen. Babcock had been engaged in any wrong transactions the president had no knowledge of it."

According to historian Timothy Rives, Grant's deposition was "[A] litany of *disremembrances* . . . The President applied his ignorance and poor memory to more than thirty-five questions regarding Babcock's relationship with the Whiskey Ring conspirators . . . Grant's legendary photographic memory consistently failed him throughout most of the deposition, but it did not fail him when it came to Babcock. The President had no trouble remembering his aide's fidelity and efficiency nor in testifying to his universally good reputation among men of affairs."

Historian Rives continues:

> The [prosecutor's] "hands off Grant" strategy marked the triumph of the defense team and signaled the effective end of the prosecution. Months of political intimidation in the wake of the Avery trial and Senator Henderson's "attack" on Grant had forced the prosecutors to the President's defense. Thus, on the morning of February 12, 1876, instead of pursuing the evidence wherever it led, instead of pressing the sort of question made famous by Senator Howard Baker during the Senate Watergate Hearings a century later—"What did the President know and when did he know it?"—the attorneys representing the United States of America were reduced to little more than gathering character references on behalf of their opponents.[214]

---

[214] Timothy Rives, "Grant, Babcock & the Whiskey Ring: Part 2" *Prologue Magazine* Vol. 32, No. 3 (Fall 2000) Available: http://bit.ly/2iIEVJy [Accessed: January 2, 2018]

After reading Grant's deposition aloud, Babcock's defense team erroneously gave jurors the impression that the prosecutors were really attacking President Grant personally but were trying to get at him indirectly by limiting their formal charges to Babcock. Some of the jurors were moved to tears when one defense counsel compared the President to Christ as he commented upon the deposition by saying, "The President ... now stands fully vindicated. There were no more flowers of rhetoric in his deposition than in Christ's Sermon on the Mount." A defense co-counsel later proclaimed, "[The prosecutors] evidently felt that every stab they gave this defendant [Babcock] is really thrust through him at the President himself." He falsely added that the zealous drive of the government lawyers was due to "their avowed hostility toward President Grant."

Ironically, despite his forbearance toward Grant during the trial, Treasury Secretary Bristow may well have privately concluded that the President was as guilty as Babcock. After A. E. Willson replaced the treasury department's chief clerk—a convicted Ring participant—Willson wrote future Supreme Court Justice John Harlan three days before Babcock's trial began, "What has hurt Bristow worst of all ... is the final conviction that Grant himself is in the Ring and knows all about [it.]"

The trial judge's jury instructions also helped Babcock. He told them that the cryptic language in the telegrams between McDonald and Babcock should not be ascribed a sinister interpretation if an innocent one was equally plausible. Additionally, he prevented the jury from seeing one of Babcock incriminating telegrams, even though signed in Babcock's own name. The judge's flimsy excuse for the exclusion was that there was no proof that Babcock had sent it because nobody could locate the original telegram order form. Consequently, on February 25, 1876 Babcock won acquittal. He was lucky. Eventually over one hundred others were convicted of participating in the Whiskey Ring, which became yet another symbol of Republican Party corruption following the Civil War.

After dodging a legal bullet in St. Louis Babcock presumed that he would be returning to the White House to continue as the President's gatekeeper. But Secretary Fish objected, and it was not to be. Grant instead gave the post to his own son, Ulysses, Jr. He did, however, unwisely allow Babcock to remain the superintendent of public buildings in Washington. Grant also made him a lighthouse inspector along the Southern Atlantic coast, which was a job that would keep the former personal secretary out of Washington for long stretches of time.[215]

But less than a month after his St. Louis acquittal Babcock was indicted in an unrelated conspiracy in the capital city. He was charged with helping corrupt Washington builders—accused of winning lucrative contracts on public works via pay-offs to "Boss" Shepherd—in an evidence-planting scheme. As explained in chapter nine, Shepherd controlled the city until he bankrupted it in 1874. According to one Bristow biographer, Babcock used his influence to help Shepherd become the capital city's political kingpin. Although Shepherd and his construction company cohorts beautified the city, the cost was staggering. Moreover, most of the

Orville Babcock

---

[215] Charles Calhoun, *The Presidency of Ulysses S.* Grant, 521, 524-25; Timothy Rives, "Grant, Babcock & the Whiskey Ring: Part 2" *Prologue Magazine* Vol. 32, No. 3 (Fall 2000) Available: http://bit.ly/2iIEVJy [Accessed: January 2, 2018]; Max Skidmore, *History? Because its Here* "General Grant, General Babcock, and Journalist Colony: A Study in Scandal & Friendship" Available: http://bit.ly/2EsU5wV [Accessed: January 1, 2018]

profit allegedly went to a cabal of contractors and government officials including Shepherd and Babcock. Partly due to a fear of losing their homes in tax deficiency sales caused by the high taxes required to finance Shepherd's program, Washington's property owners were outraged.

Among the angered residents who helped expose Shepherd's misdeeds was Columbus Alexander. Ring members decided to retaliate against Alexander by framing him for evidence theft. Specifically, Alexander had been complaining that one major contractor was submitting false records to the prosecution. He repeatedly demanded that the true records be produced. Ring members responded by hatching a comical plan to secretly put the valid records into Alexander's home in order to leave the false impression that he had been hiding them all along while accusing others of failing to produce them. It was a botched affair from beginning to end. Ultimately two of the participants confessed to the conspiracy thereby verifying Alexander's innocence.[216]

Babcock was accused of helping to recruit crooked secret service agents into the farce. At the time, most of the service's agents were stationed in New York where they focused on catching counterfeiters instead of acting as presidential bodyguards. Although Babcock was once again acquitted, historian Ellis Oberholtzer later wrote, "the jury had been packed in the interests of the men who were being tried." Ten years after the incident Babcock drowned during a Florida lighthouse inspection trip.[217]

The month following his June 1876 resignation as Treasury Secretary, Benjamin Bristow took the stand before a congressional inquiry into the Whiskey Ring prosecution. When he was peppered with questions that suggested his interrogators suspected Grant of

---

[216] Ted Rockwell Tosh, *The Life and Times of Benjamin Helm Bristow* (New York: Page Publishing, 2015), Kindle Location, 6717, 6763-6782

[217] Ellis Oberholtzer, *A History of the United States: 1872-78* Available: http://bit.ly/2ArZ4KR [Accessed: January 4, 2018]; Ted Rockwell Tosh, *The Life and Times of Benjamin Helm Bristow*, Kindle Location, 6768, 8196

complicity, Bristow steadfastly refused to answer on the grounds that conversations between the President and a member of the Executive Branch were privileged. Ultimately his stance would become known as the principle of "executive privilege."

Years later Bristow told St. Louis Ring prosecutor David Dyer that Grant had summoned Bristow to his New York City home shortly before the ex-President moved to Mount McGregor to finish his memoirs during his fatal illness. While meeting with Dyer, Bristow told the former prosecutor that Grant had beckoned him in order to apologize for his treatment of Bristow while the latter was pushing the Whiskey Ring investigation.[218]

The House investigations into Grant Administration corruption during the Forty-Fourth congress encouraged by Democrats were not the only consequence of the Party's sweep of the 1874 elections. Since the Republicans controlled the Forty-Third Congress, they resolved to use its lame duck session to promote their agenda one final time.

---

[218] Charles Calhoun, *The Presidency of Ulysses S. Grant*, 544; Ted Rockwell Tosh, *The Life and Times of Benjamin Helm Bristow*, Kindle Location, 8424-29, 11, 406

CHAPTER 13: HOLLOW VICTORY

REPUBLICANS SET AMBITIOUS GOALS for the lame duck session of the Forty-Third Congress, which would extend from December 7, 1874 to March 4, 1875. Since their Party would lose control of the House but still hold the presidency and the Senate in the Forty-Fourth Congress, House Republicans aimed to quickly pass bills that would improve GOP prospects in the next general election in 1876. According to historian William Gillette they hoped to:

1. Adopt a new civil rights law in order to keep Southern blacks loyal to the Republican Party.
2. Pass voter enforcement legislation to optimize Republican prospects in locations where the Party felt their constituents were discouraged from voting, or where their votes were vulnerable to undercounting due to fraud.
3. Pass a constitutional amendment to change—in the Party's favor—the methods of electing a President in the House of Representatives in the event of a disputed general election in 1876 and beyond.
4. Outlaw the Democratic government elected in Arkansas in 1874.
5. Admit to the Senate a black Louisiana Republican whose 1872 election was disputed.
6. Reestablish military or territorial provisional governments in Southern states where 1876 Republican election prospects looked poor.
7. Admit Colorado and New Mexico as states because both were expected to provide Republican senators, congressmen, and electoral votes.

8. Obtain a full two years of financial appropriations for the U. S. Army in order to deny Democrats the ability to block future provisional governments in the South or military intervention in the region's elections.
9. Investigate the new Democratic state governments in the South in order to justify denying their legitimacy and to showcase allegations of white violence that might be used as publicity against Democrats in the 1876 presidential campaign.[219]

The GOP would get Colorado, but not New Mexico. They would fail in Louisiana and Arkansas. There would be no new provisional governments and no new constitutional amendment. Although Congress passed a new civil rights act, it would fall short of expectations in practice.

The resulting 1875 Civil Rights Act was a final tribute to Republican Massachusetts Senator Charles Sumner who had died the preceding year at age sixty-three. Sumner was long an outspoken advocate for black equality. At age twenty-seven in 1838 he took an educational trip to Europe. While attending lectures at the Sorbonne he noticed mulattos in the audience. He particularly noted that they seemed to be treated as equals in French society despite their darker skin. When he returned home, he was convinced that the American tendency to see blacks as inferior was learned behavior.

In 1848 he helped organize the Free Soil Party, which evolved into the Republican Party in 1856. In 1851 Sumner won a Senate seat where he promoted African American interests for the next twenty-three years. After the Civil War he repeatedly opined that era's federal civil rights laws did not go far enough. Landmark achievements such as the 1866 Civil Rights Act and the Thirteenth, Fourteenth, and Fifteenth Amendments, he judged to be inadequate. He wanted the end of slavery to be coupled with an end to racial

---

[219] William Gillette, *Retreat from Reconstruction*, 260

segregation. Thus, in 1872 he introduced a bill to require social equality for blacks and whites in public places. The bill also mandated that legal complaints for non-compliance be adjudicated in federal courts, instead of state courts. Although the 1872 bill failed, Congress passed a modified version on March 1, 1875, partly as a memorial to Sumner.[220]

During the three months preceding its passage, the bill was enmeshed in a wrangling over terms. The Senate version most closely followed Sumner's intent. It required integration for all public accommodations including schools. Since even Grant opposed ending racial segregation in public schools, however, the House bill dropped the provision as it did a requirement that cemeteries be integrated. The House bill also imposed lower penalties for non-compliance, with some fines dropping from $5,000 to $500. It did, however, require equal rights in accommodations for travel, dining, lodging, and amusements. Finally, it guaranteed blacks equal rights to be jurors.

Eventually, the Senate adopted the House version, which was signed by President Grant. Historian Gillette writes that the Republicans "had a number of reasons for passing the . . . [House] bill including their interest in insuring their party's future by strengthening the loyalty of blacks . . . and . . . an assurance that the final bill was innocuous. Indeed the widely understood assumption that the measure would never operate effectively was the reason the bill had passed." In short, Republicans believed that "It would not provoke lasting resentment among the whites and . . . the Negroes would be grateful to the party." As a result, Republican backers of the 1875 Civil Rights Act "had created little more than an illusion of achievement." The *Boston Post,* for example, wrote that the act was "a shallow trick to make the blacks of the South believe the

---

[220] Michael Holt, *By One Vote: The Disputed Presidential Election of* 1876, 17; Anonymous, *Wikipedia* "Charles Sumner" Available: http://bit.ly/2m6p8He [Accessed: January 6, 2018]

Administration party [is] its best friend, while actually doing nothing for them which is more than a nominal service."[221]

A number of black leaders were not fooled. The black-owned *San Francisco Elevator* denounced the small statutory fines and the failure to integrate public schools. Most other blacks voicing complaints, such as the secretary of Pennsylvania's Equal Rights League, objected for the same two reasons. A few Southern Republicans even resigned from the Party.

A number of white Republican newspapers also criticized the act. The *Philadelphia Press* commented that the rights to a seat in the opera house or parlor car were marginal in comparison the benefits that might have been gained by school integration. *Harper's Weekly* also complained about the failure to require integrated schools. The *Golden Age* presciently foretold that the coercive aspects of the act would aggravate racial disharmony in the South. The *New York Times* agreed. It warned that the act would make it difficult to recruit Southern whites to the Republican Party while simultaneously doing little to advance the social equality of Southern blacks. A few Southern states, the *Times* noted, already had such statutes but they had proven to be ineffective.[222]

Democrats, and some Republicans, doubted the act's constitutionality. Two years earlier the Supreme Court interpreted the Fourteenth Amendment by ruling in the New Orleans *Slaughterhouse* case that citizens, including blacks, derived most of their civil rights from the states as opposed to the federal government. Before the 1875 Civil Rights Act was even a month old a Memphis federal judge instructed a jury that the law was an "almost grotesque exercise of national authority" in violation of state's rights.

---

[221] William Gillette, *Retreat from Reconstruction*, 263-64, 270-71, 274
[222] *Ibid.*, 264, 273-75

In 1883 the Supreme Court basically agreed by ruling that the act was unconstitutional.[223]

More important than the Civil Rights Act *per se* was the attempt by Republicans to pass an enforcement bill, termed a "Force Bill" by its opponents. If enacted, the bill would have facilitated the enforcement of civil rights under the Sumner legacy act. Having evolved from the findings of a House investigation into the 1874 Alabama elections, the bill would have permitted federal supervision of elections in geographic areas where the President judged that free elections were at risk. He could even suspend the writ of *habeas corpus* thereby enabling federal marshals to temporarily jail anyone without charging those arrested with a crime.

Although represented as a noble bill to enforce racial equality, it undoubtedly had a coupled political objective too. The *National Republican* newspaper plainly wrote that the bill "is required to preserve [for] the Republican party the electoral votes of the Southern States. Remember that if the Democrats carry all of the Southern States . . . [they] will require only fifty Democratic electoral votes from the Northern States to elect a Democratic President."[224]

The Force Bill failed to pass because Congress worried that it gave the federal government too much control over elections. It empowered the President to unilaterally judge whether a situation justified *habeas corpus* suspension. It also allowed him to appoint federal marshals to supervise the elections and even the counting of votes. Democrats complained that its "purpose was not to protect elections, but to win them." The *New Orleans Picayune* warned that Grant's partisan interference in Louisiana elections and her state government since 1872 suggested that federal usurpations might happen anywhere. Indeed, Northern Democrats had noticed that Grant's policing of polls was not restricted to the South. He had also

---

[223] Charles Calhoun, *The Presidency of Ulysses S. Grant*, 453, 479; Eric Foner, *Reconstruction: The Unfinished Revolution*, 556
[224] Robert Selph Henry, *The Story of Reconstruction*, 541

posted federal marshals in Northern cities as a way to deter immigrant voting.

Notable Republicans also opposed the bill. They included such leaders as future President James A. Garfield and Speaker of the House James G. Blaine. Because so many Northerners opposed the Force Bill, argued Garfield and Blaine, enactment of it would cause the Republicans to lose more votes in the North than they would gain in the South. Similarly, the *Boston Advertiser* wrote, "The partisan madness that stakes all. . . on the [Force Bill] . . . is the madness of suicide." The owner of the *Chicago Tribune* warned fellow Republicans that since "we" might become the future minority Party; "we have no business to be [presently] making such oppressive coercive laws."[225]

Since the end of the Civil War, Democrats had warned of creeping federal intrusion into state's rights. They reminded the public that Republics do not last, as the ancient examples of Greece and Rome demonstrated. It was not uncommon for a military hero to become a dictator as Caesar did in Rome and the Macedonian Philip did in Greece. In 1874 the publisher of the *New York Herald*, James Gordon Bennett, suspected that Grant had dictatorial ambitions, which would be triggered by a third presidential term in 1876. After winning a third term, Bennett speculated, Grant might try to hold the office for the rest of his life. The *Herald* labeled the dreaded concept, "Caesarism."

Republicans had themselves helped fan the flames of such worry. For example, they had similarly accused President Andrew Johnson of trying to become a despot. Moreover, as explained in chapter eight, Grant had arbitrarily selected governors in the disputed 1872 elections in Arkansas and Louisiana. He had even tried to reverse his Arkansas choice in December 1874 as the Force Bill was under

---

[225] Robert Selph Henry, *The Story of Reconstruction*, 541; Mark Summers, *The Era of Good Stealings*, 249; William Gillette, *Retreat From Reconstruction*, 283-86, 288-90, 293; Michael Holt, *By One Vote: The Disputed Presidential Election of 1876*, 34

consideration. And in January 1875 federal troops barged into the Louisiana legislature to forcibly remove selected Democrats, as also explained in chapter eight.

Although concerns that Grant wanted to become "Ulysses the First" may have been invalid, the worries were genuine. Frank Blair, who was the vice-presidential candidate on the 1868 Democratic ticket when Grant first won the presidency, once warned that if Grant ever got into the White House, he'd never leave. The growing scandal disclosures of his Administration fed speculation that Grant was becoming habituated to profiting from high government office. Similarly, his political appointments for family members and friends suggested lucrative nepotism-based corruption. The son of James Polk's vice president, George Dallas, wrote a Philadelphia congressman that he believed that Grant intended to hold his office by voter fraud or "Army support wherever requisite."[226]

In fact, Grant's 1874 refusal to disavow a run for a third term in 1876 contributed to his Party's weak showing in the 1874 elections. By coincidence, that campaign provided the first illustration of the Republican Party symbolized as an elephant, which appeared in a *Harper's Weekly* cartoon. It depicts a frightened Republican elephant running toward a pit of chaos as a Democratic donkey disguised as a lion scares everyone by warning of an approaching third presidential term for Grant.

The general concern over possible power consolidation in the executive branch led one Republican congressman in the lame duck session to introduce a constitutional amendment to limit future Presidents to a single term. It failed to win enough support to override an anticipated Grant veto. When a Democratic congressman introduced a resolution proclaiming that no man should be President

---

[226] Mark Summers, *The Era of Good Stealings*, 252

for more than two terms, all but eighteen House Republicans voted for it.[227]

Even many Northern politicians became concerned enough about Grant despotism to defeat the Force Bill. As historian Mark Summers puts it:

> Had the issue been simply one of the South itself, the bill would have had a rough time, but Grant's ambitions complicated the problem [even more.] Given Caesar's weapons, might he not be a Caesar in practice? Using the powers of appointment, to say nothing of the military authority of the measure, the President could . . . dominate the South in 1876. Indeed, since the Force Bill set no boundaries to its operation, what would stop Grant from jailing leading Democrats of the North?[228]

As a result, historian Gillette concluded that in 1875, "many Republicans . . . were anxious to conserve party power, to preserve at least the northern party, and to scale down both federal activity in the South and the northern Republicans' responsibility for southern reconstruction." The retreat disillusioned Southern blacks. One example was Booker T. Washington who ultimately became one of the most famous freedmen. In remarking upon Republican Reconstruction years later he wrote: "In many cases it seemed to me that the ignorance of my race was being used as a tool with which to help white men into office, and that there was an element in the North which wanted to punish the Southern white men by forcing the Negro into positions over the head of the Southern whites."[229]

---

[227] Jimmy Stamp, *Simthsonian.com* "Political Animals" (October 22, 2012) Available: http://bit.ly/2m6rLb5 [Accessed: 1/7/2018]; Mark Summers, *The Era of Good Stealings*, 255-56

[228] Mark Summers, *The Era of Good Stealings*, 256-57

[229] Booker T. Washington, *Up From Slavery* (New York: A. L. Burton & Co., 1900), 84; William Gillette, *Retreat From Reconstruction*, 294

The Republicans got the 1875 Civil Rights Act, but they were unable to arm it with powerful statutory enforcement provisions due to divisions within their own Party. As a result, the Party had accomplished little during the Forty-Third Congress toward improving its Southern prospects for the approaching 1876 election. To win the presidency next time, they'd need to restore public confidence in the Party's integrity.

CHAPTER 14: 1876 PRESIDENTIAL ELECTION

ON DECEMBER 6, 1876 thirty-eight states submitted to Washington their electoral votes for selecting the winning presidential and vice-presidential candidates to be inaugurated in March 1877. Four of the states tendered two, or more, ballot packets containing conflicting results. Consequently, there could be only one of two alternative ways to choose the next President.

First, the disputed returns could be discarded. Since neither candidate would then have a majority, the House of Representatives would select the winner as stipulated in the Twelfth Amendment. Due to the outcomes of the 1874 congressional elections the resulting Democratically controlled House would undoubtedly put their candidate into the White House. Second, the disputed returns might be settled by choosing only one packet for each state submitting multiple returns. In the second scenario, Republicans could win only if the choices in all four disputed states were in their favor.[230]

This is how the situation came to pass.

Almost three weeks before the Republican National Convention was scheduled to begin in Cincinnati on June 14, 1876, the Pennsylvania state GOP convention pronounced themselves, "unalterably opposed" to a third presidential term for "any person." Since the Keystone State was America's second most populous state, President Grant could not ignore the declaration. Thus, under pressure, he reluctantly disclaimed interest in a third term. After

---

[230] Michael F. Holt, "By One Vote." *Lecture, The Presidency: University of Virginia (C-SPAN)* March 4, 2011 Available: http://cs.pn/2AYWAnN [Accessed: January 14, 2018]

pointedly stating that nobody could be denied a third term except by an amendment to the constitution he added, "I am not, nor have I ever been, a candidate for re-nomination. I would not accept a nomination if it were tendered, unless it should come under such circumstances as to make it an imperative duty—circumstances not likely to arise."[231]

After Grant removed himself from consideration, the leading Republican candidates were, in rank order, James G. Blaine, Oliver Morton, Benjamin Bristow, and Roscoe Conkling. Blaine, who had been Speaker of the House for most of Grant's presidency, captured 38% of the delegates on the first ballot. But he was suspected of chronically accepting railroad industry payoffs at a time when the Party needed a candidate who could deny connections with such

Rutherford Hayes

mischief. Southerners favored Morton because the Indiana senator outspokenly supported blacks, but he only polled 16% of the delegates on the first ballot. He also had little appeal outside the South because the Party was decreasingly inclined to use federal troops to keep carpetbag regimes in office. Bristow was the favorite of reformers but, as noted, Grant worked against him. Instead Grant backed New York Senator Conkling who had loyally supported his Administration during the past eight years. But most delegates wanted to avoid choosing a candidate with links to the scandal infested Grant presidency.

---

[231] Michael F. Holt, *By One Vote: The Disputed Presidential Election of 1876*, 34

As a result, on the seventh ballot the convention chose dark horse Rutherford B. Hayes of Ohio. During the Civil War, Hayes enlisted in the Union army as a major, was wounded in battle and eventually rose to the rank of major general. After the war he became an Ohio congressman until moving into the governor's office in 1868 where he served two consecutive two-year terms until 1872. Thereafter he was an independent businessman until 1875 when nominated a third time for governor. He barely beat his Democratic opponent but given the Democratic sweep in the congressional elections the preceding year, Hayes's victory was a hopeful sign to the conventioneers gathered in Cincinnati only five months after Hayes won back the Ohio governor's office.[232]

After the 17 June nomination, Hayes's first objective was to pen an acceptance letter detailing his campaign positions. He felt it especially important to release the letter before the Liberal Republicans, who had opposed Grant with their own candidate in 1872, held their nominating convention set for 26 July. The GOP's Cincinnati platform was not enough. Hayes needed to address three fundamental Liberal Republican priorities if he were to win back the Party's disaffected wing.

First was honest government. The Liberals were appalled at the corruption during Grant's terms and reasoned that political patronage was a major cause. Consequently, they favored civil service reforms that would put the most qualified persons on the federal payroll without regard to Party affiliation. Second, they objected to the increasing centralization of power in the federal government. This led them to advocate more self-government among the Southern states. They concluded that the reason the carpetbag regimes could not remain in power without armed federal intervention was because the carpetbaggers were hopelessly corrupted. Third, the Liberals wanted paper money to be redeemable for specie at face value.

---

[232] Michael F. Holt, *By One Vote*, 54, 65, 70, 73-76, 80

Hayes's 8 July acceptance letter did the job. On 20 July the Liberal Republican National Committee chairman cancelled their convention. On the foremost matter of civil service reform Hayes wrote, "[The spoils] system destroys the independence of the separate departments of the government . . . It is a temptation to dishonesty; . . . in every way it degrades the civil service and character of the government . . . It ought to be abolished." In order to set an example that a future President be "under no temptation to use the patronage of his office to promote his own re-election," Hayes pledged his "inflexible purpose" to serve only a single term if elected.[233]

As for specie redemption, Hayes wrote: "I regard laws . . . relating to the payment of public indebtedness, [greenbacks] included, as . . . a moral obligation . . . which must be kept." He identified the fluctuating greenback-to-gold values as an "uncertainty" that was "one of the great obstacles to a . . . return to prosperity." He added, "That uncertainty can be ended in but one way—the resumption of specie payments." Thus, specie redemption was central to his economic recovery plan.

Notwithstanding the standard Republican rhetoric for equal rights, Hayes had a new GOP message for white Southerners. "With a recognition of . . . [black civil rights] fully accorded, it will be practicable to promote . . . by all agencies of the General Government the efforts of the [Southern] people . . . to obtain for themselves the blessings of honest and capable local government. If elected, I shall consider it my ardent desire to labor . . . for . . . this end." The statement was about as close as any Republican—outside the Liberal wing—could come to admitting that carpetbaggers were the problem, instead of the solution. Moreover, it implied that Hayes would allow Southerners to reestablish honest state governments without armed

---

[233] Michael F. Holt, *By One Vote*, 123; Rutherford B. Hayes, *Letters and Messages: 1877-1881* (Washington, D. C.: U. S. Government Printing Office, 1881), 5-6

federal interference designed to artificially keep the carpetbaggers in power.[234]

Democrats opened their St. Louis convention on 27 June, which was ten days after the Republicans nominated Hayes. There was little doubt from the beginning that the Party would choose New York Governor Samuel J. Tilden as their candidate, even though he would have to win a two-thirds majority of delegates. Although they felt confident that most any Democratic candidate could win the ninety-five electoral votes of the former Confederate states in the general election, the delegates realized that they could not win the presidency without carrying New York's thirty-five votes. A total of 185 would be needed to win.

Moreover, Tilden had impeccable credentials as a foe of political corruption, even when the enemies were within his own Party. Most famously, as chairman of New York's Democratic Party he played a key role in bringing down William "Boss" Tweed who headed the Executive Committee of New York City's Democratic Party, commonly known as the Tammany Hall political machine.

This is what happened.

At age thirty-three in 1860 Tweed gained control of Tammany's general committee, which enabled him to control the Party's nominations to all city positions. He soon opened a law office so that he could collect fees for "legal services," which were basically bribes paid by politicians and vendors to the city government. By 1868 he gained near-absolute power over Tammany Hall. He was thus able to dominate the Democratic Party in New York, city and state. During the next three years his candidates were elected mayor of New York City, governor of the state, and speaker of the state assembly.

At his urging, in 1870 the city adopted a new charter, which enabled Tweed to control its treasury. He and his Ring of associates

---

[234] Rutherford B. Hayes, *Letters and Messages: 1877-1881*, 6-7; Michael F. Holt, *By One Vote*, 124

started pillaging the city by selling it overpriced goods and services through Ring-controlled suppliers. Voting irregularities, which had long been common, multiplied.

A prime example of Tweed thievery involved the construction of the New York County courthouse. Originally budgeted at $250,000 when construction began in 1862 the structure cost over $14 million to complete over ten years. Carpenters earned $2.1 million for $30,000 worth of work. Furniture cost $1.6 million. Carpeting totaled $4.8 million, which was reportedly enough to cover the entire city. When an electric fire alarm contractor submitted an estimate of $60,000 for his work Tweed asked, "If we get you a contract for $450,000 will you give us $225,000?" When later asked to provide a written report explaining why the building was taking so long to complete, copies were printed by a Tweed-owned company for a cost of $7,700.

Finally, investigative journalists at the *New York Times* and *Harper's Weekly* targeted Tweed in 1871. Somehow the *Times* gained access to Tweed's books but could not decipher them. As an experienced railroad attorney and dealmaker, however, Tilden understood complex accounting. He unraveled the books and traced the money trail of kickbacks and padded construction contracts to the bank accounts of Tweed and his Ring members.

Next Tilden organized a slate of seventy candidates to oppose Tweed's toadies in the November 1871 elections. Tilden's candidates won every state assembly and senate seat from metropolitan New York except Tweed's own. Finally, Tilden persuaded Governor John Hoffman to appoint a special prosecutor to investigate Tweed who was convicted of forgery and larceny in 1873. As a reward, in 1874 New Yorkers elected Tilden as governor with a 50,000-vote margin. The following year the Democratic margin would drop to 15,000 without him on the ticket.[235]

---

[235] Editors, *Encyclopedia Britannica* "William Mager Tweed" Available: http://bit.ly/2D5K47R [Accessed: January 15, 2018]; Michael F. Holt, *By One Vote*, 99-100,

Once in office Tilden promoted a number of antimonopoly initiatives. Among them was a fight to break-up a Ring that monopolized business on New York State canals, such as the Erie Canal. He appointed a commission that put an end to the frauds, which he estimated had cost the state $5 million in revenue over the preceding five years. When editorializing early in 1876 about the culture of corruption in Washington, the Democratic *New York World* wrote, "Would to God that some Hercules might arise and cleanse *that* Augean stable as the city and state of New York are cleansing."236

At age 62 Tilden was eight years older than Hayes. Unlike Hayes he did not serve in the army during the Civil War. In fact, during the secession crisis he urged that the cotton states be allowed to leave peaceably, although he stood behind the war effort once the shooting started. Also, unlike Hayes, he was a lifelong bachelor. But Tilden was an intellectual powerhouse who accumulated a fortune in railroad legal work including mergers and Wall Street financings. By 1876 he was chiefly known as a champion of honest government. About a month after Hayes released his "acceptance" letter Tilden published his own on 10 August to clarify his political positions beyond the messaging contained in the Democratic Party platform. Like Hayes, Tilden wanted to win-over the Liberal Republicans. 237

109; Roy Morris, Jr. *Fraud of the Century*, (New York: Simon & Schuster, 2003) 100; George Martin, *Causes and Conflicts* (New York: Fordham University Press, 1997), 63

236 Roy Morris, Jr. *Fraud of the Century*, 104

237 Michael F. Holt, *By One Vote*, 120

Tilden Presidential Campaign

Unlike Hayes's, however, Tilden's letter provided thoughtful analysis. First, he urged that taxes be cut in order to help lift the economy out of depression. He estimated that the federal government had taken $4.5 billion away from private citizens in the form of taxes during the preceding decade. To that he added an estimated $3.0 billion in state taxes. Republicans, he argued, had wasted it on bloated federal payrolls, government-funded boondoggles and sheer waste. In short, he believed the economy would do better if the public got to keep more of its own money.

A second cause of the depression, he reasoned, was the "systematic and insupportable misgovernment imposed on the South." The carpetbag regimes had over-issued worthless bonds that destroyed the creditworthiness of the affected Southern states. Oppressive property taxes impoverished the residents and decimated real estate values. While echoing Hayes's stance on civil rights, Tilden was more pointed in criticizing carpetbagger corruption.

Although he agreed with most Northeasterners that a return to specie redemption for paper currency would help end the depression, he addressed the matter creatively. He suggested that the treasury sell—for gold—the U. S. Government bonds that the national banks had deposited as reserves with the comptroller of the currency. Such sales would enable the treasury to use the incremental gold for redeeming greenbacks. While the treasury would continue to pay interest on the bonds, the payments would go to the new bondholder—those who bought the bonds for gold—instead of to the banks. Tilden's plan would flood the treasury with gold and likely avoid any contraction of the paper money supply. If implemented Tilden's suggestion might have pleased everyone on either side of the redemption debate, except the owners of national banks. (The banks would no longer be paid interest on the bonds they had deposited as bank reserves, because their reserves would have essentially been converted into non-interest-bearing gold.)[238]

Despite the conciliatory wording of his acceptance letter, in practice Hayes's campaign emphasized "bloody shirt" rhetoric. It was a form of hate-speech containing impassioned oratory about the bloody sacrifices Northern soldiers made to defeat the Confederacy. Such demagoguery was designed to sustain the hatreds and prejudices of the Civil War against the South. Six weeks after releasing his letter Hayes told his campaigners, "our main issue must be *it is not safe to allow the rebellion to come into power."* That same month he wrote congressman, and future President James A. Garfield, *"the danger of giving the rebels the government,* is the topic that people are most interested in."[239]

The second Republican Platform plank . . . "charge[ed] the Democratic party as being the same in character and spirit as when it sympathized with treason." The politician who nominated Hayes at the Cincinnati convention, for example, later addressed a Union

---

[238]*Ibid.,* 135-137
[239] *Ibid.,* 124, 130

veterans convention by stating, "I am opposed to the Democratic Party . . . Every state that seceded . . . was a Democratic State . . . Every man that tried to destroy this nation was a Democrat. Every enemy this Republic had for twenty years was a Democrat. Every man who shot Union soldiers was a Democrat." Similar speakers portrayed everyone who starved prisoners at the Andersonville prisoner of war camp as a Democrat and all of Lincoln's assassins as Democrats. And so on.[240]

Tilden's running mate, Indiana Governor Thomas Hendricks, responded, "I would regard the man who would arouse . . . sectional antagonisms among his countrymen as a dangerous enemy to his country. The strife between sections and between races will cease as soon as the power for evil [i.e. federal usurpation of states' rights] is taken away from a party that makes political gain out of scenes of violence and bloodshed."[241]

Hayes's campaign strategy led to a sharp sectional divide in the election results. On first count, Tilden carried every state south of the Ohio and Potomac Rivers, except South Carolina where elections were held under the glitter of federal bayonets. In the North, Tilden carried Missouri, Indiana, New York, Maryland, Delaware, New Jersey, and Connecticut. All the other states north of the Ohio and Potomac Rivers went to Hayes along with the three far western states, Nevada, California, and Oregon. Colorado, which had only been admitted earlier in the year, also voted for Hayes. If the count had remained unchanged, Tilden would have become President with 196 electoral votes to 173 for Hayes. As implied at the start of this chapter, however, the count got revised.

Although Democrats regained power in most of the ex-Confederate states prior to 1876, carpetbaggers still controlled the election machinery in Florida, Louisiana, and South Carolina. Each of the three had Republican-dominated returning boards authorized

---

[240] *Ibid.*, 85, 158
[241] *Ibid.*, 139

to count the ballots. The despotic boards could generally contrive reasons to discard most any votes they wanted to exclude. The Florida board, for example, rejected the Key West returns where Tilden got 401 votes and Hayes only 59.

Therefore, Democrats in each pertinent state objected to the returning board tallies. They sent competing electoral counts, endorsed by a friendly state official in each case, to Washington. A total of nineteen electoral votes were thus disputed. Additionally, a technical challenge to one Oregon Republican elector prompted that state to send two rival packets to Washington. The narrative explaining how the three carpetbag states reached their Republican vote totals is a fascinating drama but is ultimately immaterial because of the wholly predictable self-interested results of the partisan returning boards.[242]

President Grant also played a role in trying to prevent a Tilden sweep in the South. About three weeks before South Carolina's 7 November election day, he sent more than 1,100 additional federal troops into the state. Even though Grant publicly rationalized that South Carolina was in state of virtual insurrection, the district commander disagreed and told the President he did not need any more troops. Even some Northerners objected. On 19 October the *Nation* editorialized, "The soldiers who are now making arrests for 'intimidation' in South Carolina, and who are to preserve order on Election Day, are really an armed force in service . . . of one of the parties to the political contest." Similarly, an Indiana Republican judge worried that "the use of bayonets in connection with the election [is] a dangerous thing. How long will it be before the same thing is resorted to in the North?"[243]

On 10 November Grant sent two telegrams to Commander of the Army, General William T. Sherman. The messages, which were also released to the press, ordered Sherman to send additional federal

---

[242] Michael F. Holt, *By One Vote*, 185, 192; Roy Morris, Jr. *Fraud of the Century*, 160, 174-75
[243] Roy Morris, Jr. *Fraud of the Century*, 160

troops to the capital cities of Florida and Louisiana—Tallahassee and New Orleans, respectively. He officially instructed the troops to ensure that the returning boards were "unmolested in the performance of their duties." Although he added, "the military [should] have nothing to do with counting the vote," there can be little doubt that Grant understood that "unmolested" boards were almost certain to report the results that the GOP wanted, regardless of the true vote.

But Grant did even more to help Hayes. Immediately after the election he contacted leading Republicans and urged that they travel to New Orleans and Tallahassee in order to protect Party interests. Among those he contacted were future Presidents James A. Garfield and Benjamin Harrison. Ultimately twenty-five prominent Northern Republicans showed up in New Orleans and a smaller number in Tallahassee. Some arrived with suitcases full of cash or assurances of federal sinecures for cooperative local politicians.[244]

Recognizing the inevitable, Congress began considering plans to settle the election in Washington. To repeat, if the returns for any state were discarded neither candidate would have a majority. That would force the election into the House of Representatives where a solid Democratic majority would likely put Tilden in the White House. Thus, Republicans were nearly certain to challenge the constitutionality of throwing out the returns of any state, even though they did precisely that with Louisiana's disputed electoral votes back in 1872 when the incremental votes were unnecessary to obtain Grant's reelection victory.[245]

In December 1876 each congressional chamber organized a committee to derive a solution. Toward the end of January in 1877 they agreed to organize an arbitration board, known as the Electoral Commission. An authorizing bill passed in both the Republican-dominated Senate and Democratic-dominated House. President

---

[244] Michael F. Holt, *By One Vote*, 178-180
[245] William Hesseltine, *Grant The Politician*, 344

Grant signed it on 29 January. The Commission was empowered to determine which of the competing electoral accounts from each of the disputed states were valid. Its decisions could only be overruled by majority votes in both congressional chambers.

The new Commission was to have a total of fifteen members to be composed of five from each of the Senate, House, and Supreme Court. By mutual agreement the Senate would provide three Republicans and two Democrats, while the House would supply three Democrats and two Republicans. Four of the Supreme Court members were identified by name in the bill and those four were to choose the fifth Court member. Nearly everyone assumed that Justice David Davis would thus be selected. Although Lincoln appointed Davis to the Court, the justice supported the Liberal wing of the Party in 1872. He was therefore assumed to be nearly neutral.

But shortly before Grant signed the bill, a coalition of Democrats and Independents in the Illinois legislature elected Davis to the U. S. Senate. Consequently, Davis declined to join the Commission because he felt that the public might doubt his objectivity. As a result, the Commission's four stipulated Court members invited Justice Joseph P. Bradley to join them. He had been appointed to the Court by Grant in 1870 but was from New Jersey whereas two of the other possible choices were from Hayes's home state of Ohio. Nonetheless, after surveying informed politicos in Washington about the likely result of the Bradley selection, Hayes's son Webb wired his father, "The bets are five-to-one that the next president will be Hayes."[246]

The curtain on the drama went up when the electoral vote counting began on 1 February before a joint audience that included all the senators and congressmen. The results of each state were counted in alphabetical order until the roll call reached Florida. Republicans objected to the state's Tilden returns and Democrats objected to its Hayes return. The joint meeting adjourned, to be resumed after the Commission announced its Florida decision. The

---

[246] Michael F. Holt, *By One Vote*, 213, 220, 224; Roy Morris, Jr., *Fraud of the Century*, 219

commissioners started hearing oral arguments on 2 February and finished on 5 February. The next day nearly all of the Commission's congressional members voiced their predictably partisan remarks. The Supreme Court members, including Bradley, would speak on 7 February.

Bradley had visitors on the night of 6 February. One was John Stevens who was a friend to both Bradley and Abram Hewitt who chaired the national Democratic committee. According to Hewitt, Stevens read Bradley's opinion and later told Hewitt that the justice had sided with Tilden. But after Stevens left Bradley's home, a pair of New Jersey politicos visited the judge. One was a Commission member and the other was Grant's navy secretary. They urged Bradley to change his mind. The following morning observers also noticed the carriage of railroad mogul Tom Scott in front of Bradley's home. Scott opposed Tilden because he expected Tilden to resist federal subsidies for Scott's transcontinental Texas & Pacific Railroad, which was then little more than a paper company.[247]

The lynchpin of Bradley's 7 February opinion held that the Commission should accept the tally provided by Florida's returning board without investigating how the board obtained its results. Commissioners should not, he opined, investigate complaints that the board fraudulently excluded legitimate votes in order to insure a Hayes victory. He held to the same opinion respecting Louisiana and South Carolina. Thus, the Commission voted eight-to-seven to accept the Hayes electors from the three disputed Southern states.

Bradley strangely took the opposite position on Oregon. Instead of merely choosing one of the disputed packets he felt that the Commission should evaluate the reasons the state submitted conflicting results. In the end, the commissioners voted eight-to-seven to accept the envelope submitted by Oregon's attorney general instead of her governor, which was directly opposite the circumstances in the Florida case. All three of Oregon's electoral

247 Michael F. Holt, *By One Vote*, 225, 229

votes went to Hayes. He was inaugurated President on March 5, 1877 with 185 electoral votes compared to 184 for Tilden. Grant's presidency was over.[248]

---

[248] Roy Morris, Jr., *Fraud of the Century*, 229

CHAPTER 15: EPILOGUE

WHEN PRESIDENT GRANT LEFT OFFICE in March 1877 he may have disliked politics and politicians more than ever, particularly considering the unethical conduct of some of his closest friends. He wanted to get away and headed first for Europe almost without a plan. The day after he sailed from Philadelphia on May 17, 1877 aboard the steamer *Indiana* he remarked that he "felt better than he had" since the start of the Civil War, merely to be free of the responsibilities of the past sixteen years. Originally, he intended to visit only the major European capitals, but his investments back in America were proving to be profitable and he was able to stay abroad much longer than initially planned. He did not get back to America for another twenty-eight months when he arrived in San Francisco after a tour around the world. No previous ex-President had traveled so extensively.

At his first stop in Liverpool, Grant was greeted by the city's mayor, other dignitaries and an enthusiastic crowd. But even while he was a sensation among the English working classes, he wrote brother-in-law Abel Corbin about America's 1877 railroad strike, "My judgment is that it should have been put down with a strong hand and so summarily as to prevent a like occurrence for a generation." His 1871 Ku Klux Klan Act gave the federal government to power to do precisely that because the strike interfered with postal deliveries.

Although he was scheduled to meet the Queen and the Prince of Wales, the American minister was not satisfied with the terms. Since he was not a sovereign, Grant would rank below royalty. When Ambassador Edwards Pierrepont complained that Grant should be treated as an ex-sovereign, British officials replied, "The Americans gave their ex-Presidents no rank; why should we?" Although the local

American dignitaries were annoyed by the reception protocol, Grant later said, "I received nothing but kindness from every Englishman from the head of the nation on down."[249]

From England the Grants went to Belgium and then to Alsace and Switzerland. In October 1877 they visited Paris but did not have a good time because the French suspected that Grant was sympathetic to the Prussians during the 1870 Franco-Prussian War. Next the U. S. Navy put a warship at his disposal that transported the Grant family to Naples, Sicily, Egypt and other spots around the Mediterranean. He saw the pyramids, visited the Holy Land and returned to Italy for an audience with the Pope. In Venice he reportedly remarked that the city ". . . would be a fine place if it were drained." In Berlin he met Bismarck. He went on to Denmark, Norway, Sweden and Russia. He eventually saw Spain, Portugal and Ireland before departing for the Orient in January 1878. In Asia he stopped first in India, and then went on to Siam and China. He finished in Japan where he met the Emperor.[250]

Meanwhile, with his tacit approval, friends back home were laying plans to get him elected as President for a third term in 1880. Although he was greeted fervently upon returning to America on September 20, 1879, his advisors worried that the enthusiasm might die down during the remaining nine months until the June 1880 Republican convention. Roscoe Conkling became his campaign manager and would lead Grant's attack against the New York senator's old foe, James G. Blaine. Victory at the convention required 378 delegates. If Conkling could get the convention to adopt the "unit rule" Grant would likely win on the first ballot because many of his delegates were from populous states. (The unit rule would require that all of each state's votes go to the candidate supported by the majority of the applicable state's delegates.)

Unfortunately for Grant the convention declined to adopt the rule. As a result, he got 304 votes on the first ballot compared to 284 for Blaine, which left 167 votes scattered among lesser candidates. As

---

[249] W. E. Woodward, *Meet General Grant*, (New York: Literary Guild, 1928), 457-463
[250] *Ibid.*, 468-72

with Hayes in 1876, the convention eventually settled on another Ohio dark horse, James A. Garfield. Grant felt humiliated and characteristically blamed his friends. "They should not have put my name in nomination unless they felt perfectly sure of my success." He petulantly failed to send a congratulatory letter or telegram to Garfield, although he knew him well. As noted in chapter three, about a decade earlier he had even thanked then-Congressman Garfield for managing the Gould-Fisk Gold Corner investigation in a manner that minimized damage to Grant and the Republican Party. He even toyed with supporting Garfield's Democratic opponent during the summer before finally endorsing Garfield.[251]

Next, Grant focused on his finances. He had about $100,000, which would have enabled him to live satisfactorily in a place like Galena, but he wanted more. Fortunately, a group of business leaders, including Jay Gould, raised a $250,000 fund for him to be managed by trustees. It gave him an annual income of about $15,000. A year later, in the fall of 1880, he yielded to temptation and joined his son Buck as a partner in the Grant & Ward investment bank. Unfortunately, the bank ran a Ponzi scheme orchestrated by Buck's partner, Ferdinand Ward. Grant invested $100,000 into the firm before Ward contacted him with an emergency request on May 4, 1884 to invest another $150,000 because Grant & Ward was short on cash, supposedly only temporarily. Grant hastily borrowed the $150,000 needed to cover the cash shortage from William Vanderbilt. But the shortage was not temporary. Grant & Ward was bankrupt.

---

[251] *Ibid.*, 474-75

Grant's Final Days

The $250,000 fund that originally paid him $15,000 a year might have saved Grant financially, but the trustees told him it had no more money because they had invested in speculative railroad stocks. Ulysses Grant was less than penniless; he was deeply in debt. In the end, Grant & Ward had $17 million in liabilities and only $67,000 in assets. The former President sold all of his personal assets or pledged them to Vanderbilt but was still in debt. In November 1884, six months after the Grant & Ward collapse, Mark Twain gave Grant a $25,000 advance for rights to publish the general's memoirs. Grant finished them less than a week before he died of throat cancer at Mount McGregor, New York on July 23, 1885. Julia Grant's first royalty check for the memoirs of $250,000 was the largest such check paid by an American publisher up to that time. She would eventually receive royalties totaling $450,000, which is equivalent to $11 million at this writing.[252]

THE END

---

[252] William McFeely, *Grant*, 490-91; W. E. Woodward, *Meet General Grant*, 486-87, 489-90; Marszalek, John and Calhoun, Charles "A House Divided" Interview by Bjorn Skaptason, *Abraham Lincoln Bookstore*, October 14, 2017 Available: https://youtu.be/6kcgtX-nr7s [Accessed: January 18, 2018]

BIBLIOGRAPHY

MEMOIRS, DIARIES AND PERSONAL PAPERS

_____. *Letters of Ulysses S. Grant to His Father and His Youngest Sister, 1857-78.* http://bit.ly/2GJ5NEP

Hayes, Rutherford B. *Letters and Messages: 1877-1881.* Washington, D. C.: U. S. Government Printing Office, 1881.

Simon, John Y., Editor *The Papers of Ulysses S. Grant: Vol. 27. 1988 ed.* Carbondale: Southern Illinois University Press, 2005.

_____. Editor *The Papers of Ulysses S. Grant; Vo. 22. 1988 ed.* Carbondale: Southern Illinois University Press, 1967.

Welles, Gideon. *Diary: Volume 3.* Boston: Houghton Mifflin, 1911.

HISTORICAL DOCUMENTS

U. S. House of Representatives. *Gold Panic Investigation, Forty-First Congress, Second Session, Report Number 31.* March 1, 1870. http://bit.ly/2vEJoTD

BOOKS

Adams, Henry. *Historical Essays.* "The New York Gold Conspiracy." New York: C. Scribner's & Sons, 1891.

_____. *The Education of Henry Adams.* Boston: Houghton Mifflin, 1918.

Agar, Herbert. *The Price of Union.* Boston: Houghton Mifflin, 1950.

Ambrose, Stephen. *Nothing Like It In The World.* New York: Touchstone, 2000.

Anders, Curt. *Powerlust.* Garrison, N.Y.: Highland Outpost Press, 2010.

Barreyre, Nicolas. *Gold and Freedom: The Political Economy of Reconstruction*. Charlottesville: University of Virginia Press, 2015.

Beale, Howard K. *The Critical Year*. New York: Frederick Unger, 1958.

Beatty, Jack. *Age of Betrayal*. New York: Alfred A. Knopf, 2007.

Blum, Edward. *Reforging the White Republic*. Baton Rouge: LSU Press, 2005.

Borneman, Walter. *Iron Horse*. Boston: Little Brown & Company, 2014.

_____. *Rival Rails*. New York: Random House, 2010.

Bowers, Claude. *The Tragic Era*. Cambridge, Ma.: Riverside Press, 1929.

Brands, H. W. *American Colossus*. New York: Anchor Books, 2010.

_____. *Greenback Planet*. Austin: University of Texas Press, 2011.

_____. *The Man Who Saved the Union: Ulysses Grant in War and Peace*. New York: Random House, 2012.

Brown, Dee. *Bury My Heart at Wounded Knee*. New York: Holt Reinhardt & Winston, 1971.

Calhoun, Charles. *The Presidency of Ulysses S. Grant*. Lawrence: University Press of Kansas, 2017.

Castel, Albert. *The Presidency of Andrew Johnson*. Lawrence: University Press of Kansas, 1979.

Chernow, Ron. *The House of Morgan*. New York: Grove Press, 2001.

_____. *Grant*. New York: Penguin Press, 2017.

Coulter, Merton. *The South During Reconstruction*. Baton Rouge: LSU Press, 1947.

Craughwell, Thomas J. *Presidential Payola* (Vancouver, British Columbia: Fair Winds Press, 2011), 34

Craven, Avery. *Reconstruction: The Ending of the Civil War*. New York: Holt, Reinhart & Winston, 1969.

Cozzens, Peter. *The Earth is Weeping: The Epic Story of the Indian Wars for the American West*. New York: Alfred Knopf, 2016.

Davis, Gene. *High Crimes and Misdemeanors.* New York: William Morrow, 1977.

Davis, William C. *Jefferson Davis: The Man and His Hour.* New York: HarperCollins, 1991.

DeBlack, Thomas. *With Fire and Sword: Arkansas, 1861-1874.* Fayetteville: University of Arkansas Press, 2003.

Donovan, James. *A Terrible Glory.* Boston: Little Brown & Company, 2008.

Ezell, John. *The South Since 1865.* New York: Macmillan Publishing, 1963.

Foner, Eric. *Reconstruction: The Unfinished Revolution.* New York: Harper & Row, 1988.

Gillette, William. *Retreat from Reconstruction.* Baton Rouge: LSU Press, 1979.

Gray, John S. *Centennial Campaign: The 1876 Sioux War.* Norman: University of Oklahoma Press, 1988.

Guelzo, Allen. *Redeeming the Great Emancipator.* Cambridge: Harvard University Press, 2016.

Hacker, Louis and Benjamin Kendrick. *The United States Since 1865.* New York: Appleton-Century-Crofts, 1949.

Hearn, Chester G. *Gray Raiders of the Sea.* Camden, Me.: International Marine Publishing, 1992.

Henry, Robert Selph. *The Story of Reconstruction.* Indianapolis, In.: Bobbs-Merrill, 1938.

Hesseltine, William B. *Ulysses Grant Politician.* New York: Dodd Meade & Company, 1935.

Holt, Michael F. *By One Vote: The Disputed Presidential Election of 1876.* Lawrence: University Press of Kansas, 2008.

Hummel, Jeffrey R. *Emancipating Slaves, Enslaving Free Men.* Chicago: Open Court,   1996.

Johnson, Ludwell. *Division and Reunion.* New York: John Wiley & Sons, 1978.

Josephson, Matthew. *The Robber Barons*. San Diego, Ca.: Harcourt Brace & Co., 1962.

_____. *The Politicos*. New York: Harcourt, Brace, 1958.

Kirshner, Ralph. *The Class of 1861: Custer, Ames, and Their Classmates After West   Point*. Carbondale: Southern Illinois University, 1999.

Lane, Charles. *The Day Freedom Died*. New York: Henry Holt, 2009.

Leigh, Philip. *Trading With the Enemy*. Yardley, Pa.: Westholme Publishing, 2013.

McDonough, James Lee. *William Tecumseh Sherman: In the Service of My Country*.   New York: W. W. Norton, 2016.

McFeely, William. *Grant: A Biography*. New York: W. W. Norton, 1981.

Martin, Edward. *A Complete and Graphic Account of the Credit Mobilier   Investigations: Chapter 7*. New York: Continental and National Publishing Companies, 1873. http://bit.ly/2nzA57q

Martin, George *Causes and Conflicts*. New York: Fordham University Press, 1997

Miles, Donald. *Cinco de Mayo*. Lincoln, Nebraska, iUniverse, 2006.

Moneyhon, Carl H. *The Impact of the Civil War and Reconstruction in Arkansas*. Baton Rouge: LSU Press, 1994.

Morison, Samuel and Henry Commager. *The Growth of the American Republic: Volume Two: Fourth Edition*. New York: Oxford Press, 1950.

Morris, Roy *Fraud of the Century*. New York: Simon & Schuster, 2003.

Nevins, Allan. *The Emergence of Modern America*. New York, Macmillan, 1927.

_____. *Hamilton Fish: The Inner History of the Grant Administration: Volume 1*. New York: Frederick Ungar Publishing, 1957.

Nugent, Walter. *Money and American Society: 1865-1880*. New York: The Free Press, 1968.

Oberholtzer, Ellis. *A History of the United States: 1872-78*. New York, Macmillan Company, 1926. http://bit.ly/2ArZ4KR

Pfaelzer, Jean. *Driven Out: The Forgotten War Against Chinese Americans*. Berkeley: University of California Press, 2008.

Philbrick, Nathaniel. *The Last Stand*. New York: Viking, 2010.

Randall, James and David Donald. *The Civil War and Reconstruction*. Boston: D. C. Heath & Company, 1961.

Rhodes, John Ford. *History of the United States: 1850 – 1877 Vol. VII.* http://bit.ly/2DML3NK

Rose, Joseph. *Grant Under Fire*. New York: Alderhanna Publishing, 2015.

Rothbard, Murray. *A History of Money and Banking in the United States*. Auburn, Ala.: Ludwig von Mises Institute, 2002.

Simkins, Francis and Charles Roland. *A History of the South*. New York: Alfred A. Knopf, 1973.

Simpson, Brooks. *Ulysses S. Grant: Triumph Over Adversity. 1822-1865*. Boston: Houghton Mifflin, 2000.

_____. *The Reconstruction Presidents*. Lawrence: University Press of Kansas, 1998.

Smith, Jean Edward. *Grant*. New York: Simon & Schuster, 2001.

Soennichsen, John. *The Chinese Exclusion Act of 1882*. Santa Barbara, Calif.: Greenwood, 2011.

Stampp, Kenneth. *The Era of Reconstruction*. New York: Alfred Q. Knopf, 1965.

Summers, Mark. *The Era of Good Stealings*. Oxford: Oxford University Press, 1993.

Tosh, Ted Rockwell. *The Life and Times of Benjamin Helm Bristow*. New York: Page Publishing, 2015.

Tuchinsky, Adam-Max. *Horace Greeley's New York Tribune*. Ithaca, N.Y.: Cornel University Press, 2009.

Tunnell, Ted *Crucible of Reconstruction*. Baton Rouge: LSU Press, 1984.

Tyler, S. Lyman. *A History of Indian Policy*. Washington, D. C.: Bureau of Indian Affairs, 1979. http://bit.ly/2EcX50D

Unger, Irwin. *The Greenback Era*. Princeton, N. J.: Princeton University Press, 1964.

Utley, Robert. *Custer Battlefield: Official National Park Handbook*. Washington, D. C.: U. S. Government Printing Office, 1988.

Wang, Xi *The Trial of Democracy: Black Suffrage and Northern Republicans: 1860-1910*. Athens, Ga.: University of Georgia Press, 1997

Washington, Booker T. *Up From Slavery*. New York: A. L. Burton & Co., 1900.

Webb, Walter. *Divided We Stand*. New York: Farrar & Reinhart, 1937.

White, Richard. *The Republic for Which it Stands*. Oxford: Oxford University Press, 2017.

_____. *Railroaded*. New York: W. W. Norton, 2011.

White, Ronald C. *American Ulysses: A Life of U. S. Grant*. New York: Random House, 2016.

Wildenthal, Bryan. *North American Sovereignty on Trial* (Santa Barbara, Ca.: ABC-CLIO, 2003).

Woodward, W. E. *Meet General Grant*. New York: Literary Guild of America, 1928.

ARTICLES

Allen, Cain. "Land Fraud Trial of Senator John Mitchell." *The Oregon History Project* http://bit.ly/2BmTnCZ

Bingham, Tom. "The Alabama Claims Arbitration." *International and Comparative Law Journal*, 54, no. 1 (Jan. 2005). 1-25

Bragg, William H. "Reconstruction in Georgia." *New Georgia Encyclopedia* (10/19/2016). http://bit.ly/2xbUwdY

Chamberlain, Daniel. "Reconstruction in South Carolina." *Atlantic Monthly*, (April, 1901). http://bit.ly/2DnK6b4

Craughwell, Thomas. "Top Ten Mistakes by U. S. Presidents: Number Nine." *Encyclopedia Britannica Blog*. http://bit.ly/2wzNrTL

Finn J. D. "Oregon Man's Supreme Court Confirmation Scotched by His Wife." *Offbeat Oregon History*. (April 16, 2012). http://bit.ly/2nJAaW1

Frommer, Frederic. "Black Hills Are Beyond Price to Sioux." *Los Angeles Times*. (August 19, 2001) http://lat.ms/2yoo96M

Gelderman, Carol. "Cruikshank Case." *knowlouisiana.org Encyclopedia of Louisiana*, (September 4, 2013). http://bit.ly/2AMzgOm

Greenbaum, Mark. "The Civil War's War on Fraud." *Opinionator: Disunion (blog). New York Times,* March 7, 2013. http://nyti.ms/2zPQplW

Guyatt, Nicholas. "America's Conservatory: Race, Reconstruction, and the Santo Domingo Debate." *The Journal of American History,* 97, no. 4, (March, 2011). 974-1000

Harpers Weekly, "A Fable—With a Modern Application" (March 25, 1882). http://nyti.ms/2jhTaXj

Henry, Robert Selph. "The Railroad Land Grant Legend in American History Texts." *The Mississippi Valley Historical Review* 32 no. 3, (Sep. 1945). 171-194

Hesseltine, William. B. "Economic Factors in the Abandonment of Reconstruction." *The Mississippi Valley Historical Review* 22, no. 2 (September, 1935) 191-210

Lane, Charles. "Edward Henry Durell: A Study in Reputation." *13 Green Bag 2D* (Winter, 2010). 153-168 http://bit.ly/2A5syzA

Nast, Thomas. "Preserved Lumber." *Harpers Weekly* (June 20, 1885) http://bit.ly/2lkAWVU

Peck, Garrett. "The Seneca Stone Ring Scandal." *Boundary Stones: WETA's Local Blog*. http://bit.ly/2Bdo5hG

Richardson, John. "Alexander R. Shepherd and the Race Issue in Washington." *Washington History* 22 (2010). http://bit.ly/2APksfc

Rives, Timothy. "Grant, Babcock & the Whiskey Ring; Part 1." *Prologue Magazine:* Vol. 32, No. 3 (Fall 2000) http://bit.ly/2CAJpvr

_____. "Grant, Babcock & the Whiskey Ring: Part 2." *Prologue Magazine:* Vol. 32, No. 3 (Fall 2000) http://bit.ly/2iIEVJy

Rodrigue, John C. "Freedman's Savings & Trust Company." *Encyclopedia.biz.* http://bit.ly/2koHd1p

Skidmore, Max. "General Grant, General Babcock, and Journalist Colony: A Study in Scandal & Friendship." *History? Because it's Here.* http://bit.ly/2EsU5wV

Smith, Marian L. "Race, Nationality and Reality." *Prologue Magazine,* (Summer 2002). http://bit.ly/2zF30Jm

Soodalter, Ron. "The Union's 'Shoddy' Aristocracy." *Opinionator: Disunion (blog).* New York Times, May 9, 2011. http://nyti.ms/2ANwOa8

Stiles, T. J. "Ulysses S. Grant: New Biography of 'A Nobody form Nowhere.'" *The New York Times,* October 19, 2016. http://nyti.ms/2xNTi51

Terry, John. "Portland Mayor George Williams Faced Charges in Court." *The Oregonian.* http://bit.ly/2BQl6bm

Watts, Dale. "How Bloody Was Bleeding Kansas?" *Kansas History: A Journal of the Central Plains, 18, no. 2,* (Summer 1995). 116-129

Wilentz, Sean. "The Return of Ulysses," *New Republic,* January 25, 2010 http://bit.ly/2ilsgw2

Woodward, C. Van. "The Lowest Ebb" *American Heritage* 8, no. 3 (April, 1957): http://bit.ly/2ydpIdA

MISCELLANEOUS

Anonymous. "Charles Sumner." *Wikipedia* http://bit.ly/2m6p8He

BlackPast.org. "Freedman's Savings Bank & Trust: 1865 – 1874." http://bit.ly/2ALzCSC

DeBlack, Thomas. "The End of Reconstruction in Arkansas." *Lecture.* http://bit.ly/2AHsVUq

Encyclopedia Britannica. "U. S Presidential Election of 1860." http://bit.ly/2zh2Ab6

Encyclopedia Britannica. "U. S. Presidential Election of 1876." http://bit.ly/2lhQpoV

Encyclopedia Britannica. "William Mager Tweed." http://bit.ly/2D5K47R

Encyclopedia.com. "Railroads: Federal Land Grants." *Gale Encyclopedia of U.S. Economic History* 2000. http://bit.ly/2DF8CsK

Federal Reserve Bank of Minneapolis. "Consumer Price Index." http://bit.ly/1FTcHOC

Granthomepage.com. "Chronology." http://bit.ly/1QNXvhe

Holt, Michael F. "By One Vote." *Lecture, The Presidency: University of Virginia. (C-SPAN* March 4, 2011). http://cs.pn/2AYWAnN

Lehrman Information Institute: The Gold Standard Now. "The Legal Tender Cases." (February 7, 2012). http://bit.ly/2vNiRaw

Marszalek, John & Chas. Calhoun. "A House Divided" Interview by Bjorn Skaptason. *Abraham Lincoln Bookstore.* October 14, 2017 https://youtu.be/6kcgtX-nr7s

Mooney, John. "The Brooks-Baxter War." http://bit.ly/2zOU6MX

New York Times. "On this Day: September 9, 1869." http://nyti.ms/2ww6xtE

Pierce, James A. "From McMath to Rockefeller: Arkansas Governors and Illegal Gambling in Postwar Hot Springs, 1945 – 1970." *Thesis for Master's Degree* (University of Arkansas, 2008), 1-126

Public Broadcasting System. "A Long History of Racial Preferences – For Whites." http://to.pbs.org/1HMtoBf

Revolvy. "Annexation of Santo Domingo." http://bit.ly/2vXuOpa

Richards, Mark David. "Touring Hidden Washington: Living in the Shadow of Congress." http://bit.ly/2kqkjXQ

Stamp, Jimmy. "Political Animals." *Simthsonian.com* (October 22, 2012). http://bit.ly/2m6rLb5

Treasury.gov *Historical Debt Outstanding.* http://bit.ly/2B0Lqmv

Tulane University *Media Nola.* "1872 Gubernatorial Election." http://bit.ly/2xIJj1V

Uenuma, Francine and Mike Fritz. "Why the Sioux are Refusing $1.3 Billion." *PBS News Hour.* (8-24-2011). http://to.pbs.org/1GECxYi

United States Senate. "James Patterson Expulsion Case." http://bit.ly/2nmEwlK

INDEX

ABOUT THE AUTHOR

PHIL LEIGH holds an MBA from Northwestern University and a B.S. in Electrical Engineering from Florida Institute of Technology. The *New York Times* published twenty-four of his articles on the Civil War during the Sesquicentennial. He's authored five earlier books on the Civil War and Reconstruction including: *The Confederacy at Flood Tide, Trading With the Enemy, Co. Aytch, Lee's Lost Dispatch* and *Southern Reconstruction.* Last year Shotwell published his book about Hot Springs, Arkansas during the gangster era: *The Devil's Town.*

For more information on the author, please visit Mr. Leigh's blog on Civil War Chat and his Author Page at Amazon.

ShotwellPublishing.com

CPSIA information can be obtained
at www.ICGtesting.com
Printed in the USA
LVHW032124051220
673449LV00005B/815

9 781947 660182